business
and
professional
speaking

second edition

business and professional speaking

william s. tacey
professor emeritus **university of pittsburgh**

wcb
wm. c. brown company publishers
dubuque, iowa

To the hundreds and hundreds of business and professional men and women who have studied in my classes or have called upon me as a consultant and who have taught me much about business and professional speaking.

contents

Business and Professional Speaking is designed to help people to perfect their oral communication skills. Each part of the book is based upon the author's many years of experience in teaching, from first grade through the other eleven grades, undergraduate and graduate university classes, adult education, and as a communications consultant in business and industry. Correlated with experience in teaching has been a study of the writing of authorities in the field.

Emphasis in parts of the book is placed upon public speaking, in answer to an expressed demand from most of those business and professional women and men whom the author has taught. Regardless, however, of whether the audience is one or one thousand, the principles of communication are much the same—one person speaks, and each person in the audience listens, appraises, and responds.

The book is designed to be used either as a textbook in speech communication classes or for private study by those who wish to improve their communication skills.

Speech classes often do not afford enough opportunity for practice. Materials provided at chapter ends may well be used for supplementary assignments. Or, they are useful for the person who chooses to study by himself. Because only the rudiments of the subject can be covered by a brief text, attention is directed to the bibliographies. Those interested in serious study will want to read a large number of the references.

The style of writing was chosen for ease in reading. One reader reported having read the first half of the book in one sitting. To some, the contents may seem disarmingly simple, and such readers are cautioned against deceiving themselves. A consulting engineer on the fourth reading said that he had discovered much that had eluded him previously. A profusion of examples is used so that recall of them may make the impact of the principles they illustrate more permanent.

Photographs have been added to this edition both for illustration and study. All photos have been furnished by institutions and corporations and depict actual scenes where women and men are communicating orally.

In response to requests of readers of the first edition, two chapters have been added: "Group Discussion" and "Parliamentary Procedure." In discussion the use of reflective thinking is emphasized as a means of reaching consensus, in contrast to debate in which intentional thought is required.

Advice given on parliamentary procedure has grown out of the author's long years of experience as an officer of numerous organizations and service as a professional parliamentarian for local, state, and national organizations. Authorities such as Henry Robert and Alice Sturgis have been drawn upon liberally. While some memorization of rules is necessary, the study of principles is emphasized. For with an understanding of what the principles of the democratic process are, derivation of the rules and their application become more readily comprehensible.

As with any textbook, the success of *Business and Professional Speaking* depends upon the diligence of the reader. With thoughtful reading and much practice a reader may expect to improve materially his communication skills.

Speech was made to open man to
man, and not to hide him; to promote
commerce, and not to betray it.
David Lloyd

Business Is Based on Oral Communication

Ask any business executive, supervisor, or professional man what is his greatest problem, and you will hear him snap: "Communications." Further elaboration may reveal "My people don't understand me" or "I can't get the information I want" or "We waste too much time in meetings just talking aimlessly."

Wherever an inquirer goes, whether it be among members of management or labor unions, among professional men or women, the plea is usually the same—"Help us to communicate." Aid is needed in improving instruction, in giving orders, and in conducting interviews—hiring, corrective, or terminal. Men need help in translating the office or trade jargon into a language which the layman—or boss drafted from the layman's ranks—may understand. Subordinates need to understand the significance of the information they have. They need to know that their superiors must have it if they are to make intelligent decisions. All who wish to speak publicly can use help. The physician not only must understand what his patients tell him, but also must be able to give from his great store of information about the human body and disease a comprehensible set of instructions and to persuade the patient to follow them. Any physician knows that merely stating facts or directions will not be enough to win the patient's cooperation. Motivation is necessary, and human speech is the most frequently used medium to generate it.

1

To motivate one's listener is to persuade to action or belief or both. Telling is usually not enough, a reason must be given. Listeners may hear and understand, but remain unimpressed. Motivating appeals need to be used to bring about the desired response. A manager usually needs to go far beyond a general statement announcing that he welcomes information from subordinates. Their interests lie in their own assigned tasks, and if they are to be led to communicate upward they must be shown the relevance to what they are already engaged in.

Just as the physician must rely on speaking and listening to deal with his patients, so must the attorney, the banker, the certified public accountant, the engineer, the nurse, and the teacher rely on speaking and listening in order to relate to their fellowmen, whether they be colleagues or clients, customers, patients, or students. At every level of activity engaged in by business or professional people, the act of oral communication is of extreme importance. Business transactions may succeed or fail, lawsuits may be won or lost, and patients may recover or die, depending upon how well the business or professional person as speaker transmits ideas and information and how effectively a listener hears and understands.

A sales manager's income increases to the degree that salesmen can be led to produce. Sales persons who listen well are more apt to understand not only what the boss wants, but also what customers are telling them. A politician's progress will depend as much upon his ability to understand what the voters tell him as upon his ability to explain his platform.

Everyone should know more about the theory as well as the practice of communication, for even among people of adequate intelligence and sophistication, communication confusion can create serious problems. One of the greatest of these sometimes occurs because we think communication is complete when we have *told* someone what we want done. Skilled observers tell us that in addition to what we say, we also communicate nonverbally other messages which may negate what we say. Smiling broadly as we call an old friend an insulting name probably will not get us into trouble, but having a preoccupied manner as we give an order may cause our wishes not to be carried out. Pleading poverty while stylishly dressed may be as unconvincing as the message of the high school student who says: "I don't need no more English courses." In both instances, signals of which we are unaware are apt to take precedence in the mind of the listener over the words which we speak.

The man or woman who works in the middle or upper ranks of a modern business or professional organization spends most of his time in oral communication—talking and listening. The independent entrepreneur, whether he is the corner grocer or druggist, the village dentist or the city lawyer, depends as much upon his ability to communicate effectively as he does upon his professional knowledge. Any person who belongs to one or more organizations which hold meetings—board of directors, conference or professional association, or service club—finds it necessary to participate interminably, and often out of sheer boredom he either resigns or joins the ranks of those who demand improvement in oral communication.

Isocrates stated it well when he said: "None of the things that are done with intelligence are done without the aid of speech."

People in business and the professions seldom succeed by keeping silent. We need to expose our thoughts and desires, to share our information. Although secrecy is sometimes necessary, the airing of what we know and believe will enable us to develop our own personalities as well as help others.

One great American corporation has attempted to establish openness in communication by adopting this policy: "Any employee of this company may speak with any other employee on any subject." Although difficult to accomplish because of rigid schedules and lack of proximity and opportunity, the aim is clear—employees are expected to feel free to talk freely.

Undue attempts to be secretive or any mistaken ideas of the need to remain silent about matters of mutual concern can cause unfavorable results among the people involved. False conjecture, misunderstandings, or dangerous rumors caused by a lack of communication can often be harmful, but good talk can be designed to prevent such dangers.

Communicative Effectiveness

One's success in a chosen field depends upon skill in informing one's fellows and in understanding their statements, in persuading customers to buy or clients to act on proffered advice. His communicative effectiveness is measured in the responses he receives—not in his degree of skill in speaking nor upon the excellence of his rhetoric. How his audience responds—whether one or one thousand—is the ultimate gauge of whether the communicator is effective. What happens *within* the mind of the hearer determines the outcome of any attempt to communicate orally.

Obedience to orders and the following of instructions depend in large measure upon how they are heard and understood. The executive who thinks that subordinates do not follow orders is usually the one who is least successful in the ability to communicate. Such a person may be the one who shows contempt for the opinions of his subordinates, or the man who, when annoyed with his wife, vents his anger on his associates. He may forget that the listener's attention is on other matters, or that the

U.S. Steel News

As chief executive of a great corporation this man's position is secure and his appearance tends to indicate the fact.

scanty information given a new employee is insufficient to insure that the task will be done efficiently. Forgetting to query the listener on how he intends to carry out the assignment denies the speaker the chance to test the clarity of his order. Asking "Do you understand?" avails little, for most people are apt to answer yes, finding out too late that their understanding is incomplete. Instructions that are garbled in transmittal will be misunderstood no matter how eager the learner is to understand and to act upon them.

Without effectiveness in communications, our social relationships, including business, the professions, and government, are doomed to failure. Person-to-person relationships depend upon the ability of individuals to speak effectively and to hear intelligently.

Anne Morrow Lindberg tells us that "Good communication is as stimulating as black coffee, and just as hard to sleep after."

As our skills in building gadgetry increase, whether it be in refining the telegraph or the telephone, in multiplying Early Bird and Telstar, or sending oral messages by laser beam, our need for face-to-face communication increases. The wonders of modern science and invention merely multiply the opportunities to converse, the chances to make errors, and our obligations to increase our communicative skills.

Extension of the horizons under which a democratic way of life flourishes obligates the individual to improve his ability to talk and to listen. In industry, the "bull-of-the-woods," the foreman who ruled by physical strength and who could lick any man in the crew, has disappeared. Even the ability to do any task in the department better than any other employee is no longer a qualifying talent to win a promotion. Today's best supervisor is the person who is most skillful in leading and persuading, in learning and collating varying points of view. Such a person spends most of his time in talking and listening.

The most talented executive is the one who can marshal Aristotle's "all available means of persuasion" while addressing a sales meeting or a board of directors, or in encouraging a talented scientist to join the company's research organization. He can be equally at home in phoning a colleague or in addressing a convention of his profession's national association or the local luncheon club. In each case skill in assembling one's thoughts, putting them into understandable language, and appealing to listeners' interest will enable a person to be successful in speaking.

The physician, the dentist, the nurse, or the pharmacist will discover that knowledge of one's field and skill in its practice will be negated without equivalent skill in communicating with patients and customers. Each

Women who can speak well can more readily earn entrance to the ranks of management.

profession has its own jargon—its own vocabulary and way of speaking—which must be patiently translated and explained so that the layman may understand. "You have a carious lesion requiring restoration" may sound impressive, even frightening, to a dental patient, but it won't have much meaning until the dentist explains that a decayed tooth must be filled or restored.

Whatever one's business or profession, success in its practice depends largely upon observing and practicing the skills of oral communication. A new understanding of the dignity of the individual and of his attendant rights has both increased our opportunity for resort to persuasion and made necessary the use of persuasive means. As our understanding of people increases and the democratic principle is extended, the use of threats and violence decreases. Resorts to force are an admission that our ability to talk with people is poor, that our knowledge of persuasion is inadequate, and that we need to develop our communicative skills.

Using Communication Persuasively

In our society we settle differences by either of two means, by force or by discussion and persuasion. In business and industry we use the threat of firing less often than formerly. (For one reason, it costs too much to train people for today's complex jobs.) Besides, people do not scare as easily as they once did. Both labor and management have discovered that strikes and lockouts can be avoided through the use of less warlike means. The United Steel Workers recently signed an Experimental Negotiating Agreement whereby they are to use arbitration instead of strikes to settle disagreements. The work of the United States–sponsored Federal Mediation and Conciliation Service and of the American Arbitration Association is an example of how matters of dispute may be settled amicably. In all other areas we can rely upon reason to settle our differences. Parents and teachers find that children respond well to the use of the techniques of persuasion and secure obedience through means other than fear of punishment. When consideration is given to the needs and opinions of all the people involved, the use of force becomes unnecessary.

The development of the ability to persuade begins in infancy when we look to parents for our need satisfactions. We start to learn then of the opposing points of view which people may have and of the need for developing persuasive skills. From infancy on, hardly a day goes by that we do not attempt to win one or more points through our ability to influence others to accept our ideas.

While the salesman is often credited with using persuasion most, his attempts may be puny compared with those of the supervisor who is attempting to bring his department's production up to standard or with the labor representative trying to enroll new members or to secure a favorable response at the bargaining table. The conscious purpose of the speaker and the knowledge of how to communicate it help to determine the heights which he may attain in his effort to persuade.

Persuasion may take as many forms as there are communicators and as many degrees as there are levels of knowledge and intelligence. In a way, all forms of speaking are persuasive, the speaker's purpose being the chief determining factor.

Because persuasion is so all-pervasive, we find that we are usually engaging in it as a way of life, being almost continuously persuader or persuadee. For that reason Quintilian, the ancient rhetorician, insisted that the persuader (orator) must be a good man as well as a skillful speaker. To learn to persuade is not enough, for we must develop ethical or moral values. We must also develop an understanding of our surroundings and of the character of those whom we influence.

Resistance to Change

Most of us tend to follow an established pattern. We generally eat the same kinds of food—"I'm a meat-and-potatoes man," or Henry Luce's statement that food is only "fuel." We follow a general style in our choice of clothing. We have our favorite chair. Students tend to continue to use the same seats which they chose on the first day of class. Most of us resist changing jobs or profession, even when we learn of the profitability of doing so.

Any oral communicator needs to be acutely aware and unusually well informed of such human foibles if he is to be successful in conveying his messages. Listeners' preconceived notions and habit patterns are hard to overcome. Disturbing them may tend to make resistance to change even stronger.

To be able to effect change requires careful study of one's listeners as well as one's subject matter. To effect change is compulsory, for without it any individual or organization will soon be lost in modern society. Today, *change as inevitable* has been added to the duo *death and taxes*.

Business and Professional People and Their Problems

Problems generate speaking. Because business and professional people face problems daily, they must speak frequently in attempting to resolve them. The measure of the individual is revealed by the manner in which he reacts. Although one may wish that he might avoid problems, he should realize that as he faces them intelligently he often attains his highest level of competence and attainment.

So long as man reacted unintelligently to his environmental problems, he made little progress. Ignoring nature's elements or accepting placidly the onslaught of disease kept him at the animal level. Only as he learned to protect himself from the weather and disease did he begin his slow march toward civilization.

The presence of problems and man's determination to solve them can be the great motivating force that leads our civilization to greatness. Having to fight for survival and to meet emergencies seems to bring out in us our best abilities. For weakness we substitute strength, our ability to think is stimulated, and we burst the bonds which have restrained us, thus advancing toward a new plateau of life. Europeans, tired and discouraged by the Dark Ages, sparked the Renaissance. In the 1960s the world's youth, upset by war and other evidences of inhumane practices, began to oppose the "Establishment" whom they blame for many of the world's social ills. Americans thrilled at the precision and timing dis-

Honoring a colleague affords a chance to display friendship and concern, helpful ingredients in any communicative situation.

played by the thousands involved in the first successful lunar flight of our astronauts. The very difficulty of the problem inspired our scientists and technicians to succeed.

In our civilization, unsolved problems are as harmful to us as were the wars of the Dark Ages or as the diseases of nineteenth-century America. The ancient Romans demanded their bread and circuses while ignoring the moral corruption and decay of their government. Other civilizations have all been destroyed, either when they proved unable to solve their problems or when they concentrated on those that were of less importance. Not a few governments have been overthrown when they put curbs on the freedom of their citizens to speak. We sympathize with the citizens of any country whose invasion by an aggressor puts an end to a government founded on the principles of freedom.

Problems which people face in their ordinary existence range from family matters to corporation finance, from auto repairs to labor disputes, and from incompetency of employees to the meeting of competition. How such problems are met and disposed of tends to determine how successful we become in our business or profession. To ignore problems may be no more fatal than to choose only minor ones for solution. The executive who for days studies how to decorate an office while ignoring the welfare of subordinates may be greatly upset when a strike is called. To be successful an executive must set priorities for solving problems.

In his speaking, man must learn first to identify and describe problems as they exist. The antebellum slave owners failed to realize that the plantation economy was in serious economic and sociologic difficulty. Not until war had destroyed the slave system did they realize how deep-seated were their problems.

What socioeconomic problems are we overlooking today? Recognition of them, meeting, and solving them will determine how much longer our economic and political system may survive. Does the hippies' protest indicate that our society has discarded worthwhile values? Are we relying upon scientific discoveries to the exclusion of those of the philosophers or historian? Have we opposed Communism so vigorously and single-mindedly that we have forgotten what we stand *for*? In our popular distrust of intellectualism have we overlooked or rejected more competent leadership than we have been relying upon? Are we so concerned with profits, taxes, and comforts that we are refusing to consider the warnings of the ecologists? The importance of the problems is that their solution tends to create new sources of strength and to open new vistas into which our lives may expand. To ignore problems is to welcome failure and disaster. We are reminded that President Thomas Jefferson called democracy an experiment to test man's ability to govern himself.

By speaking we can make ourselves and our fellows vividly aware of what we face, of what our aims or goals need to be, and of the choice of methods to be employed in realizing our aims. To locate and define our problems is the necessary first step in achieving their solution. Through study and talking we can take this first step, and by improving our skills as speakers and listeners we can approach our problems more effectively.

Solving the Problems of Business and the Professions

In our age the opportunities—and the responsibilities—for speaking were never before so great. We have a higher degree of literacy than ever before; we have every conceivable kind of organization for men, women, and children, and most of them hold frequent meetings affording platforms for business and professional people; we have a communication system that can put us in instant touch with any part of the globe. Our opportunities for learning and study are unparalleled. Knowledge of any subject and advice from any field are ours for the asking. Audiences everywhere are prepared to listen attentively and with respect. Precedents have been established for the substitution of reasonable discourse for physical force. Corporations and professional organizations have wisely formed speaker's bureaus to supply the demand for speakers and to express opinion.

As great as the opportunity for speaking is the obligation. In ancient Greece and Rome, the educated citizenry were required to speak out as occasions arose. Only when the opportunities to speak were denied and force of arms was substituted for free discussion did the ancient civilizations begin to decline. Today's business and professional executives are equally obligated, and many speak ably to our mutual gain.

A common complaint of business executives is that information does not reach them, that their subordinates remain silent or speak conservatively, even when questioned or when given assurance that frank talk is desired. In contrast, many subordinates discover that promotion is often earned through their ability to speak intelligently and forcefully in handling problems for their employers. The reward of promotion comes because they have fulfilled their obligation to speak effectively when the occasion arose.

A test of one's value as a member of his community—business, professional, or political—is his willingness and ability to speak out on matters of mutual concern. Whether in conferences or at conventions, at Parent Teacher Association or school board meetings, or before a city council (and business and professional executives may be participants in all of them), the responsible person meets his citizenship requirements by

A self-assured member of management. What observation can you make of his stance? What may be the effect of his grasp on the lectern or of holding the spectacles?

Westinghouse Nuclear Energy Division

sharing his knowledge and demonstrating his speech skills, not for the sake of exhibiting them, but to help him and his associates arrive at a sensible solution of whatever problem they may be discussing.

The need to speak may often not be apparent. How few businessmen saw the need in 1928 and 1929 to speak about the flaws in our economic system, yet the signs of coming failure were there for those who would observe closely. Perhaps the debacle of the stock market crash and ensuing depression of the 1930s might have been averted had the problem been pointed out to us with sufficient skill and effectiveness. Only after poverty had brought us to a realization of our economic problem did we begin to take remedial steps. The disastrous riots in the Negro ghettos during "the long hot summers" of the 1960s resulted from our hesitancy in facing the socioeconomic problems which have beset the Negro since slavery days. Might we not reduce the senseless slaughter of people on our highways if those of us who are able would speak loudly and vigorously against it? By our silence we condone "the vast wasteland" of television programming, the rape of our natural resources, including the pollution of air and water, our outmoded local governments, the insolent disregard of the consumer's rights by many of our giant corporations, and the political practices which have led to such corruption as the Watergate episode has revealed.

Conversation in social functions may be as valuable in business and the professions as the oral communications used in more formal situations.

To be ready to meet the need to speak one must study and prepare constantly. The employee who must remain tongue-tied from want of information when the boss asks a question hasn't been doing enough homework. The specialist who knows all about a topic and yet remains silent when asked to stand and say "a few words" before a group of peers has delayed learning how to overcome fear of speaking. Being content to air one's personal minor problems, whether they are limited to a bad golf slice or the difficulty of finding a competent barber or hairdresser, precludes attention to matters of broader importance.

As a nation we have created a government which we believe to be worthy of survival. We are equally proud of our economic system. Realistically, we must recognize the flaws and inequities of both, constantly facing up to our problems and attempting to discover worthy solutions. As we develop skill in speaking, we come closer to maintaining our political and economic systems, for in a democratic society such as ours we substitute talk for force. Only through a competent and informed *vox populi* can we hope to achieve the ultimate in our society.

Conclusion

Business and professional people recognize and admit that they have problems in communication. With their admission they recognize that the ability to communicate accurately and well is indispensable for success in their undertakings. Not so many are aware that they have need of understanding the *theory* of communication as well as a need to develop skill in *practice*.

Without effectiveness in communications we are foredoomed to failure since our person-to-person relationships depend largely upon our ability to speak effectively and to listen intelligently. Opportunities and need for communication increase daily as we discover new ways for coming into direct contact with our fellowmen.

Persuasion is our strongest weapon for settling disputes amicably. Almost constantly we find ourselves as persuader or persuadee. The theory and techniques of persuasion have been discovered and are available to those of us who are willing to study and master them.

As problems arise, the need for speaking increases, for most problems can be faced intelligently only at the level of discussion. Problems have served as the motivating force which has led mankind to greatness. Resort to war is an admission that we lack the ability to communicate effectively. Through oral communication we can define our problems and work toward their solution.

Coupled with increased opportunity for speaking is an increased obligation for speaking ethically. Parallel with this obligation is the responsibility for constant study of one's subject matter in order to be prepared to speak and to listen when occasion arises. By acting as responsible citizens we help to preserve and protect our democratic society.

FOR DISCUSSION

1. What is your definition of "communication"?
2. Is there a distinction between "communication" and "communications"?
3. What are your principal problems in oral communication?
4. Is there anything about your habits of thinking, talking, or listening which may complicate your problems?

---

* These questions, the Problems and Exercises, and the Bibliography, together with those elsewhere in the book, are designed primarily for private study and should be used whether or not formally assigned.

5. In what ways is the act of communication a system of solving problems?
6. How may you measure the effectiveness of any talking (informal or formal) which you may do?
7. Which is the most frequent cause of workers to disobey—willful disobedience or lack of understanding? Why?
8. How may one listen intelligently? (See Chapter 8.)
9. What change in philosophy has tended to reduce the use of threats as a means of accomplishing our ends?
10. What is the meaning of "persuasion"?
11. Why is an appeal to the listener's interests imperative?
12. Do you agree or disagree with Quintilian's definition—"an orator is a good man speaking well"? Why?
13. How may one's choice of problems indicate one's stature as an individual?
14. What current problems do we need to direct our attention to?
15. How does one find time to attack important problems?
16. In what ways does a democratic society depend upon an informed, articulate electorate?

PROBLEMS AND EXERCISES

1. Interview two or more business and professional executives to ask them what problems of communication they have with associates, with clients or customers, and with subordinates.
2. Whisper a 15- to 25-word message to a classmate who will whisper it to the second, continuing around the room until the last one whispers it to you. Write on the board the original message and the whispered one. If there is a variance, try to discover the reasons.
3. Send five people out of the room. Show a sixth a fairly complicated picture depicting people performing various actions. Call in person number one, and with the picture hidden, have number six describe it to number one. Then have number one describe it to number two, two to three, three to four, four to five. How accurate are the descriptions? Why?
4. Remove your coat, then ask a classmate to stand in the back of the room and give you oral instructions on how to put it on. Follow what he says literally, not drawing on your long practice in wearing a coat.
5. Prepare a five-minute speech in which you use the technical language of your business or profession before a lay audience. Quiz your audience to learn if any terms were not understood.
6. Relate an experience in which you had a "violent argument." Explain wherein your communications broke down.

7. Attempt to persuade the next five people you see to donate a dollar to your favorite charity. Make a list of all the means used to persuade them. Which were successful? Which not? Why?

8. Make a list of the problems which the United States has solved since 1900. Make a second list of those not solved which have existed since 1900. Of those solved what have the effects on our civilization been? And similarly, those not solved?

9. Make a list of all the opportunities which you evaded during the past year when you might have spoken on a problem related to your business, profession, or local civic matters.

10. Prepare a ten-minute speech dealing with an appropriate problem to be given before a local audience.

11. Choose a problem of immediate concern in your business or profession. Prepare a presentation in which you will outline the problem and offer a solution for it.

BIBLIOGRAPHY

Books

BAKER, VIRGIL L., and EUBANKS, RALPH T. *Speech in Personal and Public Affairs*, N. Y.: David McKay Co., Inc., 1965.

BOIS, J. SAMUEL. *The Art of Awareness*. Dubuque, Ia.: Wm. C. Brown Company Publishers, 1966.

BORMANN, ERNEST G.; HOWELL, WILLIAM S.; NICHOLS, RALPH G.; and SHAPIRO, GEORGE L. *Interpersonal Communication in the Modern Organization*. Englewood Cliffs, N. J.: Prentice-Hall, Inc., 1969, chaps. 1–3.

BREMBECK, WINSTON LAMONT, and HOWELL, WILLIAM SMILEY. *Persuasion: A Means of Social Control*. Englewood Cliffs, N. J.: Prentice-Hall, Inc., 1952, chap. 24.

BRIGANCE, WILLIAM NORWOOD. *Speech: Its Techniques and Disciplines in a Free Society*. 2d ed. N. Y.: Appleton-Century-Crofts, 1952, 1961.

BROOKS, WILLIAM D. *Speech Communication*. Dubuque, Ia.: Wm. C. Brown Company Publishers, 1971.

Communication (a *Scientific American* Book). San Francisco: W. H. Freeman and Company Publishers, 1972. (Eleven articles reprinted from the September 1972 issue of *Scientific American*, which was devoted to the subject of communication.)

DIETRICH, JOHN E., and BROOKS, KEITH. *Practical Speaking for the Technical Man*. Englewood Cliffs, N. J.: Prentice-Hall, Inc., 1958, chaps. 1, 9.

DOOHER, M. JOSEPH, and MARQUIS, VIVIENNE, eds. *Effective Communication on the Job*. N. Y.: American Management Associations, Inc., 1956.

EISENSON, JON; AUER, J. JEFFERY; and IRWIN, JOHN V. *The Psychology of Communication*. N. Y.: Appleton-Century-Crofts, 1963, pp. 3–10.

ESKELIN, NEIL. *How to Make Money Speaking in Public*. West Nyack, N. Y.: Parker Publishing Company, 1969.

GOLDHABER, GERALD M. *Organizational Communication*. Dubuque, Ia.: Wm. C. Brown Company Publishers, 1974.

HUSEMAN, RICHARD C.; LOGUE, CARL M.; and FRESHLEY, DWIGHT L. *Readings in Interpersonal and Organizational Communication*. Boston: Holbrook Press, Inc., 1969, pts. 1, 2.

JANDT, FRED E. *Conflict Resolution Through Communication*. N. Y.: Harper & Row, Publishers, 1973.

JOHNSON, DAVID W. *Reaching Out: Interpersonal Effectiveness and Self Actualization*. Englewood Cliffs, N. J.: Prentice-Hall, Inc., 1972.

JOHNSON, WENDELL. *People in Quandaries.* N. Y.: Harper & Row, Publishers, 1946.

LEAVITT, HAROLD J. *Managerial Psychology.* Chicago: University of Chicago Press, 1969, pp. 138–52.

MARTIN, ROBERT C., et al. *Practical Speech for Modern Business.* N. Y.: Appleton-Century-Crofts, 1963, chap. 12.

McCARTHY, MARY. *The Groves of Academe.* N. Y.: New American Library, Inc., 1963, p. 63.

MENNINGER, WILLIAM C., and LEVINSON, HARRY. *Human Understanding in Industry.* Chicago: Science Research Associates Inc., 1956.

MERRIHUE, WILLARD U. *Managing by Communication.* N. Y.: McGraw-Hill Book Company, 1960.

MORTENSON, C. DAVID. *Basic Readings in Communication Theory.* N. Y.: Harper & Row, Publishers, 1973.

OLIVER, ROBERT T. *The Psychology of Persuasive Speech.* 2d ed. N. Y.: David McKay Co., Inc., 1957, chap. 2.

PACE, R. WAYNE, and BOREN, ROBERT R. *The Human Transaction: Facets, Functions, and Forms of Interpersonal Communication.* Glenview, Ill.: Scott, Foresman and Company, 1973.

PACE, R. WAYNE; BOREN, R.; and PETERSON, BRENT D. *A Scientific Introduction to Speech Communication.* Belmont, Cal.: Wadsworth Publishing Co. Inc., 1974.

REDDING, W. CHARLES, and SANBORN, GEORGE A., eds. *Business and Industrial Communication: A Source Book.* N. Y.: Harper & Row, Publishers, 1964, chap. 1.

SANBORN, GEORGE A. "Communication in Business." In *Industrial Communication: A Source Book,* ed. W. Charles Redding and George A. Sanborn, chap. 1. N. Y.: Harper & Row, Publishers, 1964.

SANDFORD, WILLIAM PHILLIPS, and YEAGER, WILLARD HAYES. *Effective Business Speech.* 4th ed. N. Y.: McGraw-Hill Book Company, 1960, chap. 1.

U.S. NAVY, DEPARTMENT OF SPEECH BUREAU. *Speaker's Guide.* NAVSO P3000, 6–1966, Office of Information (OI–450) Department of the Navy. Washington, D.C. 20350.

WALTER, OTIS M., and SCOTT, ROBERT L. *Thinking and Speaking.* 3rd ed. N. Y.: The Macmillan Company, 1973, chap. 8.

WEAVER, CARL H., and STRASBAUGH, WARREN L. *Fundamentals of Speech Communication.* N. Y.: American Book Company, 1964, chap. 1.

WEINBERG, HARRY L. *Levels of Knowledge and Existence.* N. Y.: Harper & Row, Publishers, 1959, chap. 8.

WEINBURG, JOHN, and WILMOT, WILLIAM W. *The Personal Communication Process.* N. Y.: John Wiley & Sons, Inc., 1973.

WEISS, HAROLD, and McGRATH, J. B., JR. *Technically Speaking.* N. Y.: McGraw-Hill Book Company, 1963, chap. 1.

WILMOT, WILLIAM W. *Communication Involvement: Personal Perspectives.* N. Y.: John Wiley & Sons, Inc., 1974.

ZELKO, HAROLD P., and DANCE, FRANK E. X. *Business and Professional Speech Communication.* N. Y.: Holt, Rinehart and Winston, Inc., 1965, chaps. 1, 2, 3.

Periodicals

ADAMS, RICHARD P. "On the Necessity of Literature." *AAUP Bulletin* 60 (1974):24–26.

"Aftermath of the Boycotts." *Chain Store Age* 43 (January 1967):27–29.

BARNLUND, DEAN C. "Toward a Meaning-Centered Philosophy of Communication." *Journal of Communication* 11 (1962):197–211.

BASSETT, G. A. "What Is Communication and How Can I Do It Better?" *Management Review* 63 (February 1974):25–32.

BENSAHEL, J. G. "Playing Roles to Convey Your Ideas." *International Management* 28 (June 1973):32–34.

BROMAGE, M. C. "In Justification of Jargon." *Michigan Business Review* 20 (July 1968):20–23.

COLLIER, J. J. "Live Lectures." *New York Times Magazine,* March 3, 1974, p. 14.

ELY, H. B. "Communications — Some Basic Principles." *Graphic Arts Monthly* 40 (December 1968):42–47.

GENEEN, HAROLD S. "The Human Element in Communications." *California Management Review* 9 (Winter 1966).

GRALA, WILLIAM. "Industry's Best Defense: The Speakers' Bureau." *Public Relations Journal* 20 (1964):12–13.

GRICKSCHEIT, G. M., and CRISSY, W. J. E. "Improving Interpersonal Communication Skills." *Michigan State University Business Topics* 21 (Autumn 1973):63–68.

HARDO, JOSEPH A. "Why Interpersonal Communication?" *The Speech Teacher* 31 (January 1972): 1–6.

HICKS, MASON. "Speech Training in Business and Industry." *Journal of Communication* 5(1955): 161–68.

HOLLINGWORTH, J. E. "Oral Briefing: A Tool for More Effective Decision Making." *Management Review* 57 (August 1968):2–10.

HULETT, J. EDWARD, JR. "A Symbolic Interactionist Model of Human Communication." *AV Communication Review* 14 (Spring 1966):5.

KLOTSCHE, J. MARTIN. "The Importance of Communication in Today's World." *Central States Speech Journal* 11 (November 1962):322.

LANGER, SUSANNE K. "The Origins of Speech and Its Communicative Function." *Quarterly Journal of Speech* 46 (April 1960):121.

LILLYWHITE, HEROLD. "Toward a Philosophy of Communication." *Journal of Communication* 2 (1952):29–32.

LINK, A. W. "Plain Talk about Communicating in Business."*Business Management* 25 (April 1964).

MASTERS, WILLIAM H., and JOHNSON, VIRGINIA E. "Touching—And Being Touched." *Redbook*, 1972; condensed in *Reader's Digest*, December 1972, pp. 66–69.

MEDLIN, JOHN. "Individual Responsibility Versus Group Decisions." *Administrative Management* 28 (January 1967):24–30.

MORGAN, J. B. "Communication Is the Alpha and Omega." *Office* 61 (February 1965).

NILSEN, THOMAS R. "On Defining Communication." *The Speech Teacher* 6 (1957):10–17.

"Managers Are Made." *Royal Bank of Canada Newsletter* 54 (June 1973).

"Selective Dissemination of Information." *Business Management* 31 (December 1966):49–51.

SHERRILL, ROBERT. "How to Bend Your Elbow Without Putting Your Foot in Your Mouth." *Lithopinion* 8 (Fall 1973):56–61.

SMITH, DAVID H. "There Is No White Horse: A First Step Toward Improving Communication in Business." *Speech Journal*, Southern Connecticut State College, 5 (1969):35–38.

STEWART, JOHN. "An Interpersonal Approach to the Basic Course." *The Speech Teacher* 31 (January 1972):7–14.

WERTZ, JACQUES B. "The Anatomy of a Thought." *The Toastmaster* 40 (June 1974):16–19.

WIETING, MAURICE C. "When Neighbors Meet." *Adult Leadership* 15 (March 1967):323.

ZIMMERER, THOMAS W. "Is Your Leadership Thinking Up to Date?" *The Toastmaster* 40 (June 1974):26–29. Reprinted from *Association Management*, September 1972.

Films

"The Communication of Purpose." Forty minutes, black and white.

"Conflict." A two-part film designed to develop an awareness and understanding of the causes and consequences of interpersonal conflict. Thirty-four minutes, color.

"Is It Always Right to Be Right?" To demonstrate the importance of openness and receptivity. Eight minutes, color.

"A Measure of Understanding." How to clear up conflicting double messages and improve communications. Twenty-nine minutes, color.

"The Rewards of Rewarding." To show psychological behavior techniques for improving personnel relations. Twenty-four minutes, color.

"The Telephone at Work." Fifteen minutes, color.

"Person to Person Communication." Fourteen minutes.

"The Uncalculated Risk." To show how communications break down when actions are based on guesses rather than facts. Twenty-six minutes, color.

"The Way I See It." To illustrate how people's perceptions differ. Twenty-three minutes.

"The Will to Work." To explain the factors of motivation. Twenty-six minutes, color.

All films may be obtained from Roundtable Films, Inc., 113 North San Vicente Boulevard, Beverly Hills, Cal. 90211.

2

In their declamations and speeches
they made use of words to veil
and muffle their design.

Plutarch

Bars, Blockades, and Red Lights in Communication

"You didn't tell me"; "I didn't understand"; "That's the last time I'll try to do business with you."

These are examples of statements which are apt to be made when our attempts at communication fail. Errors are committed, time is lost, new starts must be made, and feelings are often irreparably hurt. In most instances, failure results despite the best of good intentions and the ultimate in goodwill.

What stops our communications?

We often put up needless bars when we try to broadcast on the wrong wavelength. The telecaster who insists on using a UHF transmitter when the only receivers in his broadcast area are designed for VHF is foredoomed to failure. The speaker who is adamant in refusing to study and respect his hearers' peculiarities is predestined to equal inglorious failure. A speaker who addressed an audience in English when most of the listeners understood only Polish failed despite his carefully prepared and well-rehearsed speech. One or two simple questions asked in advance could have alerted him to the need for an interpreter. An equally strong barrier is set up by the speaker who talks in such a low voice that few listeners can hear him. The simple expedient of posting a friend in the back of the room to serve as a monitor or of watching his listeners closely can help remove such an obvious barrier.

18

Parents and their children often cannot communicate because they are broadcasting on different wavelengths—"speaking at cross-purposes" some call it. Examples drawn from "when I was a boy" fall on deaf ears because current circumstances are so different. Even though child and adult use the same words, their meanings may be dissimilar. Witness the man's definition of "square" in contrast to the child's contemptuous use of it. What adult can hope to keep abreast of the teenager's rapidly changing slang? And yet with patience and careful study, both adults and children can overcome the communication barriers between them. The first step is to recognize that they exist, then to discover which wavelength each is on. The same careful approach is needed no matter whom we attempt to talk with if we are not to find ourselves failing to communicate.

A steel mill foreman was faced by an angry workman whose complaint was "I can't make out on my machine." The foreman began to question him carefully: "Have you oiled it correctly? Are the blades sharp?" Despite his attempts, the man's anger increased. "Don't you think I know how to take care of my machine?" he yelled.

The foreman was puzzled, for the man was the best machine operator on the job, earning the highest rate of pay. He kept encouraging the workman to talk, finally agreeing to look over the machine later in the day. As the complaining man turned to leave the office, he suddenly stopped, faced his foreman, and blurted out, "No man in my circumstances can afford to pay $100 a month on a new car."

At last the barrier which had been effectively stopping all communication between man and foreman was down. Now that the source of trouble was known, getting the car refinanced at the credit union solved the problem. From then on "making out" on the machine was again possible. Family spats, labor disputes, or neighborhood quarrels can often be as easily resolved if only disputants will seek to discover how to talk with each other. The engineer who describes in technical language before a woman's club the operation of an automatic transmission; the physician who talks about carbon monoxide, phenols, and aldehydes to smokers who differentiate only between Kools, Kents, and Camels; the policeman who yells to a black man, "Move along, boy," all have one matter in common—certain failure until they remove the communication barriers by studying and adapting to their audience's interests and needs.

The Act of Oral Communication

The act of oral communication is composed of three elements: the listener, the message, and the speaker. An ancient recipe for rabbit stew began: "First you must get a rabbit." To be a successful communicator one must first get a listener. He is the object of our communication; he is the one who is to be led to respond. The listener is the decoder of our message. How he decodes it depends largely upon our skill in encoding it to suit his needs and interests. A needless bar is set up when the speaker overlooks the listener's abilities, personal foibles, and interests.

The diagram below represents what happens when one person attempts to talk with another. The arrows indicate that there is continuous action and reaction (feedback). For both speaker and listener there must be adaptation to the other, and the circular response is continuous. Vertical dotted lines indicate the distractions which occur. (Communications theorists call the interference "noise.")

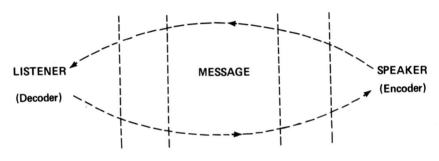

The Act of Interpersonal Communication

The message or code, adapted to the listener, conveys the speaker's thoughts which are to be transmitted. While adapted to suit the listener, the code is used solely for the purpose of accomplishing what the speaker wants. Through its use the speaker drives as unerringly toward his target as does the missile which is attracted by the heat of its intended target engines. As unerringly must the speaker concentrate on the listener or listeners of the moment, rather than some vague "average audience." The listener, if he is to accomplish his purpose, must be active in attending to what the speaker is saying and in showing his response. As the quality of an actor's work increases when he hears the expected applause, so does the speaker's effort improve as he gets a favorable response—at least courteous attention.

EMOTIONAL BARRIERS Failure to study the listener will cause bars to be erected; some are emotional. Common ones are fear, embarrassment, anger, or jealousy. They may afflict the speaker as well as the listener. The patient who is afraid that his doctor is going to tell

Westinghouse Nuclear Energy Division

Concentrating on the use of machines and written messages may lead either to improved or decreased ability to communicate orally. Can you explain how this can be?

him that he has a fatal disease will not be able to listen to a discussion on the pros and cons of socialized medicine. A speaker with an advanced case of stage fright will have difficulty concentrating on persuading his audience to accept his ideas. The old maxim describes love as blind, but may it not also be inarticulate, especially when in the presence of the object of affection? Angry crowds may soon degenerate into mobs, completely unable to listen intelligently. Angry individuals may as easily forget reason and resort to force.

Conversely, emotions, when intelligently controlled, may be used to heighten and strengthen one's message. The speaker who gets "warmed up" may find himself much more effective than he who remains coolly calculating in his manner. His own enthusiasm and emotions are contagious, leading the listener to feel as he does and helping to persuade him to respond as the speaker wishes.

At the same time, the speaker needs to be aiding listeners to put their emotions to better use. Open admission of speech fright often is useful in developing a sense of empathy in the audience, thus leading to a decrease in the speech fright symptoms. Showing concern for the listeners and their interests can win favor. A few words of sympathy or expression of good cheer or declaration of understanding can help listeners to believe that they can trust the speaker. Obviously such methods can be effective only if completely honest and sincere.

PHYSICAL BARRIERS Physical barriers such as speaking out of hearing range, voice defects, deafness, or conflicting sounds may stop communication. Before the days of the public address system, those on the fringes of large crowds expected to barely hear the orator. Today some may not hear because the man with the mike may expect more than the amplifier is capable of giving, thus not reaching as many people as he anticipates. Acoustic properties of rooms are puzzling, often making sounds inaudible even when speaker and listener seem to be close enough for easy hearing. Such speech defects as stuttering or lisping may attract so much attention as to distract the listener's attention from the speaker's message.

"I guess you preached a good sermon," a slightly deaf man remarked to the preacher as he was leaving church one Sunday. "Where did you

Note the possible hindrances to successful communication: the microphone partially hides the speaker's face, people standing behind the speaker, part of the audience not easily visible to the speaker.

Possible distractions to listeners: loud tie, big name tag, and bald head reflecting light. Are they sufficient for a speaker to be concerned about? Why?

sit?" the preacher asked. "Why, right there in the back pew where I always do," came the indignant reply.

Deafness, especially when coupled with unwillingness to move near the speaker or to wear a hearing aid, can be a severe block to any speaking situation. Speakers who refuse to recognize that some of their listeners (almost anyone over forty) have a hearing loss are culpable. We are all familiar with the person who, when asked to repeat a statement, does so without increasing the loudness of his tone, or with the one who, when he hears "Louder!" shouted from the back of the room, speaks the next few sentences in greater volume, but soon lapses into his previous inaudible tone.

A hard-of-hearing speaker may either speak so softly that he cannot easily be heard, or so loudly that his vocal sound becomes distracting.

When President Lincoln spoke at the dedication of the site of the Battle of Gettysburg, only a few hundred of the thousands who were there could hear him, for no public address system—not even a bullhorn—had yet been invented.

SOCIAL BARRIERS   Conflicting social views between listener and speaker may set up impassable barriers. The worker who believes the boss to be exploitative may purposely misinterpret most messages. The boss who feels only contempt for "foreigners" will misunderstand whatever one of them may tell him. Admiral C. Turner Joy, who served as chief United Nations Delegate during the Korean Armistice negotiations with the Communists at Panmunjom, has written a revealing book, *How Communists Negotiate*.[1] The book delineates clearly the effect of major social and political differences between two groups attempting to reach an important agreement which would stop the Korean War. The Communist delegates had the ability to exhibit "persistence and an unruffled demeanor in the face of logic. . . ." They relied on tedious delays to weaken the opposition and staged incidents which they hoped would strengthen their bargaining position. Withdrawal of abominable red herrings was promised on condition that the United Nations would grant other unpalatable concessions. Joy reports that in their discussion about prisoners of war "They lied; they blustered; they became vindictive; they welshed; they twisted, distorted, and denied truth; they delayed; they threatened."

While we hope that such extremes are uncommon in business and professional speaking, some of the attempts to communicate at the time of race riots and student demonstrations during the 1960s seemed almost futile. Invited speakers were interrupted and not permitted to speak. At times during negotiations when demands were not instantly satisfied disorders resumed. Such tactics are reminiscent of those employed by the Communists at Panmunjom and are equally hurtful to successful communication.

Semantic blockades to communication occur whenever words used by a speaker are interpreted in contrary fashion by a listener. An ultraconservative person may react violently to the word *union* whether it be credit union, union suit, or labor union. To one who is fearful, *snake* becomes abhorrent. Such people have never learned Korsybski's General Semantics dictum "that the map is not the territory."[2] For such persons the connota-

1. C. Turner Joy, *How Communists Negotiate* (New York: The Macmillan Company, 1955).

2. Alfred Korsybski, *Science and Sanity* (Lakeville, Conn.: International Non-Aristotelian Library Publishing Company, 1933).

tion of words is so strong as to block effectively whatever message the speaker means for them to denote. The signal which the word serves to give them immediately sets up a prejudiced reaction. For such people the *word* becomes the *object,* the map the territory, and the picture an actual snake.

A group of Presbyterian young people once petitioned their church session for permission to have "dancing" in the church social hall on Saturday nights. They reasoned that it would be wholesome recreation for all who participated, that it would add to the attractiveness of the church's program for youth, and that it might attract more young people from the community. On hearing the request, the church elders rose up in righteous indignation, centering all of their objections on the evils of "dancing."

The young people withdrew in confusion. Six months later, having acquired some good advice, they again presented their petition. Following the same line of arguments previously used, they ended with a plea to be allowed to engage in "folk games" in the social hall. The elders smiled benignly and immediately granted permission. The next Saturday night a few of the elders who had so outspokenly disapproved of "dancing" previously were found in the social hall teaching the youngsters a favorite folk game—"square dancing."

In the California state colleges and universities, students pay modest "fees." Early in his administration, Governor Ronald Reagan proposed that students pay "tuition." The ensuing uproar was loud and prolonged. Opposition on the campuses, from both students and faculty, was near-universal. Had the Reagan proposal been for increased "fees" the opposition might have been much less. The hated word "tuition" with all of its unwanted connotation caused a signal reaction.

The remedy for overcoming social barriers is to discover how "the other half lives," or at least thinks, and to be able to adapt to circumstances in the new social environment. For example, the proverbial generation gap tends to disappear as members of different generations attempt to understand each other's viewpoints.

Semantic Blockades

The semantic blockade is equally great when caused by lack of knowledge of the idiom used. Such a phrase as "empty gasoline tank" conveys no notion of danger to the uninitiated. Only when he explores the interior with a lighted match does he learn that "empty" has a different meaning when applied to gasoline tanks from which liquid gasoline has been drained but which is still "full" of explosive vapor.

The United States Steel Corporation's Fairless Works was built on land formerly used for truck gardening. Many of the new employees hired had never before been inside a steel mill but had worked previously on the truck farms. During a preoperations training session for foremen, one of the men advised his colleagues: "You'd better explain to your men what you mean when you tell them what to expect when they hear a *loud noise.* If you don't, the first time some molten steel falls into a puddle of water you'd better hurry out of the way. For if you don't, you'll be trampled to death by a herd of ex–lettuce pickers."

At the time that the Fine Arts Building was being erected at the Carnegie Institute of Technology (now Carnegie-Mellon University) plans were submitted to the donor, Andrew Carnegie. He believed the theatre to be a wicked institution, and when he found that one was to be constructed, he vetoed the plans saying, "It is not elevating, and a college campus is no place for a theatre." The architect returned the same plans to Mr. Carnegie, but where he had previously read "theatre" he now found "Dramatic Laboratory," and quickly approved the plans.

Near the end of World War II, the Japanese were called upon to surrender. Apparently they did not intend to ignore the demand, but wished to use it as a basis for negotiation and needed time to reply. The answer given by then Premier Suzuki was "makusatsu"—*to withhold comment.* In another context it can mean ignore but has no exact counterpart in English. When translated by the Allies, the word used was *ignore* —a fatal mistake which led to the A-bombing of Hiroshima and Nagasaki.

A much less serious example of semantic confusion happened in a hospital when a patient asked for a drink of water. Finding it lukewarm he asked for ice. The nurse refused because, she said, "Your chart says 'no solids.' "

A study of general semantics can be of inestimable value in discovering how apparently "simple English" can vary so greatly in meaning among people all of whom seem to be speaking the same language. More use of questions to discover the meanings of others—rather than instant denials or ready refutation—can help remove semantic blockades. For example, an Australian lad tried to compliment an American girl by saying, "You sing just like a jackass." If, instead of feeling insulted, she had asked "What do you mean?" she might have learned that he was comparing her voice to that of an Australian song bird, rather than to that of an American "Rocky Mountain canary," as she so mistakenly thought. This example is illustrative at once of social and semantic blockades.

When we remember that the same words have many different meanings for different people, we can more easily avoid semantic blockades.

Each listener perceives what he sees or hears through his own experiences and background. A psychologist asked several American and

Mexican teachers to look into a device that showed simultaneously a different picture to each eye. One eye saw a picture of a baseball player, the other of a bullfighter. Most Americans in the experiment saw the baseball player, most Mexicans the bullfighter.

Personality Red Lights

The personality of the speaker can stop communication as surely as red lights stop traffic on Fifth Avenue. The absentminded-appearing listener discourages the subordinate with an important message to tell. Equally effective in its capacity to discourage communication is the show of anger when one hears bad news, especially when he gives the impression that he somehow blames the teller for originating it. In Shakespeare's *Antony and Cleopatra,* Cleopatra flogs the news-bearer who tells her of Antony's death.

"My door is always open," boasts an executive of a large company, and yet his manner is as forbidding as any locked and bolted door. Abrupt, quick to judge, impatient and ready to interrupt, he stifles the attempt of all but the most hardy to talk with him. Every action seems to say, "I'm busy, so don't delay me. My work is so important that I haven't time to listen unless what you have to say is really important. Since I'm already so well informed, there's little you can tell me. Anyhow, my mind is already made up." Open door or not, such an executive may expect few messages to come from his subordinates. Such a person has set up a communications traffic light which is permanently red.

Doubtless an executive so ill-attuned to others would not realize the negative message which he is sending. One might be astounded to learn that what is done negates all of the words, that subordinates are motivated to avoid the boss at all costs, to communicate only when commanded, perhaps even dissuaded from listening.

Another red light of equal effectiveness is the negative personality which shows little interest, no enthusiasm, or no evidence of encouragement to fellow communicators. A man with such a personality seldom generates ideas himself or inspires them in others. Few look to him for leadership. His manner seems to indicate: "I have nothing to say. Why do you bother to talk with me? Why should I want to listen? No matter what you say, it will not matter to me." The negative person neither inspires a speaker nor commands the attention of any listener.

In contrast, a vivacious woman, able to display much enthusiasm and interest, can inspire even the most doltish lout to express himself.

An annoying type of personality red light is the *scatterbrain* who can never seem to keep his mind focused on one thought at a time. Asked for information, he clutters his answer with the most extraneous remarks until his questioner nearly forgets what was asked for. When supposedly listening to a communication, he may interrupt with references to unrelated incidents excited in him by what he hears. Sievelike, his mind cannot concentrate, either to relay information and ideas or to receive them.

The *one-track mind* is another communication red light. Unable to adapt, its owner can hear and appraise only what is on his one track. He will not listen to contrary ideas. When such a man was asked if he had heard Vice-President Rockefeller speak in his town last week, he replied: "Of course not, I'm a Democrat."

Audience Analysis

In addressing any audience, whether as few as one or as many as a thousand, we must first remember that it is made up of individuals, each bringing with him the result of all his learning and experience. To recognize that phenomenon is to take the first step toward removing the bars,

Obviously the listener is more interested in his award than in what the speaker may be saying. What might the speaker do to recapture the listener's attention?

blockades, and red lights from the broad avenues of our communications. Because each auditor is an individual, we should be aware of generalizing too hurriedly about his beliefs or sympathies. For example, one might be lead to say: "This is an all-Catholic audience. They are opposed to most forms of birth control." Yet we learn that some Catholic women use the "pill" regularly, and numerous priests have written books and articles in opposition to the Church's policy of forbidding all forms of birth control except the rhythm method. For these reasons our generalization must be greatly modified, and our speech composition changed accordingly.

Before deciding what to say to people, we can learn much from *observation*. The little man who sits erect, right hand tucked into the front of his coat, and facing a bust of Napoleon on his desk won't take kindly to adverse criticism of "the little corporal." The woman who is obviously fiftyish, but dressed like a college coed, evidently believes that she is retaining her long-departed youth. The men who are dressed in work or sport

Pennsylvania's Governor Milton Shapp is shown here in a characteristic pose. What kind of function do the equipment and decorations indicate?

clothes but with sullen looks on their faces as they file into the meeting room seem to be in dead earnest about what they expect. However, their mood may keep them from taking any interest in what they hear from the speaker's platform. In contrast, the crowd of laughing people who are engaging in mild horseplay, and who are slow to come to order, cannot instantly adapt to serious remarks on any subject.

Reading appropriate information can be enlightening. To scan the platform of a political party, the creed of a service club, or the printed reports of an organization of professional men can give a speaker insight that will be invaluable to him as he prepares to speak and while he is speaking.

The favorite ploy of a mill superintendent, when not wanting to listen to an expected complaint, was to ask his caller to guess the area of the irregularly shaped glass in his office window. One of his visitors, who had heard how a friend had been put off once in that manner, answered, "The area is 9.26 square feet. Now this is the reason I came to see you. . . ." A young insurance agent once met with a high school faculty to present a plan for a group policy. As he finished his presentation, the teachers turned to one of their number who immediately began to ask a series of highly technical questions which the agent deftly fielded. When he had satisfactorily answered the final question, he grinned and said, "Mr. Hyde, I'm glad that you came to this meeting, for you brought up several points which I might not have thought of explaining." Only then did he reveal, as the caller in the mill superintendent's office had done, that he had *asked questions* before coming to speak, another effective way of learning about one's audience.

The principal reason for learning all about your audience beforehand is to help you speak more successfully. You are in a position similar to the fisherman who asks, "What are they biting on today?" or "Did you see that big steelhead in Bent Tree Pool this morning?" Both speaker and fisherman hope that they won't have to fall back on a lame explanation about "the big one that got away."

Questions to Ask

In studying the audience, here are some of the questions for which the speaker should seek answers:

1. How many people will be present?
2. How will they be distributed as to age, sex, and level of education?
3. May they be expected to be relaxed, tired by having heard several preceding speeches, hungry or surfeited by a big dinner?

4. In what kind of room will the speaking be done—size, shape, seating arrangements, ventilation, lighting?
5. What is the mental ability of the listener(s)? How much interest is there in the topic to be discussed?
6. What beliefs regarding the subject are held? What general and specific attitudes?
7. What group loyalties may serve as barriers? Or what group loyalties may be used as persuasive weapons?
8. How liberal or how conservative is the audience in its views on the speaker's subject?
9. What expressions of opinion have members of the audience given publicly anent the speaker's subject?
10. What is the probable distribution of those *favoring* the speaker's viewpoint, those *opposed,* and those who are *neutral?*
11. What are the lines of argument and what evidence has proved effective previously in persuading listeners to adopt the views which they now hold?
12. Is the speaker believed by the audience to be an authority on his subject? Is he expected to "talk their language"?
13. Has the speaker discovered his own prejudices and biases in relation to those of his audience?

Conclusion

To be effective in oral communication we must understand that it requires a circular response with both speaker and listener participating. Each must react to the cues, both verbal and nonverbal, which he perceives in the other.

In any attempt at oral communication, the speaker must be aware that he faces many barriers, mainly physical, social, and psychological. To the degree that he can overcome both those existing in himself and in his audience, he is more apt to accomplish his purpose.

Some of the difficulties which must be overcome include differences in language, contrasts in ages and social situations, reliance on jargon which is not familiar to the uninitiated, semantic misunderstandings, and personality faults.

One of the effective means of overcoming barriers in oral communication is to observe and analyze the audience in advance. Through observation, reading, and asking questions, much helpful information about the listener may be obtained. By studying the listener and preparing the message to suit his interests and needs, the speaker can put himself into a more advantageous position to make his speaking effective.

FOR DISCUSSION

1. What are the effects of a breakdown in our interpersonal communications?
2. How is it possible for people to talk at cross-purposes?
3. Why is it advisable to start with the listener instead of oneself when communicating orally?
4. How can one focus on the listener's needs and interests, yet not deviate from his own goal in speaking?
5. How may our own inner conflicts act as a barrier to successful communication?
6. How can one translate technical language or trade jargon without talking down to the uninitiated listener?
7. "Never underestimate a listener's ignorance nor overestimate his intelligence." How can you use this information in your attempts to communicate?
8. What is the importance of feedback in communication?
9. What is the significance of "noise" according to communication theorists?
10. What steps might one take to discover what his own personality "red lights" are which may be hindering his effectiveness?
11. How can we deal with the "scatterbrain" and with the "one-track" mind"—whether our own or another's?
12. What is the meaning and significance of audience analysis?
13. Suppose you are asked to give a persuasive speech about your business or profession in a neighboring city. What advance information should you have about the audience before writing the speech?
14. What sources of information might prove to be reliable?

PROBLEMS AND EXERCISES

1. Why do business and professional executives feel so keenly their problems of communication? Interview five or more to learn their answers.
2. Observe several families in which there are teenage children to discover what barriers there may be in their attempts to communicate. List them.
3. Listen to a dispute or "argument" between two or more people. Make a list of all the barriers which seem to prevent agreement. Is failure to listen one of them?
4. For one week keep a record of all instances in which you misunderstand someone or in which others misunderstand you. Analyze each to determine how misunderstandings might have been prevented.

5. Attend a lecture for the primary purpose of observing the listeners. Make notes of all observable signs of feedback which you notice. In what ways did the speaker react, or fail to react, to it?
6. Recall the last time that you made a speech before an audience. In one column list all the barriers to effectiveness which you were responsible for and in a second column all of those caused by the audience. How might you have anticipated and avoided most of them?
7. Read accounts of several of the ghetto riots and campus disorders of recent years. Analyze them to discover where and how faulty communications were involved.
8. Read accounts of labor disputes, especially those involving strikes, and analyze them similarly.
9. Make a list of all of the ways in which you react to "signals" rather than rationally. How can you overcome the problem?
10. Analyze your own listening habits. In what ways might they be improved?
11. Seek an audience with a person of some prominence, such as a mayor, corporation president, or bishop. Discover in advance all that you can that would be pertinent to the subject of the interview and plan your questions accordingly.
12. Choose an audience, such as a luncheon club, before which you want to speak. Analyze the audience.

BIBLIOGRAPHY

Books

Bois, Samuel J. *The Art of Awareness.* Dubuque, Ia.: Wm. C. Brown Company Publishers, 1966, chap. 9.

Bormann, Ernest G.; Howell, William S.; Nichols, Ralph G.; Shapiro, George L. *Interpersonal Communication in the Modern Organization.* Englewood Cliffs, N. J.: Prentice-Hall, Inc., 1969, chap. 9.

Clevenger, Theodore, Jr. *Audience Analysis.* Indianapolis: The Bobbs-Merrill Co., Inc., 1966.

Dietrich, John E., and Brooks, Keith. *Practical Speaking for the Technical Man.* Englewood Cliffs, N. J.: Prentice-Hall, Inc., 1958, chap. 4.

Eisenson, Jon; Auer, J. Jeffery; and Irwin, John V. *The Psychology of Communication.* N. Y.: Appleton-Century-Crofts, 1963, chap. 19.

Hayakawa, S. I. *Language in Action.* N. Y.: Harcourt, Brace and Co., 1946.

Johnson, Wendell. *People in Quandaries.* N. Y.: Harper & Row, Publishers, 1946.

LaRusso, Dominic. *Basic Skills of Oral Communication.* Dubuque, Ia.: Wm. C. Brown Company Publishers, 1967, pp. 38–45.

Nichols, Ralph G., and Stevens, Leonard A. *Are You Listening?* N. Y.: McGraw-Hill Book Company, 1957.

Oliver, Robert T. *The Psychology of Persuasive Speech.* 2d ed. N. Y.: Longmans, Green and Co., 1957, pp. 80–82.

Oliver, Robert T.; Zelko, Harold P.; and Holtzman, Paul D. *Communicative Speaking and Listening.* 4th ed. N. Y.: Holt, Rinehart and Winston, Inc., 1968, pp. 56–59, 66–67, 106, 213, 239, 244–45.

REDDING, CHARLES W., and SANBORN, GEORGE A., eds. *Business and Industrial Communication: A Source Book.* N. Y.: Harper & Row, Publishers, 1964, chap. 4.

WEINBERG, HARRY L. *Levels of Knowledge and Existence.* N. Y.: Harper & Row, Publishers, 1959, chap. 8.

WISEMAN, GORDON, and BAKER, LARRY. *Speech: Interpersonal Communication.* San Francisco: Chandler Publishing Co., 1967, pp. 53–55, 72, 143–44.

ZELKO, HAROLD P., and DANCE, FRANK E. X. *Business and Professional Speech Communication.* N. Y.: Holt, Rinehart and Winston, Inc., 1965, pp. 136–40.

Periodicals

BACH, ROBERT O. "Communication: The Art of Understanding and Being Understood." *AV Communication Review* 12 (Fall 1964):358.

BRODEN, F. W., and TRUTTER, J. I. "Why Communication Goes Haywire." *Supervisory Management* 12 (January 1967):9–12.

BROWN, DAVID S. "Some Feedback on Feedback." *Adult Leadership* 15 (January 1967):225.

CATHEY, P. J. "Learn About Ego-Speak—Why No One Listens to You." *Iron Age* 212 (November 1, 1973):37–38.

COUSINS, NORMAN. "Education and the Clarifying Experience." *Perspectives in Education,* Teachers College, Columbia University, 2 (Winter 1969):1–5.

D'APRIX, R. "Why Leonardo and the Boss Aren't Speaking." *Management Review* 62 (May 1973): 49–51.

FERNO, JACOB. "Speakers Are Made, Not Born." *Personnel Journal* 46 (March 1967):174.

GOETZINGER, C., and VALENTINE, M. "Problems in Executive Interpersonal Communicating." *Personnel Administration,* March 1964, pp. 24–29.

HARRISON, J. C. "Serviceman's Biggest Problem: Ineptitude of Communicating." *Air Conditioning, Heating and Refrigeration News* 130 (December 3, 1973).

HOOGERSTRAAT, WAYNE E. "Memory: The Lost Canon." *Quarterly Journal of Speech* 46 (April 1960):141.

———. "Why Doesn't Anyone Understand Me?" *Supervisory Management* 11 (May 1966):20–21.

———. "When You Can't Tell Them Everything: Advice for the Supervisor Who Must Withhold Certain Information from Employees." *Supervisory Management* 9 (May 1964):16–19.

"How to Keep Your Foot Out of Your Mouth." *Business Management* 26 (November 1964):57–63.

HUNSICKER, F. R. "How to Approach Communication Difficulties." *Personnel Journal* 51 (1972): 680–83.

KELLY, CHARLES M. "The Myth of the 'Key Communicator.'" *Personnel Journal* 45 (January 1966):39.

KNAPP, MARK L. "Industrial Speakers Bureaus." *Personnel Journal* 46 (February 1967):92.

LESLEY, P. "Why the Public Isn't Listening." *Industry Week* 179 (November 19, 1973):34.

LEVINSON, R. E. "Executives Can't Communicate." *Dun's Review and Modern Industry* 100 (December 1972):19–20.

MARINE, DONALD R. "An Investigation of Intra-Speaker Reliability." *Speech Teacher* 14 (March 1965):128.

MARSHALL, D. B. "Do You Talk to Yourself at Meetings?" *Sales Management* 93 (September 1964): 75–76.

MAYER, D. P. "But I Thought You Said." *Supervisory Management* 11 (December 1966):15–19.

MILLER, GERALD R., and HEWGILL, MURRAY A. "The Effect of Variation in Nonfluency on Audience Rating of Source Credibility." *Quarterly Journal of Speech* 1 (February 1964):36.

MORTON, R. B. "Leveling with Others on the Job." *Personnel* 43 (November 1966):65–70.

NORBERG, KENNETH. "Visual Perception Theory and Instructional Communication." *AV Communication Review* 14 (Fall 1966):301.

O'DONNELL, WILLIAM. "The Real Problem in Communications." *Personnel Journal* 46 (January 1967):50.

OLSON, DONALD O. "Confusion in Arrangement." *Speech Teacher* 13 (September 1964):216.

"Political Euphemisms Debase and Deceive." *Christian Century* 91 (January 23, 1974):60–61.

TACEY, WILLIAM S. "What Stops Our Communications." *Advanced Management* 25 (April 1960): 17–19.

TROMBOLD, G. J. "How Well Do You Communicate?" *Office* 59 (January 1964):174.

Films

"The Bob Knowlton Story." A case study showing disastrous results of poor communication. Twenty-eight minutes.

"A Case of Insubordination." Case studies in perception, communications, and handling conflict. Twenty minutes.

"I Just Work Here." To show importance of attitude. Seventeen minutes.

"A Measure of Understanding." To show how to clear up conflicting double messages. Twenty-nine minutes, color.

"Overcoming Resistance to Change." Thirty minutes.

"Person to Person Communication." Fourteen minutes.

"Talkback: A Study in Communication." Eighteen minutes, black and white.

"The Uncalculated Risk." To show how communications break down when actions are based on guesses rather than facts. Twenty-six minutes, color.

"The Way I See It." To illustrate how people's perceptions differ. Twenty-three minutes.

"Who Killed the Sale?" Twenty-one minutes, color.

All films may be obtained from Roundtable Films, Inc., 113 North San Vicente Boulevard, Beverly Hills, Cal. 90211.

Face-to-Face Communication

Communicating face-to-face both simplifies and complicates one's problems. Being able to see a listener helps the speaker to note reactions more quickly and gives him a chance to adapt to the listener's response. The observant speaker is alert to the feedback which his listeners give him, whether it is in angry retorts or blissful sleep. He responds on cue by altering his seemingly harsh words or by apologizing for any inadvertencies he may have made. For the blissful sleeper, he orders the room aired or else raises the volume of his voice and looks for means of keeping the drowsy people interested. Whatever the feedback, be it signs of boredom or quickened interest, comprehension or disagreement, confusion or satisfaction, the speaker must instantly react to it if he is to accomplish his purpose. If he is vigilant, the cues will be evident. A frown, a smile, a nodding head, a querulous glance, a dull stare, aimless doodling, or impatient squirming in one's chair are signs for the speaker to observe, to read, and to adapt to, so that he may be more successful in his speaking.

Yet the speaker may not always be successful in interpreting audience feedback nor in responding to it effectively. Sometimes he may be giving signals of which he is not aware. A necktie awry, a smudge of soot on his nose, or a distracting mannerism may negate much of what he says, and he may not correctly interpret the reasons for the signs of distaste which he notes in his listeners.

Whenever two people are together interpersonal communication is inevitable. On sight, each begins an estimate of the other, often using the other four senses too. A shapely lass may arouse a young lad's lustful daydreams; effluvia from an unwashed bum causes a companion's nose to wrinkle in disgust; persistent clicking of a woman's heels once led to her murder by an elderly neighbor with overly sensitive ears. Being crowded by the fat person who sits beside you on a bus can cause a variety of reactions. In short, people communicate as soon as they become aware of each other, even though no words or other conscious signals are exchanged.

When we consciously communicate with others we not only transmit facts and opinions, but by our choice of words, tone of voice, gestures, and other bodily action send a conglomerate of messages. For example, a simple exchange of comments on the weather may reveal whether we are cheerful or grouchy, literate or illiterate, informed or ignorant, outgoing or reserved, friendly or hostile.

In addition to visible signals which may give information *about* your message, you may also give verbal explanations. Some possible remarks are: "Please don't misunderstand," "Don't get me wrong," "You had better sit down for this," or "It's really hard to put into words."

The technical term for such information about information or the signals used by a person to show how others are expected to view his behavior is *metacommunication*.

Use All Physical and Mental Powers

Because we live in two realms of experience, the physical and the symbolic, those who would communicate successfully in face-to-face situations must expect to use all of their capabilities to the best possible advantage. A corporation executive when advised to take a second course in effective speaking demurred. "All that I could learn now would be how to act, and I don't want to become an actor." Of course his bias was unsoundly based. No conscientious speaker should expect to be or want to become an actor. Rather, he should learn to express well his deepest feelings and his most solidly based opinions in a way that will impress his listeners favorably. As he speaks, his voice reflects his emotions, his excitement, or his sorrow. In contrast, the uninspired communicator talks in a dull monotone, made duller by a monorate, and unrelieved by any change in volume. The speaker who would succeed varies his facial expression to suit his thoughts, saving his deadpan appearance for his off-hours poker game.

All of the vocal changes, the variety of facial expression, the attitude of alertness or the lack of it can have a profound effect upon one's listeners.

Westinghouse Nuclear Energy Division

In the large organizations numerous ceremonial functions must be engaged in. Proficiency in oral communication increases a worker's opportunities to participate and heightens the interest of the listeners.

Meanings which otherwise might have been lost in transmittal are caught, attention is held, and interest is developed as the speaker communicates with all of his vigorous abilities the full sense of his ideas. The interplay of his emotions is used helpfully and revealed by his voice and actions as he communes with his audience. In no true sense is he an actor portraying the part of someone else. In contrast, he is trying his best to reveal his own complete and inner self as he attempts to inform or persuade.

However, the face-to-face speaker needs to have at his command most of the tools of the actor. Emotional control, a wide vocal range and clear articulation, expressive face, and freedom of bodily action can be as useful to the effective speaker as they are to the actor. Each of them is a means of communication to be kept on tap as occasion demands, and the skilled communicator will find them reliable as he learns to use them. As he learns, he must remember that the event of communicating has small meaning in itself compared with how his listeners construe it. Their perception, their feelings, their thoughts and responses will be entirely their own, possibly coinciding with what the speaker believes he communicated but perhaps quite different.

In a Westinghouse Nuclear Energy plant instructions given to women handling materials were explicit and meaningful—a supervisor believed.

The purpose was to protect them from contamination, and the order was for each woman to wear a rubber glove on her right hand. Despite the precaution some were found to be contaminated. The fault was traced to a woman who was using her bare hand. When challenged, she showed her carefully gloved right hand. How had she contaminated the rods? She was left-handed.

Reveal Only Genuine Feelings

Any feelings or beliefs which a speaker reveals must be genuine lest the listener detect the falsity of his position. Dogs and children are supposed to be able to detect unerringly those who are trustworthy. Most listeners know as well whether the speaker is feigning interest in them or whether it is genuine. To be revealed, one's conviction must be really deep-seated, otherwise one's expression may embarrassingly reveal the shallowness of the belief or falsity of statement. Even inexperienced listeners rapidly learn to detect the telltale signs of the charlatan. What might be hidden in a letter or essay is often pitilessly displayed as one speaks, despite any conscious efforts to hide it. Based on this dictum, there is truth to the statement that the television camera is the world's best lie detector. On the screen of the receiving set the speaker stands revealed for all of us to see. Eye movements which disclose reliance on idiot cards or Tele-PrompTer, nervous twisting of the hands, the look of embarrassment as unexpected questions are asked, all may reveal that the message being given by him is not what the speaker wishes to convey. Even without benefit of TV, listeners may still notice the same kind of signs and react differently from the way the speaker intends.

Bruce Barton advised that "For good or ill, your conversation is your advertisement. Every time you open your mouth you let men look into your mind."

Being face-to-face while communicating may hinder or help one's feeling of confidence. The anonymous phone caller may be braver in his anonymity than he would be if confronted by his auditor. The speaker who talks while seated as a member of an audience may suffer less from speech fright than if he were to stand and face his fellows. Such feelings come from inexperience, immaturity of personality development (including a sense of insecurity), or lack of understanding of how to communicate since the changed circumstances vary only in degree. In each instance the speaker should consider himself to be a communicator.

Being able to see whom one is speaking to may give needed reassurance, particularly when the listener reacts approvingly. Radio announcers or teachers appearing on television often want a studio audience

Westinghouse Nuclear Energy Division

Modern technology has at once increased the need for interpersonal communication and its difficulty.

at first in order to feel more at ease. Experienced speakers want the stimulus of an audience.

The late Roy F. Bergengren, a pioneer in the credit union movement, was a powerful orator, highly persuasive, and a man of wide experience as a speaker. One night in a theatre-nightclub near Pittsburgh he was introduced to address an audience of about one thousand credit union members, the kind of people whom he knew best and with whom he was most at home. The speaker's platform was brilliantly lighted, the audience seated in semidarkness.

As Mr. Bergengren uttered the introduction of his speech, he seemed ill at ease. After a minute or two he shaded his eyes with his hands, peered into the gloom, and plaintively said, "I am told that somewhere out there in the darkness there is an audience. If there are people there, won't you please applaud so that I may know where you are."

Even with the reassurance of loud applause, the speaker missed so greatly the feedback which he was accustomed to getting from a visible audience that he was unable to speak with his usual vigor and aplomb.

The speaker needs to see the facial expression of his hearers to note how they react to his words, to deduce from their movements—shifting in their seats, nodding or shaking their heads, glancing at their neighbors—what their reaction to his words is. From the feedback which he gets the speaker adapts what he says. If the audience is sleepy, he redoubles his vigor and increases his voice volume. If they look tired or if their attention seems too intent, he rests them with a bit of humor or a lighthearted illustration. If they seem to feel too warm or too cold, he tries to have the ventilating system of the room improved. Before a hostile audience a speaker must be particularly alert, for how else can he be prepared to duck the eggs or pop bottles which may come his way?

Communication Is Complicated

Face-to-face communication is unbelievably complicated, for six different personalities are engaged whenever it occurs. First, there are the obvious two—you and I. Next, there is the person you think you are and

Westinghouse Nuclear Energy Division

As two men converse the situation is complicated by the varying estimate they have of themselves and of each other.

the person who I think that I am; there is who you think I am and the individual I think you are; and there is who I think you think you are, and who you think I think I am. Mixed among all of these conflicting personalities are the many signals which each sends to the other. Some we are aware of, such as our planned statements; others go from us without our knowledge, such as unmotivated gestures or facial expression. All of this complicates face-to-face communication, and yet above it all, we can often understand each other and win favorable responses frequently.

J. Samuel Bois explains it in another way: "A conversation," he has written, "is not so much an exchange of objective information between two persons as the encounter of two semantic reactors, of two human capsules in flight, each following its own orbit, with its mass, its momentum, its direction, and its capacity to withstand shocks."[1]

In a sense, when we talk we talk about ourselves, for each of us is a product of his own experiences, his education, his habits, his idiosyncrasies, his prejudices, and his way of thinking. Regardless of what words we speak, what we are comes through so loudly and so clearly that our listeners react to the sum total of what we are, what we appear to be, and what we say—not to our message alone. Recognition of this phenomenon can help to assure honesty and sincerity in our communications.

OBSERVE FEEDBACK   Ideally, a communicator should have his listeners wired so that their responses could be observed on appropriate meters and communications adapted to the feedback recorded by the meters.[2] Such a handy device is obviously impractical since we have not yet devised a satisfactory method of measuring human reaction to symbolic communication. The best that we can do is to use careful means of observation, study of human nature, and much trial and error.

Communicating face-to-face both simplifies and complicates one's speaking and listening. Being able to see a listener helps the speaker to note reactions more quickly and gives him a chance to adapt to the listener's response. One of the strongest arguments against trying to read a speech or looking out of the window during a conversation is that we can't observe the reaction of our listeners and adapt our message so as to accomplish our purpose more certainly. Human behavior adjusts on the basis of physical and psychological links with the environment. Com-

---

1. J. Samuel Bois, *The Art of Awareness* (Dubuque, Ia.: Wm. C. Brown Company Publishers, 1966) , p. 24.

2. *Feedback* is a term used in cybernetics where it refers to the principle of self-regulating mechanisms. Some common examples are the thermostat in the auto radiator or the light beam which signals the doors of automatic elevators.

municators are a part of that environment, and whether we are speakers or listeners we are bound to adjust to those surroundings.

When listeners nod, are they agreeing or dozing? A watchful speaker can tell at once and adjust his speaking to what he sees. Uncomfortable listeners shift frequently in their chairs, whisper to their neighbors, fuss with their clothing, or even leave when the situation becomes intolerable. Those who appreciate what they hear will show it by their facial expression or by nods of approbation, and to the joy of many a speaker, by audible expressions of approval, such as shouts or applause. In conversations, listeners may be even more demonstrative as they express their pleasure.

Not everyone is equally sensitive to feedback; the same person can't be depended upon always to react the same way. Hence we must train ourselves to be alert to response in the attempts we make to influence people's adjustments to a certain chain of interaction.

Feedback is sometimes classified as positive (that which encourages behavior in progress) and negative (that which inhibits behavior). A listener's smiling and nodding assent encourages a speaker. A frown or inattention has a negative effect. The latter may readily cause abrupt change in behavior while positive feedback will likely serve to cause one to continue even more vigorously whatever is in progress.

Whichever way his listeners react, a speaker must beware of either giving up in despair or of "playing to the gallery." His purpose in speaking should be kept foremost in mind regardless of what he sees in his audience or hears from them. To yield to discouragement when reaction seems negative may be admitting defeat, perhaps just as a listener is hoping for one more reason why he should believe. To rely on a hearer's laughter as evidence of success in speaking may be confusing skill in entertaining with effectiveness in speaking. People can laugh *at* us as well as *with* us.

In adapting to the communicative environment we may find ourselves receiving conflicting feedback from those whom we wish to impress. Such a problem is usually classified under the term *cognitive dissonance*. To resolve the problem we must seek to reduce dissonance through the generation of new communications, or new perceptions, of what we are talking about or listening to.

SELF-IDENTITY AND COMMUNICATION Most of us attempt to conduct ourselves so as to win the approval of others. Just as we react to our physical environment, so do we seek to react to our social environment. As we enter a new group, such as new class, a new job, or a party where most of those attending are strangers, we tend to seek out the "norm givers," those who seem to be the leaders. We tend then to follow the standards of dress, composure, and conversational practices which the leaders use. Frequently such persons will suggest patterns to follow, as in how guests may be expected to dress for a party or whether smoking is permitted on the job.

Attempts to discover how others act so we may emulate them, or to discover how they react to us, tend to be continuous. Many of young people's attempts to "find out who I am" are basically a search for social recognition.

As we attempt to communicate, we nearly always are thinking: "Please agree with me." "Accept me as I am." "Show me that you accept my value as a person." Affirmative confirmation is imperative because it tends to lead to freedom to be spontaneous, to be able to overlook small slights, to dare to accept and appraise feedback about oneself.

One who constantly lacks confirmation of his social status will be even more avid for information about himself, will want feedback but will fear it. Negative evaluation—no matter how slight—will prove upsetting. Self-image will deteriorate, and self-evaluation can lead to further debasement.

To restore self-esteem we try to increase the ratio of satisfactory responses to unsatisfactory by seeking those who will bolster our egos by confirming our beliefs. The practice of nondirective counseling (encouraging people to talk randomly about their interests) is sometimes used as a means of breaking the chain of need, fear, and avoidance of any feedback, even that which might prove to be image building. For the person who is attempting to improve his ability as a communicator a thorough understanding of what feedback is and of how to observe and interpret it are compulsory.

Sizing Up a Speaker

As soon as a speaker appears before a listener in a face-to-face communication situation, the latter begins to size him up and starts to react even before the conversation or speech begins. The speaker's physique, his stance, his mannerisms, and his clothing bring reaction from those who observe him. Whatever the observers may know about him, what others may say or do while waiting to listen will also cause a reaction for good or for ill. To all of these stimuli working so strongly on his hearers the speaker may be oblivious. And yet, if he is to succeed he must learn to identify and control them.

A distinguished president of one of America's great corporations in a banquet speech one night said, "He done. . . ." Immediately, a red-haired woman teacher nudged her companion. A bit later the president referred to "these kind," and the teacher muttered: "Did you hear that?" When a third grammatical error was made, the teacher indignantly said: "He's going to get a letter from me about his grammar."

Not until the president had received the letter could he have known that one of his listeners missed the importance of what he was saying, mainly because his grammar was faulty. This incident well illustrates how important it is for us to be meticulous in our face-to-face communication to be sure that every signal we give contributes to the message which we mean to convey.

Nor is displeasure with common errors in grammar limited to school-teachers. A steel mill foreman asked a young engineer for an oral report. "In his first sentence," the foreman reported, "he used two double nega-tives. The fact that a college graduate would make such inexcusable mis-takes made me so angry that I didn't hear the rest of his report." The engineer was shocked to learn that his grammatical errors were taking precedence over what he had to say about his work. The adage "What you are speaks so loudly that I cannot hear what you say" applies to every speaking situation in which we give offense, whether in grammatical errors, personality faults, or in actions which our listeners resent.

Because we are social beings, most of us like being with people. They inspire us, they please us, we enjoy their company, and social approval is compulsory for our well-being.

One-to-One Relationship

No matter how many people are in your audience, you, as speaker, have the responsibility of maintaining with each of them a one-to-one relationship. If you are successful, each person will say to himself: "I felt that he was talking directly with me." Once, after listening to a speech, two women approached the speaker. "Thank you for an interesting speech," one of them said, greeting him warmly. The second woman thoughtfully interposed: "But he didn't make a speech, he just talked with us." Such high praise is earned when a speaker seems to meet each member of his audience directly.

Speakers must remember that each listener sits on his own little island of interests. He is concerned with his family, his job, his next ap-pointment, and a myriad of other matters which may flit through his mind. Although he looks attentive, his mind may be much absorbed with his own thoughts, all of them far removed from what the speaker intends to say.

The speaker is perched on his own islet, not always aware of the fact that his listeners may not be as ready to listen as he is to speak. To be

The microphone of the public address system makes possible the reaching of larger audiences. As the size of one's audience increases, what may be the effect on the person-to-person contact?

effective he must build a bridge between his island and that of each of his listeners. While he speaks, he must continually be sure that no bridge has broken down. He must constantly look for the feedback which will give him a hint as to whether or not he is being effective. These bridges of person-to-person contact are built and maintained both by what the speaker says and by what he does. Good eye contact with each member of the audience will help listeners pay attention. Plenty of vocal variety can assure easier listening. The use of gestures for emphasis and illustration gives the added advantage of a visual signal for the supplementing of what is being said.

However, none of these in itself is significant if the speaker's message is of small worth. Face-to-face communication succeeds only in the degree that the message being transmitted has something of value for the listener. All other efforts but serve to make the transmission successful. All of the discoveries of the Bell Telephone Company and of the skillful construction of equipment by the Western Electric Company cannot improve the quality of the gossip exchanged via telephone between Grandma in Des Moines and Aunt Effie in Boston. Neither can a "presentation—replete with charts, graphs, and photos—by President Hiram, of the Winke Manufacturers' Association, succeed if he has nothing of significance to say.

Those who would communicate successfully should assume responsibility for the physical surroundings where they intend to speak. A quiet, thoughtful conversation is at best difficult in a noisy office with its jangling telephones, clattering typewriters, and interruptions by comely secretaries or importunate colleagues. Confidential matters can hardly be discussed by physicians or lawyers if waiting patients or clients can hear the conversation through open doorways or sound-leaking office walls. All such hindrances to effective communications must be considered and attended to in advance.

Sites other than crowded, noisy restaurants should be chosen if a conference, an interview, or a committee meeting is to be successful. Even with the sign language of the noisy factory to supplement the oral remarks, many of the nuances of meaning can be lost, and adjournment to a quiet corner, even if in the parking lot, is preferable.

Leave Nothing to Chance

For the public speaking situation the communicator is well advised to leave nothing to chance, much less to the willing, but inept, chairman of the meeting. Well in advance of the time for speaking, the speaker ought to know where he will be standing in relationship to his audience, whether a lectern, chalkboard (with pointer, chalk, and eraser), easel, or other needed accouterments are available and in condition for use. Public address systems and projectors should be examined and their operators consulted.

Westinghouse Nuclear Energy Division

What indicates that the two people were posing for a photograph? What change in seating arrangement would you suggest to facilitate communication?

What of the seating arrangement? The hollow square plan with the speaker in the center is probably the worst, and anyone asked to speak in such a situation should rigorously resist. To be expected to speak from the center of a long banquet table, half of the audience being on each side, is not much better. Ideally, one should have his audience arranged in front of him in a rather narrow fan-shape, the floor being raked sufficiently so as to have those in the rear elevated to let them see the speaker easily.

To ask his audience to arrange themselves in an advantageous manner is the responsibility of the speaker. If he is to speak after a dinner, perhaps the tables should be removed and the chairs rearranged. Church members notoriously fill back seats. With the aid of church officials, when expecting a small congregation to a too-large sanctuary, rear and side pews may be roped off, forcing everyone to go "front and center."

Even after a speech has begun, the speaker may profitably interrupt himself to see that his audience is comfortably seated, standees directed to vacant chairs, or those out of comfortable hearing range invited to come forward.

Lighting, heating, and ventilation need the speaker's attention. Can he see the audience and can the listeners see him? Any lights on the rostrum which shine in the listeners' eyes should be shaded or extinguished. A slightly too cool temperature is preferred to one which is slightly too hot. Conference with a janitor or hotel "engineer" can help with both heating and ventilating. Air conditioners may need to be turned on or off, windows opened or closed.

In the large auditorium of the Soldiers and Sailors Memorial Hall in Pittsburgh, Lincoln's Gettysburg Address has been patriotically printed in extra-large letters on the wall directly above the speaker's platform. No matter how rapt one's attention, nor how good his self-discipline, he frequently finds himself reading Lincoln's immortal words of 1863 instead of listening to today's speaker. At the neighboring auditorium of the Western Pennsylvania Historical Society, there is a brilliantly colored picture of a pioneer family building a log cabin. To avoid distracting listeners, the architect has thoughtfully provided heavy drapes which may be drawn during a lecture so as to provide a neutral background.

In some suburban restaurants, the luncheon table with lectern stands before a large picture window. If faced with such distractions, the audience should expect to have curtains or drapes drawn to cover the display or the window. Once the writer found that he was expected to speak while standing in bright sunlight before a large window. To the consternation of a head waitress, he insisted on having drapes drawn to cover it. With the help of a number of women, the task was accomplished amid a shower of dust. Afterward several members of the audience thanked him, saying: "You're the first speaker who ever thought of having the drapes drawn, and the first one whom we've been able to see while he spoke."

Last-Minute Checkup

A last-minute checkup on the audience can be equally helpful. Plan to arrive at the meeting place well in advance, not only to be able to see if the physical arrangements are satisfactory, but also to study members of the audience as they arrive. "Why don't you stand at the door of the dining room," the president of a woman's state association said to the banquet speaker, "and watch all the girls go by." Her thoughtfulness also included a suggestion to other officers and numerous key members that they greet the banquet speaker. By the time he was ushered to the head table, he had talked informally with twenty or more women, giving him a chance to learn more of his audience and to develop in him a feeling of being among friendly people who would appreciate his speech.

Greeting listeners before one speaks helps to break the ice, to establish rapport, and to get suggestions as to what members of the audience may be expecting. Most of the same advantages may accrue in other face-to-face situations. Arriving early for a conference allows time to become familiar with the seating arrangements and the facilities provided for personal comfort. There may even be a chance for a few minutes of friendly conversation with other conferees before serious discussion begins. Reporters tell us that some of the informal conversations at the Paris peace talks between representatives from the United States and North Vietnam were more productive than the formal confrontations. As one executive told a subordinate: "At least get there early enough so you'll have time to wipe your sweaty hand on the seat of your pants before you shake hands."

Having a few minutes to get acquainted, to learn each other's names, to explore interests, and to do some preliminary inquiring may be really advantageous when the planned discussion or conversations begin. Communications which are based upon mutual trust and regard have a far better chance of success than one in which both sides are suspicious of the motives and integrity of the other. A preliminary chat may help to develop at least an initial sense of respect and trust.

Time spent in checking the physical arrangements of the meeting site can help to assure fewer inconveniences and distractions while speaking. Not having to be interrupted by a defective public-address system or to watch the audience go to sleep because of defective ventilation can be a good reward for extra care taken beforehand. Informal conversations with one's listeners prior to a formal appearance can be equally valuable, for

by conversing the speaker may more successfully present himself and prepare himself emotionally than if he waits for the introductory part of his
speech. Television producers early learned the value of a "warm-up" period
for the studio audience in order to get a hearty response for the show to
be telecast. Effective face-to-face communication depends upon a combination of an able speaker, well-prepared message, and a set of circumstances
which will enable the audience to see and hear without needless distractions. Speakers who are most determined to succeed will make the necessary
extra effort needed to help themselves do so.

Conclusion

Face-to-face communication gives the speaker the chance to talk
directly with his listener and at the same time to observe reactions to his
message. As he interprets this feedback, he continually adapts his message
to it.

To be successful, the communicator must bring into play all of his
mental and physical powers. While the listener pays attention to the
spoken message, he is also watching the visual signals, such as hand movements and facial expression. Each of these tells the listener something of
what the speaker is thinking. Some of what is revealed may negate the
meaning of the spoken words. To be successful, the visual messages must
supplement or illustrate whatever oral message is being given.

Regardless of how we speak or otherwise reveal our thoughts, we
in a sense are speaking about ourselves. Through our speech we reveal
our personalities and the experiences and habits which have established
them.

Not only should we assume responsibility for all of our means of
personal communication, but also for our surroundings. To be successful
we must see that the place where we are speaking is suitable for our purposes and that all of its furnishings are appropriately arranged. Time
spent in seeing that all is arranged to the advantage of speaker and listener
can help assure effectiveness of any face-to-face communication.

FOR DISCUSSION

1. Why do many people prefer a face-to-face meeting to a phone call, or
   a phone call to writing a letter?
2. What are some probable reasons for unfavorable reaction, even when
   the speaker feels nothing but goodwill toward his listeners?
3. What personality flaws make a speaker feel uncomfortable in a face-
   to-face situation?

4. Why does the experienced speaker want a studio audience when first appearing on radio or television?
5. What makes face-to-face communication complicated?
6. How does a person reveal himself by body language as he speaks— quite apart from the words he utters?
7. How do listeners reveal their reactions as they listen?
8. How can a speaker overcome a feeling of despair when listener feedback is unfavorable?
9. How can a speaker resist "playing to the gallery" when audience feedback is favorable?
10. Why should he?
11. How can we learn if listeners are laughing *at* us instead of *with* us?
12. What precautions can a speaker take as he appears at the place he is to speak so as to help assure a favorable initial impression?
13. What evidences are there that man is a social creature?
14. What application of this phenomenon can be made in face-to-face communication?
15. What are some precautions which one may take in order to prevent interruptions or negative responses during a period of communication?
16. In what ways is all of the talking we do persuasive? In what ways is some of it not?
17. How is face-to-face communication a means of seeking the confirmation of our self-image?
18. What part do efforts to help listeners "save face" play in oral communication?

PROBLEMS AND EXERCISES

1. Put yourself into a position where you feel out of place and where you seem to be unwanted. List all of the apparent reasons and describe the attitude of those who seemed to be making you unwelcome.
2. Spend an hour in a crowded airport, bus station, auditorium, or similar place observing people and making notes on how they reveal their feelings by means other than speaking.
3. Attend at least three lectures where strangers are speaking. Observe each speaker for as long as possible before he is introduced and write the impressions of him which you get as a result of your observations.
4. When the speaker starts to speak, make a list of all of the visual and oral cues which he uses. Put in separate lists those which seem to help convey his message and those which detract.
5. Observe five or more salesmen as they talk to customers. Write a list of all the evidence which they give as to their honesty and sincerity and a second list to show the opposite.

6. Observe several television performers, noting when they seem not to be communicating directly with you. What are the probable distractions which hinder their direct contact with you?

7. Seat a friend or classmate behind a screen where you cannot see him. (a) Give him instructions on how to arrange a deck of playing cards on a table. Let him ask you questions and question him to be sure he understands your instructions. (b) Perform the same exercise again but do not permit him to talk and do not ask him questions. Do you feel differently during the two exercises? If so, why?

8. Anticipate when you will make another public speaking appearance. Make a checklist of everything you will do, in addition to preparing your speech, which will help you to make it effective. Remember that careful attention to details can help increase your effectiveness.

BIBLIOGRAPHY

Books

BARKER, LARRY L., ed. *Communication Vibrations.* Englewood Cliffs, N. J.: Prentice-Hall, Inc., 1974.

BORMANN, ERNEST G., and BORMANN, NANCY C. *Speech Communication: An Interpersonal Approach.* N. Y.: Harper & Row, Publishers, 1972.

CLARK, TONY; BOCK, DOUG; and CORNETT, MIKE. *Is That You Out There? Exploring Authentic Communication.* Columbus, Ohio: Charles E. Merrill Publishing Company, 1973.

CLEVENGER, THEODORE, JR. *Audience Analysis.* Indianapolis: The Bobbs-Merrill Co., Inc., 1966.

DIETRICH, JOHN E., and BROOKS, KEITH. *Practical Speaking for the Technical Man.* Englewood Cliffs, N. J.: Prentice-Hall, Inc., 1958, chap. 8.

JENSEN, J. VERNON. *Perspectives on Oral Communication.* Boston: Holbrook Press, Inc., 1970, chap. 6.

MARTIN, HOWARD H., and ANDERSON, KENNETH E. *Speech Communication: Analysis and Readings.* Boston: Allyn & Bacon, Inc., 1968.

MONROE, ALAN H., and EHNINGER, DOUGLAS. *Principles of Speech Communication.* 6th brief ed. Glenview, Ill.: Scott, Foresman and Company, 1969.

MURRAY, ELWOOD; PHILLIPS, GERALD M.; and TRUBY, J. DAVID. *Speech: Science—Art.* Indianapolis: The Bobbs-Merrill Co., Inc., 1969.

OLIVER, ROBERT T. *Culture and Communication: The Problem of Penetrating National and Cultural Boundaries.* Springfield, Ill.: Charles C Thomas, Publisher, 1962.

PACE, R. WAYNE; PETERSON, BRENT D.; and RADCLIFFE, TERRENCE R., eds. *Communicating Interpersonally: A Reader.* Columbus, Ohio: Charles E. Merrill Publishing Company, 1973.

PACE, WAYNE, and BOREN, ROBERT R. *The Human Transaction: Facets, Functions, and Forms of Interpersonal Communication.* Glenview, Ill.: Scott, Foresman and Company, 1973.

SANDFORD, WILLIAM PHILLIPS, and YEAGER, WILLIAM HAYES. *Effective Business Speech.* 4th ed. N. Y.: McGraw-Hill Book Company, 1963, chap. 3.

SCHEFLEN, ALBERT E., with SCHEFLEN, ALICE. *Body Language and the Social Order: Communication as Behavioral Control.* Englewood Cliffs, N. J.: Prentice-Hall, Inc., 1972.

WEDGE, BRYANT M. *Visitors to the United States and How They See Us.* Princeton, N. J.: D. Van Nostrand Company, 1965, chap. 8.

WENBURG, JOHN R., and WILMOT, WILLIAM W. *The Personal Communication Process.* N. Y.: John Wiley & Sons, Inc., 1973.

ZELKO, HAROLD P., and DANCE, FRANK E. X. *Business and Professional Speech Communication.* N. Y.: Holt, Rinehart and Winston, Inc., 1965, chap. 3.

Periodicals

ANDERSON, J. "What's Blocking Upward Communications." *Personnel Administration* 31 (January 1968):5–7.

"Body Language: Student and Teacher Behavior." *Saturday Review*, May 1973, p. 78.

CATHY, P. J. "Learn about Egospeak: Why No One Listens to You." *Iron Age* 212 (November 1, 1973):37–38.

DAVIS, FLORA. "How to Read Body Language." *Reader's Digest*, December 1969, pp. 127–30.

———. "The Way We Talk 'Body Language.'" *New York Times Magazine*, May 31, 1970, pp. 8, 9, 29–34, 41–42.

DENNIS, J. M. "When Silence Is Golden." *Supervisory Management* 9 (September 1964):46–47.

GRIKSCHEIT, G. M., and CRISSEY, W. J. E. "Improving Interpersonal Communications Skill." *Michigan State University Business Topics* 21 (Autumn 1973):63–68.

HARGER, H. E. "Three Ways to Send Better." *Business Review* 23 (May 1964):144–48.

KNAPP, MARK L. "Public Speaking Training Programs in American Business & Industrial Organizations." *The Speech Teacher* 18 (March 1969):129–34.

LYNCH, EDITH M. "So You're Going to Run a Meeting." *Quarterly Journal of Speech* 45 (January 1966):22.

MAYER, D. P. "But I Thought You Said." *Supervisory Management* 11 (December 1966):15–19.

MAYFIELD, H. "Silence Can Be Costly, Too." *Supervisory Management* 13 (September 1968):6–7.

MORTON, R. B. "Leveling with Others on the Job." *Personnel* 43 (November 1966):65–70.

NILSEN, THOMAS R. "Interpersonal Communication: A Conceptual Framework." *Central States Speech Journal* 15 (February 1964):31–35.

O'DONNELL, WILLIAM. "The Real Problem in Communications." *Personnel Journal* 46 (January 1967):50.

SCHREIBER, C. "Listening, a Tool That Can Be Harmful in the Wrong Hands." *Stores* 51 (January 1969):40–42.

SHAW, C. "How to Give Oral Instructions." *Office* 60 (December 1964):71–75.

SMITH, DAVID H. "There Is No White Horse: A First Step Toward Improving Communication in Business." *Speech Journal*, Southern Connecticut College 5 (1969):35–38.

"Static in Personal Communications." *Personnel Journal* 44 (May 1965):264–65.

URIS, A. "How to Give Orders That Get Results." *Supervision*, February 1965, pp. 4–6.

WALD, R. M. "Do You Speak the Presidential Tongue." *Business Horizons* 11 (August 1968): 34–36.

WEAVER, CARL H. "The Range of the Communication Act." *Speech Journal*, Southern Connecticut State College 5 (1969):21–28.

"Why Doesn't Anyone Understand Me?" *Supervisory Management* 44 (May 1966):20–21.

YARDLEY, A. "Movement and Learning." *Today's Education* 63 (March 1974):62–64.

Films

"A Matter of Method." A case study to show importance of planning and problem solving. Sixteen minutes, plus two four-minute case studies, color.

"The Rewards of Rewarding." To show psychological behavior techniques for improving personnel relations. Twenty-four minutes, color.

"Time to Think." To be efficient and to progress, the manager must allow himself time for planning. Twenty minutes, color.

All films may be obtained from Roundtable Films, Inc., 113 North San Vicente Boulevard, Beverly Hills, Cal. 90211.

4

Your
Audio Signal

The speech habits which you form as a child continue throughout life. So unchanging are some of them that they may be used to identify you when they are presented by light waves and made visible on the screen of an oscilloscope. Some experimenters insist that one's voice waves are as certain a means of identification as are the lines and whorls on one's fingertips. In short, your voice patterns are unique. They are a part of what makes you an individual.

Because your voice is so self-revealing, it is imperative for you to be in full control of yourself. Attempts to hide anger may be unsuccessful as your voice takes on a strident note. Boredom, illness, or insincerity may be made equally evident, despite all attempts to cover them up, since you have no control over many of the muscles used in speaking, such as those of the viscera or the blood vessels. If you are frightened, much larger quantities of adrenalin are secreted and have an effect on your speaking. As you attempt to communicate, you must keep in mind that all signals are being developed within yourself, and they will tend to divulge your innermost thoughts and feelings. Any attempts to be artificial are prone to reveal themselves for what they are. That is one of the reasons why learning to develop full use of the voice involves a parallel development of the whole personality. Trying to learn a system of vocal tricks will only result in what it is—trickery.

Much about a person is revealed by his voice. Some researchers claim that the human ear is capable of making some ten thousand discriminations in the human voice. We can identify a speaker readily as male or female, young or old, often as to whether he is sick or well, even as to the frame of mind he is in. When a friend calls on the telephone, we usually recognize his voice immediately. If a stranger calls, we begin to form an attitude which may be based as much on the sound of his voice as by the words which he speaks. If the voice sounds like that of a child, we respond as we usually do when speaking to a child. If the caller's voice lacks a nasal tone on certain words, we may inquire if he has a cold. A gruff voice may alarm us; a laughing one puts us at ease. If the stranger speaks with an accent, we may recognize his country of origin. His level of articulation and pronunciation may help us guess rather accurately his level of education. In each case we are establishing a mental picture of the caller. The results are sometimes laughable, as, for instance, when the romantic lady meets for the first time the scrawny little radio announcer whom she has always pictured as "tall, dark, and handsome."

By our voices we are identified by others, and, right or wrong, our listeners develop a mental image of us based in large part upon the sounds they hear as they listen to us talk. Such judgments, of course, can be entirely wrong, since the man with the booming voice may be no more self-assertive than one with an effeminate voice. The woman who speaks with a little-girl voice may be quite mature in all other aspects and quite unaware that her voice does not match the rest of her personality.

Speech—An Overlaid Function

Young love notwithstanding, the lips have only a secondary duty for osculation and the whispering of sweet nothings into pretty ears. The lips' primary duty is to help take in food. The parts of the head, neck, and chest which we label organs of speech have primary functions quite different from the forming of speech sounds. Lungs take in oxygen for the purpose of purifying the blood, removing carbon dioxide in the process. The larynx, or Adam's apple, can close the windpipe when we subject the chest and abdomen to heavy strain as in lifting weights or taking solar plexus blows, or when eating or drinking. The velum, or soft palate, forms a closure with the pharynx for the opening between oral and nasal cavities. Teeth masticate food; the nose admits, warms, and filters air. The tongue, long identified as the primary organ of speech, has as its primary duty the tasting of food and the placing of food between the teeth where it may be chewed. Because speech is an overlaid function, each of us must be taught to talk.

The complexities of the act of speaking make learning it one of our most difficult experiences. By age three most children have learned the basic steps in sound production and articulation. A few difficult sounds, such as that of *r,* may take longer, and such noticeable defects as lisping or stuttering may persist among some ten percent of school children. As the child develops, so do his speech patterns—and his speech problems. Loss of deciduous teeth causes him concern because of whistled *s* sounds. Puberty, with its attendant psychological problems, may cause speech difficulties. Effects of traumatic experiences in childhood often persist into old age.

By the time a person has grown old enough to accept responsibility, he finds that speech involves more than physical action. Mental and psychological dimensions are discovered to be a part of the act. The need for having something to say and an awareness of listener response complicates the act of learning to speak well. A young woman in a speech class spoke bitterly of her professor. "He's unreasonable," she complained. "He expects me to stand up, think, talk, and face an audience all at the same time." For most of us the same hazards exist in our speaking whenever we find ourselves going beyond the confines of idle conversation.

What might be called the raw material of the speech sound is compressed air. Filling the lungs with air is preliminary to all else. Inert in themselves and filled with air sacs, the lungs serve only as containers. As the rib cage is lifted and expanded, a vacuum is created and air rushes in through the nasal passages—oral, too, if the mouth is open—through the bronchial tubes to fill the air sacs of the lungs. Lowering the rib cage and contracting the abdominal muscles puts the air under pressure, causing it to be exhaled. Thus, *respiration,* or breathing, is the first step in producing speech sounds. *Phonation,* or making of sound, occurs as the column of air passes through the larynx, setting in motion the vocal cords. As they approach each other and vibrate, we have a "voiced" sound. Whispering is called "unvoiced." The pharynx and oral cavities serve as *resonators* or *amplifiers,* leaving most of the task of *articulation* to the tongue, teeth, lips, lower jaw, and nose.

This brief description of *respiration, phonation, resonation,* and *articulation* is greatly oversimplified and yet contains the important aspects of speech production. While we speak almost subconsciously, we are setting into action an enormously complex and intricately designed set of nerves, muscles, and cartilages. Failure of any part through injury or disease can result in a speech impediment which may be difficult to overcome. All of us know how violent exercise shortens our breath, making speech impractical as we gasp for air. Loss of the larynx makes ordinary speech impossible, and yet many patients who have undergone a laryngectomy have learned to substitute esophageal speech, using eructations of gas from the stomach as motive power. Other compensations, such as learning to talk with dentures, must be made when nature's design has been imperfect or when disease or accident has caused alteration in our speech apparatus.

Breathing while speaking is quite unlike that done by the singer. The vocal soloist who must sustain long notes may require regular deep breathing. The speaker must inhale frequently as he usually speaks in short, irregular bursts. Lowering of the diaphragm, a muscle which is shaped like an inverted dish, increases the lung capacity, and tightening of the abdominal muscles forces air out. The technique is to take short breaths during momentary pauses, the purpose being to always have an adequate supply of air as muscles are tightened to cause exhalation. Inhaling during the pauses helps to avoid the breaking up of phrases when breath supply is short, which would cause one's meaning to be distorted.

To help control breathing while speaking avoid smoking, wear loose clothing around chest and waist, and exercise often enough to have adequate chest expansion. Hold the upper body erect and avoid clothing that is too tight.

Phonation, the making of sound in the larynx by fluttering of the vocal cords, is a part of the speech act over which we have a relatively small amount of conscious control. The teenage boy, for example, has no forewarning of when his newly developing baritone will break into a shrill soprano squeal. The cords lie crosswise in the windpipe, and their movement toward each other with a sort of vibrating flutter gives us the sound which ultimately develops into intelligible speech.

The *pitch* of people's voices varies because of the difference in length of their vocal cords. Women and children generally have high-pitched voices because of the relative shortness of their vocal cords. Those of men are appreciably longer, resulting in a lower pitch. Because the vocal cords may be moved segmentally, a person can vary his pitch from high to low at will and over the appreciably long range of an octave or more.

Although the cartilages which comprise the larynx are tough, the vocal cords are delicate. Continued abuse of them can cause permanent damage. Sometimes persistent hoarseness or huskiness is caused by nodes forming on them, necessitating surgery and prolonged vocal rest. Throat infections, particularly laryngitis, are another source of danger, and avoidance of speaking until the infection is gone is advisable.

Resonation

Resonation, or amplification of sound, takes place in the pharynx and the rest of the oral cavity. Some control over it may be had by learning to move the tongue and the lower jaw while speaking. An experiment to learn the principles involved can be conducted by holding a tuning fork over bowls of varying sizes and shapes. Variation of size and shape of the bowls will cause a corresponding change in the resonance of the sound of the tuning fork. Grandfathers of today's readers used to put their radio headsets into large cut-glass bowls so that the whole family could listen to their crystal radio sets, the bowls serving as resonating chambers just as the human mouth does as we speak.

Articulation

Usually when we say that someone speaks clearly, and we are referring to his voice, we mean that he is articulating speech sounds precisely. We can distinguish easily the difference when he says *pint* or *pine, just* or *jist, Joyce* or *joist, acidic* or *ascetic*. If he is careless in the use of his articulators, we are apt to ask him to speak more slowly when we should ask, rather, for clearer articulation.

With three exceptions all sounds in the English language are made in the mouth. The sentence, "Men sing," illustrates these three exceptions: *m, n,* and *ng,* these sounds being made through the nose. Someone with "a cold id the head" is afflicted with *de*nasality in contrast to the victim of a cleft palate who must make all sounds through his nose, resulting in the speech impediment called nasality.

In articulating speech sounds, the hard and soft palates, the pharynx, the tongue, the teeth, and both lips play an important part. Misuse of any of them can cause flawed sounds. The sound of *s,* for example, is usually made with the tip of the tongue touching the back of the front teeth. Putting the tongue between the teeth gives us a *th* sound, and if we substitute *th* for *s* we are said to be lisping. Allowing air to escape from the sides of the tongue as we say *s* results in a lateral lisp.

"I wike wabbits" is another example of sound substitution, as is that of the Japanese well-wisher who says: "Rots of ruck." Each of these difficulties arises when the speaker has not learned how to use his tongue or other speech organs to form the sounds he wishes us to hear.

All such problems are capable of correction, the substitution of new speech habits being necessary to supplant those which have been in use previously. The person who misuses his means of articulation should be strongly motivated to take the necessary steps to unlearn the old set of habits and to develop the new. Successful communication depends greatly upon clear articulation.

There are other types of slovenliness which mark faulty articulation. A common one is the omission of a vowel. This is noticeable in such words as

| leg'ble | 'cross | s'pose |
| aud'ble | vis'ted | ad'quate |

Consonants are often omitted. Perhaps the most frequently dropped are *d, t,* and *ng.* (Phoneticians write it as ŋ.)

stan'	jus'	huntin'
soun'	mus'	fishin'
thousan'	las'	somethin'

Other examples of what results when we are guilty of omitting sounds because of slovenly articulation are as follows:

r l k	*n*	*v*
gene'ally	permane't	gimme
a'right	*th*	*h*
a'cept	fift'	must'uv

Pronunciation

Closely allied to articulation is *pronunciation,* the giving of a particular accentual pattern to words. A main part of the act of pronouncing words is the putting of stress on one or more syllables. In pronouncing *Detroit,* for example, we put stress correctly on the second syllable. While there are often several ways of pronouncing a word, there is usually one which is preferred by the educated people of a community or one which is determined by the meaning of the word. *Dee'-pot* is commonly heard, but *dep'-o* is the generally preferred pronunciation of the word *depot.* Those who dream of Venice and her canals say *gon'-dola,* accenting the first syllable, but railroaders, picturing a certain type of freight car, stress the second syllable, saying *gon-dol'a.* Both pronunciations, of course, are acceptable at their time and place. Linguists help us with our pronunciations by emphasizing that spoken language takes precedence over written language and all arbitrary rules.

Speakers are judged as much by their pronunciation as by their grammar, listeners consciously or unconsciously ascribing faults in accenting words, or in making similar errors, to ignorance, slovenliness, or lack of preparation. The person who habitually says *dese, dere, dem,* or *dose* will be automatically classified as semiliterate. Saying *stastistics* may give the impression that your knowledge of statistics is as faulty as your pronunciation.

The omission of certain sounds mars otherwise good pronunciation. Do you give full value to all of the sounds in such a word as *government* or does it sound in your speaking as if spelled *guvment? Ast* is often substituted for *asked* and the *g* sound omitted from *recognized* or *length.* All are examples of the speech of the semiliterate.

Conversely, such people often add sounds which do not belong in the words they use. For them *grievance* becomes *griev-e-ance, athlete* is *athalete, film* is *fillum,* and *twice* is *twicet.* Incidentally, as you have been reading this section have you noticed that there is no *noun* in *pronunciation?*

There are three generally agreed-upon dialects in the United States —Eastern, General American, and Southern—with innumerable variations among them. The preferred pronunciation of a word will vary from one to another. *Route* may be pronounced to rhyme with *rout* in one locality but with *root* in another close by. *Either* and *neither* may be pronounced *eyether* and *nyether* by some, but others will look upon such pronunciation with the disdain which they reserve for those who say *tomahto.* Whatever is acceptable as good regional or dialectical speech may be considered proper for that area. Only when a person seeks employment on the stage or in the broadcast media may a regional dialect with its differences in pronunciation become a severe handicap.

The pronunciation of proper names presents a special problem. Natives of Calais, Maine, pronounce the name to rhyme with Dallas, while those on the Ontario side of the Canadian border sound it as though it were spelled *Callay.* Berlin, Germany, has its accent on the second syllable when spoken by most Americans, yet Berlin, New Hampshire, is called *Ber'-lin* by its Yankee inhabitants. Residents of Versailles, Pennsylvania, disregard the French *Vair-sye* and give their borough's name as it is spelled. The name *Lutz* looks easy to pronounce but can vary from *Luts* to *Loots* to *Loo-its.* In short, try not to rely on spelling or lifelong habits in your pronunciation of names of people or places as you make new acquaintances or travel to new places. The preferred pronunciation may be quite different from the one which you deduce as the correct one.

Because spoken English is a dynamic, growing language, differences in pronunciation will continue to exist. What is popular and considered to be "correct" in one generation for the pronunciation of a word may well be passé by the time our children enter college. This phenomenon has become even more noticeable as the study of structural linguistics becomes more popular and dictionary editors *describe* spoken language instead of *prescribing* it.

Vocal Variety

VOLUME   "Louder, please," comes the voice from the back row to the speaker who is content to reach only a part of his audience. Actors practice until even their stage whispers can be heard in the last seat of the top balcony.

Deny it though we may, those of us over forty have nearly all suffered some hearing loss. Certain sounds which we once heard clearly are now denied to us unless sharply amplified. Such people may accuse us of "swallowing our words" or of dropping our voices at the ends of sentences. Sometimes, when we look at notes or turn to use charts or chalk boards, we forget to increase our volume, thus giving reason for part of our speaking not to be heard.

In most situations, distracting sounds make hearing difficult. Traffic, transistor radios, jet planes, clacking typewriters, and the talking of others contribute to our difficulty in hearing. Each extraneous sound claims our attention or drowns out the sounds which we are trying to hear.

Each speaker must recognize that he may have distance, slight deafness in his listeners, or competing sounds to overcome. Consequently, he should assure himself that his volume is great enough for easy audibility. If the listener doesn't hear, it is primarily the responsibility of the speaker to make it possible for him to do so. This is particularly true when the listener's interest is not at a high level. Relying on the listener to take steps to be able to hear better is too much for us to expect of him. An inattentive listener has a ready excuse for not responding as we want by simply saying, "I couldn't hear you."

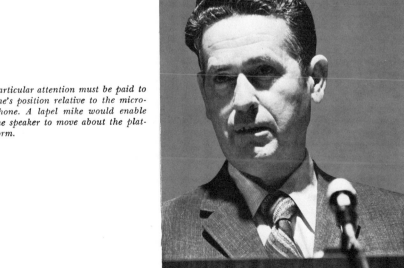

Particular attention must be paid to one's position relative to the microphone. A lapel mike would enable the speaker to move about the platform.

Recognizing that his first duty is to keep his volume high enough to be heard is the speaker's obvious responsibility. Keeping his volume high and at one level can soon cause monotony. Plenty of variety in his decibel count can help to overcome a speaker's voice when it is consistently set at one level of monotonous loudness. One's range can be from a whisper loud enough to be heard by everyone present to a shout which may startle even the most inattentive. The speaker who notes sleepy people before him can often regain their attention with a few words of his lecture effectively shouted.

Regular patterns, such as beginning each sentence in a loud voice and letting it dwindle to a low volume near its end, are to be avoided. Any form of regularity may become monotonous. Variety in volume must be achieved by the unexpected—the whispered word among several shouted ones or the series of words or phrases beginning in a low voice and rising steadily in volume until the last one is ultraloud—if it is to have a desirable effect on the audience. "First it whispers, then it shouts" was once the advertising slogan for a popular alarm clock. A speaker should remember it as a guide to increasing his vocal variety. Exciting events lose their flavor when spoken in whispers; shouting is useless for confidential speaking. And yet both have their place in conversation or in more formal speech. Try increasing volume the next time members of your audience begin to yawn.

RATE   Whether we are considered as fast or slow talkers is determined by the number of words which we speak per minute. As a convenient, but probably inaccurate, way of expressing it, we say that we speak at an average of 125 to 150 words per minute, but many of us are capable of bursts of speaking intelligibly at 300 or more words per minute. The ear and mind can assimilate information at a much higher rate. An experiment at Michigan State University well illustrates how much quicker is the ear than the voice. By means of the magic of a tape recorder a fifty-five–minute lecture was condensed to occupy but seven and one-half minutes. Two groups then listened, one to the longer, the other to the shorter version. Tests for comprehension showed no significant difference between the two groups.

Monotony of rate, or monorate, comes when a speaker sticks to approximately the same number of words each minute that he speaks. The effect is as deadening on his listeners as is any other monotonous practice. Long continued, a monorate can assure inattention with subsequent misunderstanding. Varying one's rate irregularly from ultraslow to ultrafast can make listening easier and more interesting. The pause may be used with telling effect as a way of overcoming one's monorate. Having a lengthy pause—two or three seconds—come after a burst of speed can help to assure better attention.

In contrast to writing, where space separates words, in speech we utter phrases. "Howdoyoudo?" we ask; or we say, "I'mgoingdowntown." Of course it's hard to read when the words are run together, but when spoken as a single phrase, we get instant comprehension. The speaking of single words makes understanding difficult.

Putting pauses in the right places to assure ease of comprehension is known as *phrasing*. In speaking, it has about the same function as punctuation has in writing. With suitable phrasing we enhance our meaning. Witness this sentence as spoken by a business executive: "Send me a man who reads." Do you believe that but one meaning can be taken from it? Speak the sentence as a spinster might: "Send me a man (pause) who reads?" Here is another: "The teacher said: 'The boy is a dunce.' " Now try rephrasing it by putting pauses after "teacher" and "boy."

Meanings may be as easily distorted by the speaker who reads a poem and pauses at the end of every line or who pauses the same way while reading a speech which is not typed on the page for easy reading. To be able to phrase properly while reading requires careful attention to meaning and to punctuation. "Mind your stops" was the order of the nineteenth-century teacher to his classes in oral reading. "Phrase your speech carefully," his twentieth-century counterpart advises.

PITCH   While most of us can range from alto to soprano or from bass to tenor, too many of us are content to be Jenny or Johnny One Note. From *monotone* we derive the word *monotonous* which aptly describes entirely too many of our speaking voices. Speakers who use monotones are often amazed to discover that a wide range on the musical scale is possible. The late Eleanor Roosevelt lived to middle age before she learned to vary her pitch from its squeaky and monotonous soprano range to a more agreeable series of levels. The business or professional man who studiously avoids changing his pitch imagines himself as being suitably serious, usually not realizing that he is but portraying monotony.

To get variety in pitch one must learn first what his normal range from high to low is. Usually a comfortable range is at least a half octave higher and a half octave lower than we habitually speak. Training is needed to help us change our habits so as to be able to use the complete range of which we are capable.

A high pitch used while speaking can help portray excitement; a low one can be soothing. Each can be equally impressive when used to seek variety after a series of phrases all spoken on the same pitch. Questions normally begin on a low level, rising to a higher one to indicate that an answer is expected. Statements which begin and end on approximately the same pitch tend to show an air of finality or certainty. In between, especially if the sentence is a long one, there may be much variety. Clauses, for instance, often should end on a higher note to indicate that there is more to follow.

To avoid monotony in speaking by seeking variety in volume, rate, and pitch, beginners are advised to practice on them separately. When volume can be varied from soft to low at will, without necessarily changing pitch, it is time to try learning how to vary one's rate. Developing the ability to vary pitch from high to low is perhaps most difficult of all, especially if one has no ear for music. Yet, a varied pitch is possible to achieve, and a necessity if one is to develop to the fullest extent his capacity as an interesting, easy-to-listen-to speaker.

EMPHASIS   When a person writes, he may capitalize words, underline them, use exclamation points, or insert cartoons or other illustrations to emphasize his meaning. A speaker to achieve emphasis has only his voice to rely on. It is an instrument of wide range, capable of a myriad of nuances of meaning.

"The pause that impresses" is a paraphrase of a famous soft-drink slogan. A pause not only helps to make one's meaning clear, but when used before an important statement, it can alert the audience to what is to follow. When used afterward, it gives the listener time to appraise what has just been said. When the listener has been paying close attention, he appreciates the momentary rest afforded by the pause in what he is hearing. A pause can also be useful to a speaker, giving him time to consider what to say next or to reorient himself.

Once a newly elected senator invited his family and several friends to sit in the balcony to hear his maiden speech on the floor of the senate. As he spoke he used all of his power. Reaching a high point in his speech he flung out one arm, crying: "Consider, Mr. Chairman. . . ." Then his mind went blank—as can happen to any speaker, veteran as well as amateur—as he paused with arm outstretched. During the few seconds' pause, which to the senator seemed like hours, his mind began to function again, and he was able to proceed. Afterward when his family and friends gathered to congratulate him, one of them said: "Senator, all of your speech was impressive, but the part that struck me most forcibly was where you paused with your hand outstretched, waiting to be sure that all of us would listen to what you would say next." Pauses in your speaking can be equally impressive to your listeners.

Caution: Avoid looking distressed as you pause and avoid such "word whiskers" as "uh," "er," "why-a," and the particularly annoying "you know." Calling attention to the pause distorts its meaning and detracts from the message which you intend to convey.

Variation of volume can be equally impressive. As the massive type of a newspaper's headlines compels our attention, so does the full volume of one's voice emphasize what is being uttered. Equally impressive is the small paragraph set in italics or the great truth spoken in a voice that is barely audible. Just as the glaring headlines when too often repeated lose their effect, so does the consistently loud voice or the one which continues at a barely audible level. To be impressive and to make it serve as oral punctuation, the speaker should vary his vocal volume to suit the meaning which he wishes to emphasize. To reach a climax, his voice may rise to a crescendo or drop to a softly muted sound. The method to be used will depend upon the speaker's aims, his material, and the listener.

Similarly, changes in rate can be used as a way of stressing meanings. To emphasize an important thought, speed up your rate. When the new statements follow several spoken at a slow rate, your listener will strain his attention to be sure to hear what you are saying. But keep in mind that people will not care to continue long under such strain. Vary the rate to give emphasis to your meaning. Couple the variety of rate with a discreet use of pause for the most profitable effect.

Raising the pitch of one's voice tends to emphasize the word or phrase spoken at the higher level. Combining the change in pitch with increased volume or force makes the change doubly effective. Women, in particular, should avoid allowing the voice to become shrill as the pitch is heightened for effect. As with changes in rate and volume, the use of variety in pitch is to stress one's meaning and to increase the effect of the message being communicated. To achieve vocal variety requires practice so that its use becomes nearly automatic; otherwise, attempts at using it will seem artificial and unconvincing to the listener. As you speak, your voice is conveying two messages to your listener: one of them is by sound, the other by the words which are spoken.

What you put into your voice can convey a sense of warmth or the lack of it, a sense of friendliness or austerity. By the vocal variety you use, you can not only entice your listeners to pay attention, but you can move them emotionally. Unconsciously, as they listen to you, they will be subjectively reacting to the sounds that you make, quite apart from the meaning which your words have for them. The development of all of your vocal abilities gives you a greater ability in all of your oral communication and increases the influence which you seek to assert.

Suggestions for Using Audio Aids

(For suggestions for using visual aids see Chapter 4.)

1. Instead of reading a quotation, use a tape recording of your authority's own words.
2. To recall with nostalgia the "good old days" play a record of railroad locomotive, steamboat, old auto, or farm sounds.
3. For illustrations to be used in your speech make recordings of suitable sounds or of conversations. Recordings are useful in presenting crowd noises, varying dialects, "man on the street" opinions, or the testimony of experts.
4. Use "voices from the past," such as those of Caruso, Theodore Roosevelt, Franklin Roosevelt, Edward R. Murrow's "I Can Hear It Now" records.
5. Use musical selections to enhance or illustrate what is being said.
6. Record and replay excerpts from a business conference to increase effectiveness and reliability of your own ideas.
7. Be sure that you or an assistant learns in advance how to use audio-visual equipment, such as record players, tape recorders, or projectors.
8. Set up and test all equipment at the speaking site before the audience is present.
9. Mark tapes, records, or films so as to be able to find quickly the parts to be heard.
10. Assemble in advance the equipment to be used, such as a clarinet. Tune stringed instruments.
11. Use additional amplifiers whenever necessary.
12. Instruct listeners as to what they are about to hear and use suitable transitions both before and after they listen.
13. Be careful to synchronize with the audio aid being used whatever you say, do, or show.
14. Repeat for emphasis the use of audio aids whenever advantageous.

Conclusion

Our voices serve as a positive means of identification since the patterns we learn as children remain with us all of our lives. What we call organs of speech have primary functions in breathing and eating. For that reason, children must be taught to speak.

The act of speaking involves *respiration* to insure us a supply of air, *phonation* as the outward flow of air sets into motion our vocal cords, *resonation,* or amplification of sound, in the oral and nasal cavities, and *articulation,* or shaping of sound, so as to make our words intelligible to listeners.

Because our voices are capable of an infinite variety of tones in expressing our moods and thoughts, we must learn to develop all of the means of vocal variety. The principal ways in which we can vary our voices are in volume, rate, and pitch. Each of these can be used in making the sound of our voices more interesting to the audience and also for the purpose of emphasizing what we believe to be the most important parts of what is being said.

Because we have no means of control over part of the organs of speech, we may inadvertently and unconsciously reveal through our voices some feelings which we would prefer to hide. Hence, our voices are powerful deterrents to being insincere or untruthful.

FOR DISCUSSION

1. What features of our voices distinguish us from other persons?
2. What constitutes a "dialect"?
3. What are the major differences between Eastern, General American, and Southern dialects?
4. What are some of the different variations in each?
5. What are the characteristics of your speech patterns?
6. What relationships are there between one's speech and his personality?
7. Why must a child be taught to speak?
8. Why should we, or should we not, give credence to the statement: "Anyone who has something to say can say it, therefore teaching speech is unnecessary"?
9. In what way does good speech depend upon breath control?
10. How do the vocal cords perform their function?
11. What are some of the characteristics of the resonation process?
12. What are some of the common precautions to take to assure clear articulation?
13. What is the value of vocal variety in volume, rate, and pitch?
14. What effective ways are there of using the voice for emphasis?
15. How can the voice betray our inner feelings?
16. How is the "correct" pronunciation of words determined?

PROBLEMS AND EXERCISES

1. Make a recording of your voice. With the help of your instructor or other qualified person, make an analysis of it. Can you explain why most people say of a recording: "That doesn't sound like me"?
2. Choose someone whose voice you admire and make a list of all of the qualities which make his voice admirable.
3. Read a selection of 100 or so words using first a loud volume, next a

medium, then a low volume. (Use a tape recording for the best results.)

4. Do the same in varying rates of speaking.

5. Through the use of pauses, read these sentences with as many different meanings as possible: (a) Our forefathers were passionate believers in freedom. (b) The father said to his sons Saddle me the ass.

6. By changing your pitch, give as many different interpretations as possible to this sentence: People understand me.

7. Recite the alphabet using all forms of vocal variety of which you are capable.

8. To discover the range of your natural pitch strike middle C on the piano. In unison with the sound *speak* up the scale as high as you *comfortably* can, then speak down the scale as far as you can *comfortably*. For practice read a poem of several short stanzas, first stanza at your highest pitch, next at lowest, continuing to alternate. Continue to practice until you can change easily from one pitch level to another at will. Check your progress with the tape recorder.

9. Have someone check your next speech or conversation and make a list of all false pauses and all vocalized pauses.

10. Listen to your instructor or other speaker and note all of the means by which he gets vocal emphasis for what he says.

11. Go to a courtroom or other place where persons are speaking under stress and note what their voices seem to portray.

12. Listen to popular radio or television performers and determine what vocal characteristics help to make them popular.

BIBLIOGRAPHY

Books

BLACK, JOHN W., and MOORE, WILBUR E. *Speech: Code, Meaning, and Communication.* N. Y.: McGraw-Hill Book Company, 1955, chaps. 2, 3, 4.

FAIRBANKS, GRANT. *Voice and Articulation Drillbook.* New York and London: Harper and Brothers, 1940.

HAHN, ELISE; LOMAS, CHARLES W.; HARGIS, DONALD E.; and DRAGON, DANIEL VAN. *Basic Voice Training for Speech.* N. Y.: McGraw-Hill Book Company, 1957.

JESSEL, GEORGE. *The Toastmaster General's Guide to Successful Speaking.* N. Y.: Hawthorn Books, Inc., 1969.

JUDSON, LYMAN, and WEAVER, A. T. *Voice Science.* N. Y.: Appleton-Century-Crofts, 1940.

POTTER, R. K.; KOPP, G. A.; and GREEN, H. C. *Visible Speech.* N. Y.: D. Van Nostrand Company, 1947.

OLIVER, ROBERT T.; ZELKO, HAROLD P.; and HOLTZMAN, PAUL D. *Communicative Speaking and Listening.* 4th ed. N. Y.: Holt, Rinehart and Winston, Inc., 1968, pp. 189–200.

RIZZO, RAYMOND. *The Voice as an Instrument.* N. Y.: Odyssey Press, 1969.

WEAVER, CARL H., and STRAUSBAUGH, WARREN L. *Fundamentals of Speech Communication.* N. Y.: American Book Company, 1964, chap. 11.

WILCOX, ROGER P. *Oral Reporting in Business and Industry.* Englewood Cliffs, N. J.: Prentice-Hall, Inc., 1967, pp. 284–95.

WISEMAN, GORDON, and BARKER, LARRY. *Speech: Interpersonal Communication.* San Francisco: Chandler Publishing Company, 1967, pp. 224–31.

Periodicals

BECKER, S. W. "Personality and Effective Communication in the Organization." *Personnel Administration* 27 (July 1964):28–30.

BOWERS, JOHN WAITE. "The Influence of Delivery on Attitudes Toward Concepts and Speakers." *Speech Monographs* 32 (June 1965):154.

———. "Some Correlates of Language Intensity." *Speech Monographs* 1 (December 1964).

BRODNITZ, FREIDRICH. "The Holistic Study of the Voice." *Quarterly Journal of Speech* 48:280.

CARLIN, T. W. "Making a Speech? Here's How to Put It Over." *Supervisory Management* 11 (April 1966):54–56.

"Improving Oral Communications." *Administrative Management* 26 (May 1965):16.

LONG, L. M. "Plea for the Spoken Word." *Supervision* October 1963, pp. 22–23.

NEWMAN, JOHN B. "The Linguistic View of the Voice." *Speech Teacher* 12 (November 1963):299–303.

PETERSON, GORDON E. "Some Observations on Speech." *Quarterly Journal of Speech* 44 (December 1958):402.

RASMUS, WARD. "Voice and Diction: Historical Perspective." *Quarterly Journal of Speech* 47 (October 1961):253–61.

SMITH, DONALD K. "Teaching Speech to Facilitate Understanding." *The Speech Teacher* 11 (March 1962):91.

5

Whosoever hath a good presence
and a good fashion carries continual
letters of recommendation.
Francis Bacon

Your
Video Signal

From the moment a speaker appears, his audience begins to react to his appearance. The bum begging for a quarter for a "cuppa cawfee" may incite disgust with his filthy clothes, bleary eyes, and unshaved chin. Or evidences that he has seen better days may lead his listener to pity and attendant generosity. Some people have the reputation for voting according to a candidate's looks more than to what he says. Right or wrong, we tend to judge people by the first impression that they make upon us. Any uncertainty or awkwardness, unusual table manners, or distinctly different style of dress will instantly help us form an opinion—good or bad—that will persist in our minds. The hippies, for instance, without their regulation garb of outlandish clothes, sandals or bare feet, and generally dirty appearance would cause little immediate reaction, favorable or otherwise, among those more conventionally attired. "Clothes make the man" may well be an untrue statement, but that clothes do help to cause a reaction in the observer is undeniable. Even in a day when many of us are accustomed to great informality in dress, as well as other aspects of living, we continue to be judged on our appearance. In fact, appearance is considered to be a rather accurate key to our personality.

70

Clothing

For most speaking engagements, either public or private, the speaker should be groomed with great care. Personal cleanliness is appreciated and expected by most listeners, regardless of their own habits. Men are expected to have their hair neatly combed, regardless of what style of cut they fancy. Beards or mustaches must be carefully trimmed. In most situations extremes of any sort will be a distraction, whether in hair or clothing. Dress that attracts attention to itself prevents the listener from regarding fully what is being said. Choose the type of clothing that is best suited to the occasion. Sport clothes may be quite appropriate for a job interview on a golf course but most inappropriate in an office. Even in hot weather, a jacket, white shirt, and tie are appropriate for an appearance before a luncheon club.

Women notably, and usually effectively, spend much time and expense on their appearance. A major test for appropriateness in dress is whether it suits the occasion. High style in clothing or hairdos that is suitable for a woman who is attending a banquet is out of place if she is to be a speaker at the same banquet. Large earrings, jangling bracelets, or jewelry which may evoke stares can effectively detract from what the woman speaker says in nearly any speaking situation. As she is preparing to be a speaker, she must remember that her appearance will have a profound effect upon her listeners, and she should dress accordingly.

The speaker's clothing must not attract undue attention to itself unless it is to become a part of the speech. To the burlesque comedian the baggy pants and gaudy plaid coat are necessary to enhance the ridiculousness of his humor. Neatly-fitted, conservative clothing for the serious speaker forms a sort of frame which suits the conventions and allows what he says to become dominant in the listener's mind.

Gaudy suits, flashy ties, and loudly-patterned shirts can be as distracting to listeners as are the noises of passing traffic or loud-ringing telephones. What is written here was composed after careful consideration of the current liberal attitude toward individual choice of costume. One's attire needs to be chosen with thought on how one's listeners may react to it.

Distractions can be caused by one's surroundings. What is present to divert the listener's attention? In the theatre, babies and animals are notorious scene-stealers. Any moving object near the speaker will command more of the auditor's attention than the oral message in which he is supposed to be interested. Such objects as clocks, calendars, or pictures have a distracting effect if placed so they and the speaker can be seen at the same time. "Busy" backgrounds with pictures or drawings distract. Open windows take attention from the speaker.

Facial Expression

Let your face reflect your innermost thoughts as you speak. Your facial expression should reveal to your listener almost as much about your topic as your words do. A theological seminary professor advised his students: "Let your face express your thoughts. For example, when you are preaching about heaven look happy and joyous. If preaching about hell it's all right to assume your normal expression." His advice emphasizes both the need to suit your facial expression to what is being said and to vary it to suit changes of mood and of subject matter. Some speakers who object to this philosophy, justifying their unchanging dour expression by saying that they are discussing serious matters, should realize that what appears to them to be deadly serious may seem mordantly monotonous to the listener who has to keep watching their deadpan expression.

Stance

The speaker who looks alert has an erect carriage whether sitting or standing. He keeps his back straight and his shoulders level. If standing, weight is distributed evenly on his feet and usually one foot is slightly advanced of the other to improve his balance. On the podium he avoids leaning on chair or lectern so as to free his hands for gesture and to permit easy bodily movement. The chin is held high to avoid constricting sensitive throat muscles and to permit close eye contact with listeners.

"The speaker stands with easy grace" in a manner which looks "natural" to his audience, although to the man accustomed to slumping or leaning against wall or table it may feel most unnatural. To appear natural he avoids any exaggerated posture such as the military "attention" or the "sitting-on-the-spine, feet-on-desk" pose of the tired office worker.

Bodily Action

As with all other movement, bodily action is to be used to supplement or illustrate whatever one is saying. In other words, all movement must seem to the listener to be motivated by the message which he is receiving. If he does not see the relationship between movement and message, he becomes confused. Apparently aimless walking is one example that will cause confusion, and yet it is frequently done by otherwise able speakers. Such distracting mannerisms can be overcome by assigning trusted friends or members of one's family to watch for them and to signal when they occur.

However, taking a few steps while speaking may be an advantage. When we change from one thought to another in writing, we skip a space and indent the next line, beginning its first word with a capital letter. A similar effect in speaking may be gained by the speaker's pausing, then taking a step or two to another spot on the podium before beginning his next point. Listeners may appreciate being able to see him from a new vantage point. Some speakers find it a help both to themselves and their audience to move away from the lectern so as to be able to gesture freely when their message dictates movement.

From studies made of successful business and professional people, bigness, especially in height, seems to be an advantage. Yet the advantage can be neutralized by faulty stance, such as stooped shoulders and awkward slouch, or by seeming to feel ill at ease.

Remember that any recommendations for using any parts of the body as physical reinforcement for what is said should be *adapted* rather than *adopted*. All sense of what is appropriate in dress, in facial expression, bodily action, and gestures by head and hands must come from within the speaker. Learning any of them by rote or consciously practicing them by themselves will not guarantee their effectiveness for use in conveying meanings. One must develop them so that they are used spontaneously. To be completely successful you must be like the speaker who, when praised for his vigorous, helpful gestures, exclaimed: "But I wasn't aware of using any."

Another man who spoke while standing "at attention," his hands immobile at his sides, defended his inaction by throwing up both arms in an expression of helplessness, saying: "I can't gesture when I speak." Next he pounded the table, shouting, "Gestures are wholly foreign to my nature." His experience serves to illustrate the phenomenon that we are usually most expressive when we are not aware of "making a speech" but tend to be at our best when we are eager to *communicate* our thoughts to others. Specialists in the theory of communication speak of the first situation as being "prestructured" and the latter as "semistructured." While this might be thought of as an argument for always speaking impromptu, it is a stronger argument for preparing yourself emotionally as well as intellectually in order to be able to use all of your physical powers while speaking.

Since the impulse to use gestures comes quickly, have the hands and arms free to respond. Sew up your pockets if you must learn to let your hands fall free at your sides. If lecturing, stand a half pace away from the lectern so as not to be tempted to grasp its sides. Without the hands free, speakers are apt to twitch elbows, hunch shoulders, or attempt to point with their chins as the urge to gesture arises.

Unmotivated gestures to avoid are the front handclasp, folded arms, or hands clasped over the hips. Perhaps the military influence may account for the latter, because one of the first lessons taught in military science is that a soldier should never make an advance without protecting his rear.

In advising you to keep your hands out of the positions enumerated, the purpose is not to set up rules which are to be blindly followed. It is, rather, to help the speaker learn to "talk with his hands," to supplement what he is saying, to keep his hands in position where they will be useful to his purpose in speaking. Each of the gestures described, from hands in the pockets to the rear handclasp, may readily be a supplement to what is being said. For instance, you might say "Reach into your coat pocket" or "Stand at ease," suiting your gestures to what you say. In all instances, follow the principle of using your hands to supplement and enforce what you say rather than merely expressing such an arbitrary rule as "Hold your hands at your sides."

To be effective as physical reinforcement, all gestures must be spontaneous, not a movement which is practiced in advance. Spontaneous gestures are timed to the split second; practiced gestures may come too soon or too late and so distract. The person who points, then says, "Over there," confuses his listener. One of the reasons that we laugh at a clown is because his timing is off, coming always just too soon or too late.

Such mannerisms as twisting a finger ring, buttoning or unbuttoning one's coat, holding a pen or pencil, scratching nose or chin, smoking, or rattling the change in one's pocket seem unnatural or unmotivated to the audience and should be avoided.

Among some of the good things which we have inherited from the nineteenth-century elocutionists are certain universal gestures, such as pointing, giving or receiving, rejecting, clenching the fist, cautioning, and dividing, which are generally understood regardless of the language being spoken.

Use the index finger rather than the whole hand for pointing, especially when referring to a map or chart. The open hand with palm upward illustrates giving or receiving, such as when you are offering aid or asking for support. Emphasize rejection by a sweep of the hand away from you with the palm down. We associate the clenched fist with threats or anger, and it suits violent statements admirably. Watch the policeman's upraised hand with palm facing you to denote caution. You may caution your listeners in the same way. Division may be shown by separating the hands as they are held before your chest.

The success of these and all other gestures in physical reinforcement of your efforts at interpersonal communication depends upon how graphic you make them. They must seem to the viewer to be a part of you and your message, not to call attention to themselves as separate signs, but to blend into the thoughts which you are expressing. They must illustrate the equation that one plus one equals, not two, but one—one word plus one gesture equals one impact on the listener. A technical term which well describes the effect desired is *monochromism*.

To the question of how many gestures should be used, the answer is to use as many as will properly reinforce the message being transmitted. People with a Latin- or Gallic-type temperament are apt to use many gestures, most of them highly meaningful. Those who are more placid or phlegmatic are prone to use fewer. The layman's advice, "Don't use your hands so much," might better be: "Gesture, don't gesticulate. Make your hand movements supplement and enforce what you say." Fewer gestures, well placed and emphatic, are more effective than many diffuse gestures.

Codes Represent Meaning

In any interpersonal communication, your message is conveyed by the code or codes which you use. A code is a system of symbols representing meanings which, presumably, both you as the encoder and your auditor as the decoder will understand. The *sounds* which you make represent one code. The *signs* which you make represent another. Your purpose is to strive to amplify with your visual code the same message which you give with the auditory code. That is the whole principle upon which our discussion of facial expression, bodily action, and gesture has been based. Despite one's best efforts, some aspects of the visual code will be misinterpreted, just as will parts of the auditory code, since we are making a multiband presentation. And yet we can, and must, keep trying to seek complete and accurate understanding. For that reason we should discipline ourselves not only to speak accurately and well but also to develop full control over our bodies in order to make sure that our visual code may be as accurately decoded as our audible code.

Someone has estimated that approximately eighty-four percent of our audience will understand some seventy-six percent of what we say. By learning to use all of our physical and mental abilities, we perhaps can increase, to our profit, the size of these percentages.

The Listener's Code

The listener's part of the circular response must be carefully observed by the speaker so that he may react to it profitably. What he hears may be exceedingly important, but what he can see may tell him even more accurately what his listener is thinking. One who slumps in his chair, staring dully at the speaker, may say, "I'm interested," but his actions— his visual code—belie his words.

Perhaps the man who looks at his watch while we are speaking, winds it, then holds it to his ear, is impolite. However, he doesn't need to tell us that his mind is not concentrating on what we are saying. He is as inattentive as his neighbor who reads his newspaper or their seatmate who is napping. All of these are gross symbols used by the encoders to let us know that the circle of communication has been broken, that the message may not even be reaching the ears of those for whom it is intended.

Other less gross signs to look for are uneasy body movements as though the seats were uncomfortable, toying with eyeglasses, seemingly impatient looks to one side or the other, staring at a fixed spot away from the speaker, following with the eyes any movement away from the speaker (such as the antics of a cameraman), or smiling at the small child who has attracted attention. Each of these can indicate to the speaker the need for changing his tactics so as to reestablish the circular response.

At a meeting of church fathers, the problem of parishioners sleeping during church services was brought up. One man halfheartedly suggested that they should go back to the colonial custom of having a beadle, an officer armed with a stick and charged with the duty of keeping people awake. Immediately the preacher expressed approval, saying that he could name a half dozen who ought to be poked.

"Oh, that wasn't what I intended," the maker of the suggestion explained. "I would want to have the beadle use his stick on you every time that he saw someone asleep."

When a speaker has but one listener at a time to talk with, his task of observing visual symbols is greatly decreased. Not only is his field of observation narrow, but it is much closer. Signs made by the face, such as frowns, changing expression of the eyes, hand movements, or shifting of the feet may be easily seen. If interpreted correctly, they can be of great benefit in revealing to the speaker the course of action which he should follow in making his speech effective.

Learn from Observation

What does an interesting conversationalist do with his body as he talks? Watch him, and you'll see that he is wholly involved in what he is saying. He looks alert because he is totally active, a necessary condition for successful thinking. His face is mobile, changing quickly from smile to frown, to smirk to expression of horror. The eyes roll, they wink, they

blink. The jaw opens wide or shuts with a snap. The head shakes in disbelief or nods in approval. Shoulders shrug to denote uncertainty or shake
with laughter as the belly quivers. The thigh-slapping joke brings the
hands into play and the torso rolls forward. Hands go to the knees, and
perhaps the feet leave the floor only to return with a bang of satisfaction.
Such a speaker is successful largely because *his mind is on his subject and
not on himself.*

Even as the expert conversationalist listens, he remains alert. His
body may seem to be at rest momentarily, and yet when the mind is impressed by what enters the ear, the listener sits erect, head raised, eyes
focused on the speaker. A hand may go to the chin or to the top of his
head. These movements, and many more, are repeated in infinite variety.

Such people are as they are because their minds are alert, engaging
in an activity which energizes their whole being. In contrast, we have the
person who seems to recite what he has learned; he speaks dully while his
mind is active on other matters. With a deadpan expression he drones on,
seemingly oblivious to those about him, and even to what he is saying.

Observation of both types can show you the heights to strive for and
the depths to avoid.

Empathy

As you are seated in the stadium enjoying the big game of the
season, you see the quarterback on your team fade back to pass. He hesi-
tates, unable to find a receiver who is free. Just as an opponent is about
to tackle him, the passer darts through an opening, straight-arms an opponent, falls in step behind a teammate, and is off for a ninety-yard touchdown run. Before you realize it, you are on your feet cheering lustily.
What brought you off your seat is *empathy.* As you perceived the action
on the field, you felt it. To put it into psychology terms: "Perception is a
participating function." You feel empathy with one or the other, depending on your sympathies, when you see a policeman use his nightstick on
a rioter. You empathize with the "good guys" as you watch a horse opera
on television. When you hear music or view sculpture or stand before the
Lincoln Memorial in Washington, your reactions are determined largely
by your likes or dislikes. Although you may be completely unconscious of
how you are responding, empathy has a deep and abiding effect on your
behavior. Empathy is an unusually strong determinant, and the wise
speaker seeks it in his audience.

Listeners tend to imitate the speaker. With his physical movements
he must set the kind of example with which he wants them to empathize.
Lack of physical action serves to quiet the audience physically and, ul-

timately, mentally. So if you want to put your audience to sleep, be as immobile as possible. While they may seem to be absorbing what is said, the chances are that little of it will remain in their thoughts.

All distracting movements elicit fitful, distracting responses. "Don't let him move that microphone again," an annoyed listener prays after the speaker has "adjusted" the mike for perhaps the tenth time. "If he would only stop smoking," another vainly wishes. Their empathetic reactions are destructive of the speaker's chosen aims.

To profit by the empathy of the listener, the speaker uses the kind of action which communicates the thoughts he wants his listener to have. A speaker was called on to address a college audience on a hot July afternoon. Arriving at the assembly room, he discovered that a previous speaker was dully reading a duller manuscript as the students stared at him through glazed eyes. As the second speaker was introduced, he literally ran to the front of the room. Barely responding to the chairman, he shouted: "Everybody stand up! Now take a deep breath. Breathe in, breathe out! Up on tiptoes, reach for the ceiling! Everyone sit down!"

The first words of his speech rang out loud and clear as a revivified audience sat alertly and listened. As he continued with his twenty-minute speech, he continually sought to enliven the listeners and to win their empathy. In the case of both speakers, the audience followed the actions of the speakers.

Uniting Video and Audio

One of the reasons for the greater popularity of television over radio is that we can see as well as listen. When we are given an explanation of a TV receiving set, we learn that two different sets of waves carry the message to us. One carries the audio portion of the show, another the video. Unless they somehow get out of synchronization, we sense only that someone is talking or singing. The audio and the video symbols blend so perfectly that we are not aware of their separateness. If either is missing, we become impatient and complain to the TV station or call a repairman. Listeners expect as much of a speaker in the flesh. If the speaker in either way disappoints them, they cannot conveniently call the complaint department or send for a mechanic, but they can stop listening. Someone has said that the magic number for television is seven—seven times more popular, seven times more effective than radio. Doubtless the same comparison can be made for the speaker who learns to present himself and his message visually as well as audibly to his audience. One rather safe estimate is that up to sixty-five percent of our messages in face-to-face communication are given nonverbally.

Westinghouse Nuclear Energy Division

In this situation both audible and visual signals are being used to convey a message. Note how both men's attention is converging on the visual aid.

Let Visual Aids Help You

Man was born with an effective set of visual aids—face, hands, and other body parts—for use in interpersonal communication. To supplement these, he has found that many products of the photographer, artist, sculptor, and other portrayers of the graphic arts are useful.

Visual aids are significantly helpful to a communicator because man learns more readily through visual stimuli than he does by auditory means. Researchers for the military forces estimate that up to eighty-five percent of our learning comes through the eyes. A foreman giving an assignment to one of his men in a mill soon learns that *showing* what he means as he explains the working of a machine results in more complete understanding than in telling alone. A dentist in teaching a patient proper tooth care demonstrates with a brush both within the mouth to show the feeling to be expected and outside to reinforce what he says by visual reinforcement. In oral explanations, words and phrases come one at a time, whereas the visual symbol may be perceived as a whole. The reason for this is that spoken ideas have but one dimension; what we see has two or more. Imagine a salesman being content to describe an automobile to you in words alone when he can take you to the showroom so that you may see what he is talking about. A prime advantage in all such cases, besides more complete *understanding,* is that the speaker can present his views or information with immensely greater *speed.* Thus visual aids can be used as time-saving devices, a particular value for the busy business or professional executive who is talking with even busier people.

Since effective communication is our primary aim in all speaking, we should be eager to use the visual aids which will help to increase that effectiveness. Besides the direct help which visual aids give the speaker in presenting his ideas, he finds himself able to release his tension as he performs demonstrations or handles equipment. People who are tense hold muscles rigid. To show exhibits one must move hands and arms, walk to other places in the room, and bend over to pick up objects. Such movements help the speaker to relax and to appear more at ease. At the same time, the listeners become more attentive to what is being shown rather than to any symptoms of speech fright which might be evident. A further concomitant is that planning to use objects to help put one's points across will make remembering those points easier. Because of the greater impact on learning which *seeing* gives, members of the audience will remember better the speaker's ideas.

Types of Visual Aids

Chalkboards or paper flip-over pads are probably the most universally used and most readily available of equipment suitable for use while speaking. The first requisite for the use of either is that it be so placed and so lighted as to be readily visible to everyone in the audience. Bishop Sheen had an "angel" who washed the chalkboard which he used on his TV shows. Whether you have an angel or not, keep the board clean for increased visibility. Clean erasers and a wet rag should be available as you need them. Use of chalk of varying colors can help to highlight what you write or draw. Care is needed in keeping your writing well spaced and horizontal. Make drawings simple and accurate and label the parts carefully. You will find it profitable to prepare much of your work on the chalkboard in leisure time before you speak, covering it with paper fastened with masking tape until you are ready to use it. Once what you have written or drawn has served its purpose, erase it or cover it again to keep it from distracting the listener's attention. Some lecture rooms have screens which may be used to conceal the chalkboard.

The *paper flip-over pad* is usually made of large (roughly 2½ by

4 feet) sheets of paper, bound at the narrow end to a board and mounted on an easel. Such a pad is readily portable, can be written on with crayon or felt-tipped pen, and is economical to use. Much of what is to be shown can be prepared in advance, each page being flipped over when you are ready for it.

CHARTS, GRAPHS, DIAGRAMS, AND MAPS   The conventional method is to keep a three to four relationship between length and width for all such materials as *charts*. Thus a chart planned to be four feet wide should be three feet high, the same ratio being kept for any variance in size. The paper used need not be expensive but should be tough enough to stand rough handling. Use masking tape to fasten charts, graphs, diagrams, and maps on a wall or chalkboard. If drawn or mounted on cardboard or similar material, they can be exhibited on an easel. For most purposes, getting them out of your hands can assure greater visibility and free your hands for using a pointer. Use a pointer in preference to your

U.S. Steel News

The visual aids shown here are appropriate for the purpose intended—to illustrate a talk on safety. Yet, their value might be increased if they were to be shown but one at a time.

finger to help the audience. Moving your hand vaguely toward the exhibit gives your viewer five points of reference, none of which may be the one you intend. If you point with a finger, your hand may obscure the view. For a single listener, a pen or pencil may suffice. For more people, a professional pointer with rubber tip may be best, or a dowel rod or cane may suffice. Touch the area you are drawing attention to and hold the pointer still as you speak. Slowly move to the next area, giving each listener time to focus sight and attention on it. Remember that quick and aimless movements merely confuse and distract those who are trying to follow you.

Whatever you prepare to show must be so designed as to tell effectively just what you want it to. Figures should be large, sharp, and clear. Lines, to avoid confusion, might be of different types, for example, solid, broken or dotted, or drawn with different-colored inks.

Darrell Huff in his *How to Lie with Statistics*[1] gives excellent advice on the construction of graphs to show figures in their true relationship with little exaggeration or bias.

Look for practical suggestions on the construction of charts in *Business Communication.*[2] Tools of the draftsman are recommended but are not necessary. Sharp pencils, fine-pointed pens, erasers, a ruler, and adequate working space will suffice.

For each graphic presentation there should be but one main center of interest with all other parts supplementing it. Otherwise, people will be confused by your illustration, trying perhaps to concentrate on the parts you are not talking about. To present two or more major points graphically, use a separate illustration for each. Determine in advance in what order they are to be presented—importance, size, chronology, monetary value, logical, geographical, or alphabetical. Having an orderly classification can help you in the presentation and the listener in his viewing.

Outline of maps with their main distinguishing features can be traced. Put on the map only those items which pertain to the points being illustrated. If maps are to be drawn freehand while you speak, practice beforehand until you are sure that your representation is accurate and on a correct scale.

MODELS   For some purposes, *models* such as those for a new building or of the human skeleton may be best suited. Decide whether the features of the model will be readily understood by the listener or whether

---

    1. Darrell Huff, *How to Lie with Statistics* (New York: W. W. Norton and Company, Inc., 1954).

    2. Everett C. Marston, Loring M. Thompson, and Frank Zacher, *Business Communication* (New York: The Macmillan Company, 1949) , chaps. 12–18.

the model can be conveniently handled or shown. Samples can be useful, particularly so if one can be provided for each listener to examine as you talk about it. The main features of a new product, for example, can be shown with great ease with samples for everyone to see, to taste, or to feel. Showing the actual item you are discussing greatly enhances the word description of it. Imagine being able to hold a 2,000-year-old Roman coin and say, "This might be the very coin which Jesus was shown when he advised his questioner to 'render unto Caesar that which is Caesar's.'" Such visual aids can have a greatly beneficial effect in assuring audience attention.

Distributing Materials

For sales campaigns, charity drives, or similar endeavors, *folders, pictures,* and other materials are often available. Some speakers prepare copies or outlines of their addresses for circulation. All of these have their advantages but must be used carefully if they are to be most productive. Such materials should be put in the listener's hands only at a time when his seeing or reading them will enhance what you are saying. Giving them out too soon will kill interest in your remarks. If yours is one of a series of presentations, distributing copies of your speech immediately after you have spoken may interfere with the next speaker's plans. Study the situation carefully and distribute exhibits only after you have calculated all risks and are sure that your communicative efforts will be bettered by placing materials in the listeners' hands.

Demonstrations

"How does it work?" is a natural question for a normally inquisitive man or woman. So, if your model works, start it and show it in operation. Play a tune on the musical instrument you are showing. Have a typist operate the new typewriter or have your dog perform the tricks you say he has learned. Even better is to have one or more of your listeners participate in the demonstration, both to satisfy their curiosity and to increase their interest.

In performing demonstrations be sure that all viewers can see, that you do not hide with your hands or body what you want them to see, and that the demonstration will actually aid audience understanding of what you are saying. Prepare your listeners by telling them what to look for during the demonstration, concentrate on them to note their reaction and to make complete the circular response. Parts of the operation may need to be in slow motion as you describe the action verbally and may need to

Westinghouse Nuclear Energy Division

Supervision, or the giving of instructions, can be more readily done at the work site.

be repeated for emphasis. At the end of the demonstration, use a summary transition to fix in the listeners' minds the importance of what they have seen.

Using Projectors

From the days of the primitive magic lantern to today's sophisticated video tape recorder people have been fascinated by watching shadows on a screen. Thanks to our technological skills, we have available a multitudinous assortment of *projectors* which are able to produce on a screen an even greater variety of types of "still" or "live" pictures.

Perhaps the simplest of all is the *still projector* which can put on a screen with great clarity the photographs or snapshots which we or other camera enthusiasts have prepared. Variations of this projector, when equipped with proper lenses, can show us the cross section of a slice of human tissue or the active animal life in a drop of swamp water. A great advantage of this type of projector is that the cost of slides or other materials is relatively low and new ones can be readily made for each presentation. Through the use of a tape recorder, suitable commentary may be made well in advance of the presentation to supplement what the audience sees.

Another variation of the still projector is the *overhead* type which can present material on readily made slides as large as 8½ by 11 inches. On such slides drawings may be made while the operator sits comfortably and describes what he is doing as the audience watches. Through the use of overlays, he can show steps of progression, laying each addition to the slide in place as he talks about it. Another type of overhead projector can show opaque objects such as a letter or the page of a book. Being able to operate the equipment while facing the audience gives the speaker the advantage of observing his listener to see if he is watching the screen and showing understanding of what is presented.

The use of the *motion picture projector* is limited only by the quantity and quality of the films available. The home movie camera has been simplified and reduced in price as to be within the reach of all. Professional equipment of the sixteen millimeter size is only a bit more sophisticated and correspondingly expensive. Motion picture films on thousands of subjects are available from libraries (both public and private), museums, corporations, and from most state universities and numerous other special respositories. Projectors available are suitable for audiences of any size from one to several thousand. Some projectors are so designed as to permit stopping them at any frame to show a single still picture. Almost all modern projectors are capable of showing sound pictures.

As with other complicated visual aids, the speaker must prepare his audience for what they are to see. He notifies them of what to look for, what aspects are significant for the current purpose. He may even interrupt the showing of the film to make comments, raise questions, or to repeat the showing of a few frames for emphasis. Timing is important so that remarks and showing of the film may be suited to the time limits which circumstances permit.

In preparing a message to suit the expected audience, the nonverbal (visual aids) needs to be considered at the same time that the verbal message is being composed. Otherwise, there is danger that the two will not be suitably united when presented. The preparation of visual aids takes time and must not be postponed too long. They may well serve as a stimulus to verbal preparation as their shape and structure impinge upon the encoder of the message, especially as he envisions the coming reaction of his listeners.

Characteristics of Effective Visual Aids

1. *Visibility.* A visual aid has not reached its acme of effectiveness until it is at least seen by every member of the audience. Chalk marks on a board need to be broad and heavy. Charts must be high enough and at the right angle to permit viewing. Glossy pictures need carefully placed light to prevent glaring. Models must not be hidden by the speaker's hands. *To test visibility,* try viewing exhibits from the listener's seat before attempting to use them.
2. *Accuracy.* Draw diagrams to scale. Let graphs represent figures or trends without exaggeration.[3] Make drawings look like what they are meant to represent.
3. *Clarity.* Write or print clearly. Focus projector to prevent fuzziness at edges of picture. Place labels near items they describe.
4. *Neatness.* Wash chalkboard before writing on it. Leave suitable margins at sides, top, and bottom of board or paper. Avoid marking over errors. Make clean erasures. Keep equipment looking presentable. Replace frayed cords and torn screens.
5. *Efficiency.* Prepare exhibits in advance. Keep visual aids hidden until ready for use—covers over chalkboard drawings, drapes over models. Set up projectors and screen, test and focus them beforehand. Put exhibits out of sight after use but wait until after speaking is finished before repacking or dismantling them. Test all of your plans in advance to learn of electric outlets are useable, if tape will hold exhibits on the wall, if easel will stand where needed, if pointer can be found quickly at hand, if signals for projectionist are working.
6. *Effectiveness.* Useful visual aids are those which amplify and clarify meaning. If they merely attract attention to themselves, they detract from one's meaning.

Suggestions for Using Visual Aids

(See Chapter 4 for suggestions in using audio aids.)
1. Portraying a floor plan: draw the plan on a large sheet of wrapping paper with a felt- or nylon-tipped pen.
2. For emphasis of key points or for showing successive parts of a structural model use a flannel board.
3. To show a drawing, letter, or graph on which changes are to be made as you talk about them use an overhead projector.

---

3. See Darrell Huff, *How to Lie With Statistics* (New York: W. W. Norton Company, Inc., 1954).

4. Use maps, hand-drawn or professionally made, to locate places to be discussed. A pantograph can help you draw segments needed. Use large paper.
5. Show graphs or figures on cardboard. (Backs of old show cards are suitable.)
6. If exhibits are to be distributed to members of the audience, provide enough so that each person may see the same exhibit at the same time.
7. If not everyone can see the exhibit you are holding, move about the room until the exhibit is visible to all.
8. Use a pointer (a tightly rolled sheet of paper fastened with a rubber band will often suffice) to mark what you want the audience to see on a map or chart.
9. Use masking tape or the stronger carpet tape for mounting exhibits on the wall. Cellophane tape tears paper and removes paint.
10. To show sets of figures to the audience distribute duplicated copies with computations incomplete. Asking listeners to complete the addition, and so on, will assure closer attention to the point to be made.
11. Live models require extra care. People must be coached, dogs well trained, emergencies anticipated.
12. Coach the audience in advance as to what they are to see in the motion picture film to be shown or the plant tour to be taken.
13. Show only the parts of the film or tour only the parts of the plant which are pertinent to the ideas you are presenting.
14. Allow opportunities for audience reaction, especially questions, when showing visual aids.
15. Give suitable credit to anyone who provides you with audiovisual aids and return them promptly in good condition.

Conclusion

From the instant a listener becomes aware of our presence, we begin to communicate with him, albeit unconsciously. The furniture of an office, the cut of our clothes, our stance, hairdo, and facial expression are all busy in transmitting messages to the aware observer.

When we start to speak, all of these signs will continue either to supplement or to negate what we are saying. Every facial expression, every movement of our bodies, and every gesture convey meaning to those to whom we are speaking. For that reason we must learn to direct our visual signals in a way that will supplement, illustrate, and emphasize all that we say. We must be able to direct all of our movement in such a way as to remove from our message all that is extraneous.

Visual aids to speaking are significant because most of us learn better by viewing than by listening. By their use we equip ourselves with an additional set of signals which, when properly directed, increase the listener's perception.

In using visual aids we should exercise great care in their preparation so that they may convey the impression we intend. Audiences must be instructed in what to look for and to be reminded afterward of what they have seen. Although to ourselves we may seem to be giving two messages as we "show and tell," in the listener we must create the effect of receiving but one impression—the main message which we are attempting to communicate.

To the student: Keep in mind during your study that the same principles apply whether your audience consists of one person or one thousand. Your principal aim in message preparation and presentation is to accomplish your purpose.

FOR DISCUSSION

1. What principle or principles of interpersonal communication does the choice of appropriate clothing for a speaking engagement (before one or more people) illustrate?
2. Why is the formulation of *rules* for the use of bodily action and gesture impractical?
3. The advice to "be natural" while speaking means primarily from whose viewpoint? Why?
4. What is the difference between a speaker's motivated bodily action and gesture and that which is unmotivated in respect to their effect on the audience?
5. How can the speaker prepare himself to have impulses for his physical reinforcement of his oral message come from within himself?
6. What is the potential harm in rehearsing gestures? What would be the effect of substituting breathing exercises or isometric exercises immediately before speaking?
7. How can one use gestures effectively without being aware of them?
8. What can a speaker do to prevent note cards, lectern, chairs, and the like, from causing him to use unmotivated gestures?
9. What are some gestures which would probably be understood in most parts of the Western world regardless of the languages used?
10. How can one learn to interpret accurately a listener's response by observing him?
11. How can a speaker learn to keep control of himself when he discovers that his listeners are reacting unfavorably?

12. Does the use of visual aids assure a speaker that his talk will be more effective than if he did not use them? Why?

13. Since ready visibility to the audience is a prime criterion for any visual aids used, what test or tests should a speaker put them to before he speaks?

14. What problems may a speaker who uses live models encounter?

15. What tests do you need to submit your graphs or other statistical representations to in order to avoid making them exaggerate or minimize unduly?

PROBLEMS AND EXERCISES

1. Make a checklist which you can follow before every speaking engagement. Include such items as hair combed, shoes shined, pockets emptied of whatever makes bulges, pens out of breast pocket, jangling bracelets removed, and so on.

2. Describe the way you would choose to dress for (a) a trip to a factory to meet a prospective employer, (b) a lecture which you are to give before a local woman's club, (c) a visit to a banker to apply for a loan.

3. After consulting two or three people who know you well, make a list of mannerisms which mar your speaking. How will you eliminate them?

4. Study the actions of a notably dull speaker: teacher, preacher, politician, and so on. What characteristics of his facial expression, bodily action, and gestures did you note? Write a report of your observations, including the response of listeners.

5. Observe a highly successful speaker and write a similar report.

6. Watch your classmates as they participate in class discussion or give speeches. Compile a list of all of the extraneous, unmotivated gestures which they use.

7. Watch men whose work requires them to use physical reinforcement for their communication, for example, baseball umpires, football officials, auctioneers, or traffic policemen. (One from Pittsburgh became nationally known because of his appearance on television's "Candid Camera.")

8. Watch several television performers, such as weather reporters, newscasters, and lecturers. Pay particular attention both to their visual aids and the way that they use them. Write a 300- to 500-word critique of their visual aids and techniques of using them.

9. Make a survey of your community to discover possible sources of visual aids. Include museums, libraries, commercial artists and photogra-

phers, cartographers, and industries. Write a report that would be useful for other speakers.

10. Make a similar survey of your own institution. Look for various kinds of projectors, maps, charts, chalkboards, films, cameras, models, video tapes, illustrations, model makers, or cartoonists. Write a suitable report.

BIBLIOGRAPHY

Books

BAKE, STEPHEN. *Visual Persuasion.* N. Y.: McGraw-Hill Book Company, 1971.
BIRDWHISTELL, RAY. *Kinesics and Context.* Philadelphia: University of Pennsylvania Press, 1970.
———. *Introduction to Kinesics: An Annotation System for Analysis of Body Motion and Gesture.* Washington, D. C.: Foreign Service Institute, Department of State, 1952.
BLACK, JOHN W., and MOORE, WILBUR E. *Speech: Code, Meaning, and Communication.* N. Y.: McGraw-Hill Book Company, 1955, chap. 11, pp. 314–16.
BRADLEY, BERT. *Speech Performance.* Dubuque, Ia.: Wm. C. Brown Company Publishers, 1967, chap. 4.
BRIGANCE, WILLIAM NORWOOD. *Speech: Its Techniques and Disciplines in a Free Society.* 2d ed. N. Y.: Appleton-Century-Crofts, 1961, chap. 16, pp. 264–69.
CAMPBELL, JAMES H., and HELPER, HAL W., eds. *Dimensions in Communication.* Belmont, Cal.: Wadsworth Publishing Co., Inc., 1965, pp. 158–74.
DALE, EDGAR. *Audio-Visual Methods in Teaching.* N. Y.: Holt, Rinehart and Winston, Inc., 1963.
EISENBERG, ABNE, and SMITH, RALPH. *Nonverbal Communication.* N. Y.: The Bobbs-Merrill Co., Inc., 1971.
EISENSON, JON; AUER, J. JEFFERY; and IRWIN, JOHN V. *The Psychology of Communication.* N. Y.: Appleton-Century-Crofts, 1963, chap. 2.
HASS, KENNETH B., and PACKER, HARRY Q. *Preparation and Use of Audio-Visual Aids.* Englewood Cliffs, N. J.: Prentice-Hall, Inc., 1946.
HOFFMAN, ERVING. *Presentation of the Self in Everyday Life.* N. Y.: Doubleday & Company, Inc., 1959.
HUFF, DARRELL. *How to Lie with Statistics.* N. Y.: W. W. Norton & Company, Inc., 1954.
KEMP, JEROLD E. *Planning and Producing Audio-Visual Materials.* San Francisco: Chandler Publishing Company, 1963.
KNAPP, MARK. *Nonverbal Communication in Human Interaction.* N. Y.: Holt, Rinehart and Winston, Inc., 1972.
LANGER, SUSANNE. *Philosophy in a New Key.* Cambridge, Mass.: Harvard University Press, 1942, chap. 3.
LARUSSO, DOMINIC. *Basic Skills of Oral Communication.* Dubuque, Ia.: Wm. C. Brown Company Publishers, 1967, chap. 6.
MARSTON, EVERETT C.; THOMPSON, LORING M.; and ZACHER, FRANK. *Business Communication.* N. Y.: The Macmillan Company, 1949, chaps. 11–18, pp. 378–87.
MEHRABIAN, A. *Silent Messages,* Belmont, Cal.: Wadsworth Publishing Co., Inc., 1971.
MUDD, CHARLES S., and SILLARS, MALCOLM O. *Speech Content and Communication.* San Francisco: Chandler Publishing Company, 1962, chap. 15.
OLIVER, ROBERT T.; ZELKO, HAROLD P.; and HOLTZMAN, PAUL D. *Communicative Speaking and Listening.* N. Y.: Holt, Rinehart and Winston, Inc., 1968, pp. 151–55.
STEWART, JOHN, ed. *Bridges Not Walls.* Reading, Mass.: Addison-Wesley Publishing Co., Inc., 1973.
U.S. International Cooperation Administration. *Using Visuals in Agricultural Communications.* East Lansing, Mich.: National Project in Agricultural Communications.
WALTER, OTIS M., and SCOTT, ROBERT L. *Thinking and Speaking.* 2d ed. N. Y.: The Macmillan Company, 1968, pp. 52–56, 124–30.

Weaver, Carl H., and Strausbaugh, Warren L. *Fundamentals of Speech Communication*. N. Y.: American Book Company, 1964, chap. 10.

Wilcox, Roger P. *Oral Reporting in Business and Industry*. Englewood Cliffs, N. J.: Prentice-Hall, Inc., 1967, chaps. 11, 12.

Periodicals

"Body Language: Student and Teacher Behavior." *Saturday Review*, May 1973, p. 78.

Bowers, John Waite. "Some Correlates of Language Intensity." *Quarterly Journal of Speech* 50 (December 1964):59.

———. "The Influence of Delivery on Attitudes Toward Concepts and Speakers." *Speech Monographs* 32 (June 1965):154.

Breslow, H. S. "Employee Communications: A Personnel Man's Viewpoint." *Personnel Journal* 48 (June 1969):995–97.

Cobin, Martin. Response to Eye Contact." *Quarterly Journal of Speech* 48 (December 1962): 415–18.

Ekman, P. "Constants Across Cultures in the Face and Emotion." *Journal of Personality and Social Psychology* 17 (1971):124–29.

Fennell, J. "Electronic (Convention) Aids Multiply." *Financial Post* 64 (December 26, 1970):11.

Gray, Giles Wilkeson. "What Was Elocution?" *Quarterly Journal of Speech* 46 (February 1960):1–7.

Henning, James. "How to Deliver a Speech." *Today's Speech* 3 (January 1955):3–4, 21.

Jackson, B. "Man vs. Machine: Which Makes Meetings Go?" *Financial Post* 65 (August 28, 1971):6–8.

Jones, Edward. "What It's Like to Be a Black Manager." *Harvard Business Review* 51 (July-August 1973):108–16.

"Laying the Proper Groundwork for A/V Presentations, or, If Something Can Go Wrong It Will." *Administrative Management* 34 (October 1973):80.

Lowrey, Sara. "Gesture Through Empathy." *Southern Speech Journal* 11 (January 1946):59–62.

Margarotto, C. "Towards an International Language of Gestures." *UNESCO Courier* 27 (March 1974):20–21.

Parrish, W. M. "The Concept of 'Naturalness.' " *Quarterly Journal of Speech* 37 (December 1951):448–54.

Schmidt, Ralph N. "Don't Think About Your Hands." *Today's Speech* 9 (February 1961):7, 8.

Thomas, Richard S. "Speaking with Style." *The Toastmaster* 34 (July 1968):6–9.

White, Eugene E. "Cotton Mather's Manuductio ad Ministerium." *Quarterly Journal of Speech* 59 (October 1963):317.

6

He gave man speech, and speech
created thought, which is the
measure of the universe.
Shelley

Composing
the Speech

Great speeches grow out of a burning need to speak, to share with an audience one's concern, or to try to persuade people to accept an idea or to take action. Martin Luther King's "I Have a Dream" grew out of his intense desire to better the lot of the Black American. The late Clarence Randall, former president of Inland Steel, in his famous television speech in answer to President Harry Truman's seizure of the nation's steel mills spoke from a sense of anger and outrage against what he believed to be an unconstitutional act.

Less well known Americans have spoken with equal vigor and success. The physician who deplores the lethargy of the city fathers in caring for health needs talks to the luncheon club circuit and brilliantly persuades his listeners to demand action. A dental therapist goes to a school where most of the children know little of dental care, and with a speech well adapted to the understanding of children, starts a minor revolution in oral hygiene. A lawyer, convinced of the innocence of his client, makes himself an expert on the case, and in his charge to the jury persuades them of the innocence of the accused. A businessman, knowing the needs of the poverty leagues, persuades his company to sponsor a training program for the hard-core unemployed. A mill foreman, resolving to reduce accidents, inspires his men by a series of daily three-minute speeches to protect eyes, hands, and feet because "God has made no spare parts." All of these speakers are led by their concern for their fellowmen to speak out on what they believe are important topics.

Scores more might be enumerated, such as the sales manager who sees a need to increase his company's sales or the executive who feels compelled to persuade his colleagues and superiors that their company ought to diversify its products. Scientists, although busy in their laboratories, find time to explain their findings and to urge others to engage in related research or plead for financial support. Engineers endeavor to find support for their plans to develop new structures or machines. Preachers exhort us to live the kind of lives in which we express belief.

The success of each such speaker depends upon his ability in preparing himself and his message to suit the audience and the occasion. A successful preacher, when asked how he prepared his sermons, replied: "First, I read myself full. Then, I pray myself hot. Finally, I rear back and let go." No great success will come to any speaker until he has a deep concern for his subject and a desire to imbue others with it.

Choosing a Subject

Most of the subjects about which thoughtful people are concerned are broad. The safety engineer who abhors the slaughter of one thousand or more persons weekly on our highways doesn't choose "Highway Safety" as the topic for his speech to insurance underwriters. He probably will speak instead on "The Responsibility of the Insurance Industry for Reduction of Auto Accidents." For all other audiences he will elect topics which can readily be adapted to the interests of each.

A key word for determining one's choice of subject is *appropriateness*.

1. Is it appropriate for the *speaker?* Has he had experience which qualifies him to talk on the subject? Has he observed it and studied it? Can he continue to collect suitable and necessary information?
2. Is the subject suitable for the *audience?* Should he speak on the structure and operation of the television camera to the women who are interested in improving the choice of television programs?
3. It is appropriate for the *occasion?* A political speech is generally considered unsuitable for a funeral, Mark Antony's funeral oration notwithstanding. Neither will a dolorous speech be expected on such a joyous occasion as an alumni reunion.

Purpose

The speaker's *purpose* will largely determine which aspect of his subject will be chosen. Purposes which are customary are *to inform, to*

Three microphones may indicate that the speaker is addressing at least three audiences. How does such a circumstance complicate the composition of one's speech?

instruct, to stimulate, to entertain, to convince or persuade.[1] A speech on the structure of the automatic transmission of an automobile will vary greatly from one on how to repair the same transmission. Although some elements may be common to both, a satirical speech on Los Angeles' smog will be different because of its purpose from one on persuading the electric utilities of Southern California to use nuclear fuel instead of oil for generating electricity.

A veteran sociologist confessed that for over forty years he had spoken hundreds of times but always on one or the other of but two subjects. So skillfully were they adapted to each new audience and occasion that many listeners who had heard him speak numerous times were hardly aware that they had heard the same theme before. Suiting the content of structure of the speech to the speaker's purpose and adapting it to the

---

1. Almost any speech may have a secondary, or even a third, purpose. The speech to inform may also instruct. A speech to stimulate may be entertaining. Some authorities insist that all speeches in a sense are persuasive. The speaker does well to decide what his *prime* purpose is and to subjugate all others lest he confuse both himself and his hearers.

interests and needs of the audience tend to assure the accomplishment of the speaker's purpose.

ETHICAL VALUES   To develop one's abilities as an oral communicator is not enough. A speaker must choose ethical values which will make his speaking that of a responsible person who is considerate of his fellows.

History is replete with examples of leaders who used persuasion in a disastrous manner. Hitler could sway crowds, and led a nation to its downfall with the philosophy that if you tell a big enough lie, and tell it often enough, you can persuade your followers to believe you. In an earlier age, and in a neighboring country, Napoleon Bonaparte inspired blind obedience and led France to defeat at Waterloo. In our own day we have had a plethora of demagogues and charlatans who, for their own selfish gain, deluded people through their power of oral communication.

One's ethical values as a communicator cannot be separated from one's moral character. An immoral person is apt to use his speech skills for immoral purposes just as a hunter who is immoral might use his gun to steal game or to murder his mother-in-law. A major fear in the world today is that a latter-day Hitler may set off a nuclear holocaust. The greater the skill of a scoundrel the more dangerous he is. Recent disclosures in our federal government indicate that superior intellect and several years of higher education are insufficient to guarantee moral leadership.

Dr. Robert T. Oliver, himself an able persuader, suggests seven "simple moral principles that are readily identifiable and should be easily practiced." They are:

1. Do not falsify or misrepresent evidence.
2. Do not speak with assurance on a subject on which you are actually uninformed.
3. Do not seek approval from your audience for a policy or a program by linking it in their minds with emotional values (such as patriotism or sympathy for the underprivileged) with which it has no actual connection.
4. Avoid confusing the minds of the audience about the worthiness of a point of view by "smear" attacks upon the leadership associated with it.
5. Do not delude yourself into feeling that the end justifies the means.
6. If you are activated in advocating a proposal by self-interest or by your allegiance to a particular organization, do not conceal that fact and pretend an objectivity you do not possess.
7. Do not advocate for an audience something in which you yourself do not believe.[2]

---

2. Robert T. Oliver, *The Psychology of Persuasive Speech*, 2d ed. (New York: David McKay Co., Inc., 1968).

As one's ability to persuade others increases, the conscientious speaker generally discovers that his concern for his listeners increases. The reason is that he becomes impressed with the social consequences of what he says.

IMPROMPTU, EXTEMPORANEOUS, OR MEMORIZED

Speech scholars define *impromptu* as meaning unprepared, or "off the cuff." Few speakers use this type of speech successfully. Even in informal conferences the impromptu method is not apt to be highly successful. Mark Twain once remarked that to be a successful impromptu speaker required at least two weeks of preparation—another way of saying that there's no truly impromptu speech.

Extemporaneous speaking, meaning carefully prepared—well researched, outlined, and rehearsed—has all of the claimed advantages of the impromptu method. To speak extempore assures that the speaker must think of what he is saying, can react to the feedback he gets from the audience, and is able to incorporate any recent information which becomes available. Being well prepared enables the extemporaneous speaker to keep on his topic, discourages him from making detours. Since he *sounds* impromptu as he composes his individual sentences on the spot, he seems to be speaking as if his thought had just been generated. A technical description calls the mental process "vivid realization of idea at the moment of utterance."

The *memorized,* or *manuscript,*[3] speech must be used by presidents of nations or corporations, and other leaders who must make sure that no slips will occur or state secrets be inadvertently disclosed. Unfortunately, many beginning speakers make the mistake of trying to memorize or read speeches before getting sufficient learning and experience. The results are usually a disaster and the ultimate aim of the speech not achieved.

In this book the extemporaneous method is given primary consideration. It is the principal method used by the world's greatest orators, and it is the one by which the beginning speaker can make the most rapid progress.

Getting Information

"For every pound of speech you'll need a barrel of information." Speakers who read a magazine article which interests them and then try to quote it soon reveal their ignorance when questioned by the audience. The man who spoke glibly about birds but included the "martingale"

---

3. See Chapter 7.

To insure that one's message is exact and significant, careful research is necessary.

Westinghouse Nuclear Energy Division

among those he knew revealed to his audience that he was neither an ornithologist nor an expert on the parts of a horse's harness. To be able to speak successfully on a topic, your knowledge must be both deep and broad. You must be able to draw from a stock that will give you a wide selection of facts and ideas adaptable to the audience which you are to face.

Not only must you know your subject well from your own viewpoint but also from the viewpoint of the listener.[4] Part of your study will involve learning the language of the layman to permit you to translate your own jargon so that he may understand you. Many of your illustrations, your analogies especially, must be drawn from his knowledge and experience, as well as your own, if they are to be made clear to him. An especially important part of your preparation at this stage will be a careful *analysis* of your own purpose and of all of the materials which you gather in preparation for speech making.

---

4. Review the section on *audience analysis*, pp. 28–30.

EXPERIENCE   In beginning to prepare a speech, write down a list of everything you already know about the topic selected. Draw liberally from what you have done and felt. What activities of your business or profession have you engaged in from which you may draw? What have you done as a hobby or avocation that might be related? Perhaps you've pulled a lobster trap or polished a gem-quality tourmaline. You may have restored a Model T or qualified for a Red Cross Life Saving Certificate. These are the types of experiences on which you may be able to draw in interpreting your subject to your listeners.

But beware of relying upon *your* experience alone. Even that which you've had daily for ten years may not be sufficient to draw from in making a speech. Conclusions drawn from it may be invalid, leaving you open to the charge of making hasty generalizations from too few examples. Rather, let your experience serve as the motivating influence which will help to inspire you to feel strongly about the topic and lead you to further study.

OBSERVATION   To *see* is not necessarily to *observe*. Each of us draws upon his own experience as he looks at an object. I see an ear of sweet corn as food. You look upon it as the culmination of the plant breeder's skill in hybridization. A woman fancies herself wearing the dress she sees on a model. The woman's physician husband notes the evidences of malnutrition in the model. The act of observing requires us to go beyond the casual glance, even in the examination of something we have seen frequently.

A student engineer, wishing to give a speech of information about a new bridge then under construction, spent many hours viewing the bridge from different angles, crossing and recrossing it, and studying the engineer's blueprints. The great scientist Professor Agassiz, to learn if a student was qualified to study under him, required him to spend an entire day observing a small fish which had been preserved in formaldehyde, then to report upon what he had observed.

To experience and to observe better qualifies one to know what questions to ask of authorities or specialists and what sources to read.

INTERVIEWS   No matter what subject you may choose to speak on, there is always someone who has information about it which you do not have or who has been considering your topic from a differing point of view. Previous study will enable you to ask significant questions and to explore more fully the depths of the specialist's knowledge. An advantage over reading is that you will be enabled to ask supplemental questions and to capture some of the enthusiasm of your respondent. Through conversations with others you will find that your own views will be sharpened, your thoughts quickened, and your ability to express your ideas enlarged. From others you can get suggestions as to what is available in print and what you should read to prepare yourself to speak.

READING   By the time you have examined your own knowledge, you will realize what gaps exist in it and what kinds of information you must look for. Making a list of subtopics relating to your subject will save you time as you start research in the nearest library.

A good rule of thumb to follow is to start with such general articles as those to be found in good quality encyclopedias, for example, *Encyclopedia Americana* or *Encyclopaedia Brittanica*. Usually there is a bibliography at the end of each article to give you leads for further reading. Special encyclopedias are available, including the *Encyclopedia of Educational Research* and the *Encyclopedia of the Social Sciences* or those of the Catholic and Jewish religions.

To find newspaper articles turn to the *New York Times Index*. Not only is it useful in locating articles in that famous newspaper but in others as well. Although other newspapers are not indexed by the *Times,* articles or subjects of national importance may usually be found, printed

Westinghouse Nuclear Energy Division

The Federal Register *is but one of many thousands of federal government publications available to speakers.*

on the same date or a day or two earlier or later in the newspaper files available to you. In most libraries the *Times* and certain other papers are now found on film, greatly facilitating the labor of research.

The Readers' Guide to Periodical Literature indexes articles for a great number of periodicals. For the professional journals the *Education Index, Engineering Index, Industrial Arts Index,* and others, are invaluable. Most businesses and professional journals provide annual indexes.

The federal and all state governments publish great varieties of reports and pamphlets. Many of these are on file in public and private business libraries. Federal government documents may be purchased from the United States Government Printing Office. Those from the states are generally available from the departments which publish them.

Although the use of thirty or forty references may seem impossible when preparing to give a speech, think of the results expected. Not every book or article will need to be read in its entirety. Tables of contents and indexes of books can help you discover quickly the tidbits of information which may be useful for your purpose. Most material in books and periodicals can be scanned in a minimum of time. Examining a great amount of material can help you find a good choice of suitable data adaptable to audience needs.

Taking Notes

For all of your reading, notes should be taken for use when the time for writing your speech arrives. Of all methods for recording notes, the least efficient and most cumbersome method is to use a notebook. Much to be preferred is that of using slips of paper of a uniform size, such as 4 by 6 inches. Use one slip to give the bibliographical information, including a heading under which it may be filed alphabetically, author's name, title of article or book, publisher, date, pages or chapters read, and a few sentences to help you recall the general content of what you found to be helpful.

On additional slips write the information (often quotations) which you expect to use. In the upper left corner of the slip write the author's name, book or article title, and pages where it appears. Write in the upper center of the slip a heading which will permit filing of the information under one section of your speech outline. Be careful to write but *one* item of information on each slip. If the quotation is long, continue it on the reverse side of the slip, or even onto a second slip marked "continued" and with the same heading as the first slip. Such a system enables you to sort slips rapidly and to rearrange them in any suitable combination. In contrast, notes written in a notebook are exceedingly difficult to locate quickly and can hardly be rearranged without recopying.

The same system of recording notes can be used for research done by other methods.

Outlining

The outline for a speech serves the same general function as does an architect's drawing and blueprints for a house. The outline identifies the speech purpose, its general point of view, its subordinate general statements, together with their supporting materials. Preparation of the outline leads you logically from your task of *analysis* of your information and ideas into a *synthesis* of them for the benefit of yourself and your listeners.

Once an after-dinner speaker said to the professor of speech at his side: "Tonight I intend to get a free lesson in public speaking. Please prepare to give me a critique after I finish my speech." As the speaker began, the professor wrote what seemed to be the speaker's first point, labeling it "I." and following it with support noted as "A.," "B." and "C." Suddenly he heard what seemed to be an unconnected main point and labeled it as "I." Still later a third "first" point came with neither of the first two points being in any way connected to it. The speech finally ended with an inconsequential conclusion. Silently the professor passed his "outline" to the speaker. Studying it carefully, he wrote tersely, "No wonder my listeners have trouble understanding me. I don't know what I'm talking about myself."

Although an outline for a speech will not guarantee listener understanding, it will serve to help the speaker keep to his purpose and develop his thoughts logically, just as the architect's drawing will help the contractor construct a house of an agreed-upon size with the expected number of rooms put into the prescribed relation with each other. The outline serves as a useful guide, beginning sometime while the research and study is going on, continuing during the writing and oral rehearsal, and providing the bearings needed while the speech is being delivered. At all times it should be looked upon as a useful tool, not an arbitrary device designed by speech professors to stultify the free flow of ideas. One reason that impromptu speeches are often vague, pointless, and rambling is because their author has not had time to think through his ideas and to organize his materials into a form which will seem clear to himself and his listeners. Any speech, to be successful, needs careful planning, and the outline is an unbeatable device for facilitating planning and composition.

In planning speeches, numerous thought patterns may be followed. Some of the more common ones are *problem-solution, need-satisfaction,*[5] *topical, time, space, inductive,* and *deductive.*[6] Deciding on a pattern to follow and preparing a careful outline can assure you that your thoughts are logically and understandably organized. The pattern to be used depends primarily upon the speaker's purpose and the audience which he is to address.

The specific purpose of a speech must be established before any other preparation is started. It should be written in infinitive phrase form something like this example: "To inform the members of Local 306 how observing the rules of parliamentary debate can help assure that all points of view can be expressed by members in union meetings." Once it is written, examine it carefully to determine if it expresses accurately *why* you want to speak. Revision may be necessary to be certain that the scope of the topic is narrow enough to be covered in the time alloted.

Once the specific purpose has been determined, the speaker must decide *what* to say in order to accomplish it. Call the expression of this your *subject sentence* or main idea.[7] Whatever the name used, the chief utility of both the Specific Purpose and Subject Sentence is to serve as yardsticks for measuring everything else which is to be considered for use in the speech.

The Subject Sentence should be a declarative statement which uses the same phraseology as the Specific Purpose. A Subject Sentence to suit our sample Specific Purpose would be similar to this: "Observing the rules of parliamentary debate can help assure that all points of view can be expressed by members in union meetings."

Examination of our samples will reveal that they may not be sufficiently specific to serve their purpose, especially if the time permitted for speaking is limited. Perhaps further thought will result in this revision:

Specific Purpose: "To inform the members of Local 306 that allowing but one person to speak at a time and limiting speeches to a maximum of five minutes each can help all members express their points of view at union meetings."

---

5. For a thorough discussion of this pattern (called Motivated Sequence by the authors) see Alan H. Monroe and Douglas Ehninger, *Principles of Speech,* 6th brief ed. (New York: Scott, Foresman and Company, 1969), pp. 258-77.

6. Thought pattern for speeches are discussed in William Norwood Brigance's *Speech: Its Techniques and Disciplines in a Free Society,* 2d ed. (New York: Appleton-Century-Crofts, 1961), chap. 11.

7. Some authorities combine the Specific Purpose and Subject Sentence calling it the purpose sentence. Others speak of the Subject Sentence as the topic sentence or limiting sentence.

Subject Sentence: "Allowing but one person to speak at a time and limiting each speech to five minutes can help all members express their points of view at union meetings."

Such a revision narrows the topic to manageable form. More writing and reviewing may clarify further *why* the speaker is to talk and *what* he wants to say. After several revisions the Specific Purpose and Subject Sentence will be perfected so well that they can serve effectively as yardsticks for measuring all materials to be considered for inclusion in the speech.

Once guidelines such as these have been established, the speech writer is ready to begin his outline—the development of his main thought —the one expressed in the Subject Sentence. Our example calls for a simple *topical* thought pattern. Main points in the outline might be:

I. Allowing but one person to speak at a time can help all members express their points of view at union meetings.
II. Limiting each speech to five minutes can help all members to express their points of view at union meetings.

In these examples, note that the same phraseology used in Specific Purpose and Subject Sentence is used in the outline's Main Points. The Main Points are written in parallel form, a device which helps the speaker to be sure that they expand his main idea and that they are of equal value. Once the Main Points are written, they must be tested to determine if (1) they support the main idea and (2) they further the Specific Purpose. Granted that they do, valid supporting material should be selected to change them from innocuous generalities into specific powerful entities designed to have a persuasive appeal for the listeners.

Again before going further, major revisions may be made in a minimum amount of time. Will each item of support do what it is intended to do? Are all parts of the outline related to each other? Are they put together in such a way that they clearly show the speaker's aims? If satisfactory answers cannot be given to your questions, further revisions are needed. Just as in house building, so in speech building a revision of the plans is less arduous than of the finished structure.

Once you are satisfied with your outline, you are ready to begin to write your speech using an oral style. With the outline before you in reality and your audience in your imagination, begin to address them, *speaking* aloud what you intend to say on the date of the speech. Whether or not you intend to speak from a manuscript, writing it will serve the purpose of assuring you that you have thought through the speech in its entirety at least once, good insurance that you will be more confident when you stand to speak, either from manuscript or extemporaneously.

Throughout your tasks of writing and speaking, the outline will enable you to keep clearly in mind the aim and structure of your speech and can help prevent tempting but costly digressions.

If a Problem-Solution thought pattern is to be followed, the type of outline below might be used:

> Subject: Water Pollution in Pennsylvania
>
> General purpose: to persuade
>
> Specific purpose: to persuade the members of the General Assembly, meeting in joint session, to amend the present strip mine law to include in addition to coal the mining of all minerals and to increase substantially the penalties for nonobservance of the law.
>
> Subject sentence (main idea) : Despite the good laws passed by the General Assembly in the past, our streams and rivers continue to be polluted by acid drainage from operating strip mines and can only be kept clear by means of legislation which will require mine operators, regardless of the minerals they extract, to take effective steps to prevent the drainage or else to pay fines high enough to reimburse the Commonwealth for doing so.
>
> Title: (Designed to arouse curiosity and gain attention.)
>
> Opening sentence(s): (To gain attention, stimulate interest, and to orient listeners to the problem, perhaps chosen from IA.)
>
> Closing sentence(s): (To fix the problem and the proposed solution in the minds of the listeners and to stimulate them to take the requested action.)

(Statement of problem) (Illustration)[8]	I. Pennsylvania streams and rivers are currently polluted by mine acids. A. Long stretches of the Allegheny River have such a high acid content that fish cannot live in the polluted water.
(Statistics)	1. (Write here the information you've taken from reliable sources.)
(Testimony)	2.
(Example)	B. Some parts of Slippery Rock Creek are reported as unfit for swimming and boating.
(Anecdote) (Personal Experience)	1. A camp site was abandoned. 2. My family and I no longer swim in Slippery Rock Creek.
(Fact)	C. Stocking of some streams with fish has been abandoned because fish cannot live in their waters.

(Forms of Support to be varied to suit information available and needs of speaker and listeners.)	1. (Write an enumeration of such streams
	   2. together with supporting evi-
	   3. dence.)

---

8. The purpose of writing labels in the margin is to help identify the forms of support chosen and to test for variety and quantity. Those labels used in the sample outline are merely illustrative.

(Statistics)

(Support designed
to clarify for the
listeners and to
appeal to their
interests.)

(Fact)

(Support which will
appeal to listeners
because of familiar
sources cited.)

(Fact)

D. The estimated annual dollar loss to the Common-
wealth has been computed at $_____.
   1. (Write here supporting evidence taken from
   2. bonafide and respectable
   3. sources)

E. The current strip mine laws are ineffectual because
they cover only the mining of coal and not other
minerals, such as limestone.
   1. (Write here supporting evidence such
   2. as quotes from existing laws,
   3. from official state reports, and newspaper
      accounts.)

F. The current strip mine laws are ineffectual because
penalties on mine operators for noncompliance are
not high enough to persuade them to take proper
precautions.
   1. (Write here support similar to that
   2. under E.)
   3.

(Solution)

II. To solve the problem of stream pollution in Pennsylvania the General Assembly needs to
   A. Amend the strip mine laws to cover the extraction
   of all minerals
      1. (Support to show how this
      2. will help solve the problem.)
      3.
   B. Amend the strip mine law to make the penalties
   for nonobservers so high that strip mine operators
   will be forced to comply or else reimburse the state
   enough to pay for preventing acid damage.
      1. (Support similar to that
      2. under A.)
      3.

OUTLINE VARIATIONS The *problem-solution* outline suggested can have many variations. Different audiences might make necessary
a change in Main Points as well as in forms of support. Keep in mind that
the outline is a useful tool to help you in planning your speech before you
proceed to write it or speak it. Its chief value is in helping you to clarify
your own thinking.

Outlines for speeches are as varied as the thoughts and whims of the
speaker who writes them. They may range from the detailed form given in
the previous section as an example to a hastily scribbled list of words and
phrases to be used as reminders while speaking. As a basis for choice, determine what the ultimate purpose of the outline will be. The beginning

speaker will probably have to go into much more detail than the experienced one, for the former will not have established thought patterns to rely upon. In every case, the main purpose of the outline is to serve as a guide in the development of one's ideas. Properly constructed, an outline can make the difference between audience understanding and confusion. Unless the speaker's thoughts are clarified beforehand, they are apt to sound confused. Besides, if not adequate plan for speaking has been made, important parts of the speech may be omitted or time may be wasted by ineffective interpolations. Learning to construct suitable outlines can be of inestimable value in disciplining oneself during the part of speech preparation called *synthesis*.

The complete sentence outline is of great value in guaranteeing that the writer's ideas are being clarified while writing. It also permits close examination of main ideas (few in number) and support (much) to determine if what is written actually supports the main ideas. While not properly a part of the outline, ideas for transition may be discovered while writing and inserted where suitable, labeling them as *transitions*.

Arranging main points in parallel construction will help assure that they are relatively equal. Here is an example:

   I. An educated man has command of his mother tongue.
  II. An educated man has an understanding of his environment.
 III. An educated man has the ability to use his power of learning to shape the future.

As in the selection of the components of the Subject Sentence, extra care in the choice of Main Points can result in a proper limiting of the scope of the talk. Only as many should be selected as the audience will be able to grasp—not the number the speaker may be able to put into his speech. Extra care needs to be taken to avoid writing the outline as though standing before the audience and giving the speech. Some poor outlines cover many pages, and interspersing them with a few Roman numerals or capital letters will not improve them. Some excellent outlines cover but a page or two, for the writers have avoided the temptation to write just as thoughts pop into their minds. Instead, they have carefully constructed each part in proper sequence—main points first, then support under each. To write in that order will help the process of synthesis, assuring a suitable plan to follow when time for detailed composition of the speech arrives.

Once an outline has been carefully constructed, it may be greatly reduced in length by writing single words or leading phrases which may be useable while rehearsing or even while speaking.

Speech Titles

A well-selected title, especially if advance publicity is to be given to your speech, can help prepare the audience to want to listen. Taking a tip from the novelist can be useful in selecting an attractive title. Betty McDonald wrote about the mundane *subject* of life on a chicken farm, yet the *title* of her book, *The Egg and I,* helped it to become a best-seller. How slow the sale of *Gone with the Wind* might have been had Margaret Mitchell chosen *A Civil War Story* as her title.

Even if your speech is to be on a technical subject, you can show imagination in your choice of title. *Rats, Lice and History* once drew great attention to an important book. What of "Carrots, Calories and Corn" for your speech on a limited aspect of diet control? An important feature of any speech title is that of mystifying the audience to the extent that they will want to have their curiosity allayed.

Introduction

Next to the conclusion the *introduction* of a speech is the most important single element in it. Its two main functions are (1) to get attention and arouse interest and (2) to orient the audience so that they may understand the trend your speech is to take. Skip such nonfunctional and trite phrases as "I had difficulty choosing a topic" or "Webster defines." The first is not of direct interest to anyone but you, and the second has been grossly overworked. Apologies are equally harmful to your speech purposes. Perhaps the *demonstration* of a piece of equipment will stimulate listening. Look to a subpoint under the first main point in your outline. If it is an *illustration,* relating it will save you from the sin of telling a funny, but unrelated, story. The subpoint may be an apt *quotation* which will quicken audience's interest. Other possibilities are a *startling statement,* such as "The chances are high that several of you will be maimed or killed on your way home" (speech on safe driving); *reference to the occasion;* an honest *compliment for the audience;* reference to the *common experience* of speaker and audience; reference to *special circumstances* of the audience or commentary on *special significance of the speech topic* for this audience. Whatever opening sentences you use should meet the two criteria of getting attention and orienting the listener.

Conclusion

As the farrier nails a shoe to the horse's hoof, he carefully clinches the ends so that no matter how fast the racehorse runs or trots, the shoe stays in place. In similar manner, your closing words, those which your listeners will most easily remember, must clinch what you have been saying. As the listener recalls the conclusion and the introduction, he can more surely recall the main points, thus assuring greater effectiveness of the speech.

One form is a *challenge* which calls upon each listener to dare to do what you ask. Another is a *plea,* such as an appeal for funds for charity. Use a *statement of purpose* or *personal intent* in the hopes that listeners will follow your example. For an informative speech, a *summary* may be useful because it recalls for the listener the main ideas which you have been developing. An appropriate *story* or a *quotation* are other forms which have been used with telling effect. The late Senator Robert Kennedy, when he gave his address on civil rights in Atlanta, quoted Henry Grady, young editor of the Atlanta *Constitution* during the Civil War.[9] Largely because of the Grady quotation, Kennedy's audience honored him with a standing ovation. To measure the expected effectiveness of any conclusion try to imagine just how it will make such a lasting impression on your audience that they will respond to your speech as you want them to do.

Such remarks as "I guess that about wraps it up" or "I can't think of anything else to say" or "I see that my time is up" or "In conclusion, I would like to say" have no place in your speech. They are not only ex- traneous but misdirect the listener's attention.

Avoid saying thank you. This is usually the mark of an amateur who doesn't know how to quit, and it detracts from the effect of the conclusion. Thank the audience only if you've been granted a favor, such as staying overtime.

Prepare your conclusion with utmost care, and if time runs out before your speech can end, sacrifice an earlier part in order to be able to use your conclusion for the purpose intended.

Support

"The illustration is the heart of the speech" is a commonly accepted truism in the art of speechcraft. A minimum of generalities and a max- imum of supporting materials can help assure speech effectiveness. If the support (termed by the expert in communication theory as "development material") is adequate, the listener is in a position to draw his conclusions which the illustrative material suggests. Unsupported assertions are usually

---

9. Grady's speech was given before the New England Society in New York City immediately after the Civil War. In it he made an appeal for understanding of and sympathy for the South.

so open-ended as to permit each listener to make his interpretation, often quite different from what the speaker intends. Obviously, then, you should use supporting material profusely in order to assure that the listener may understand your speech as you wish him to do. The principal purposes of support in a speech are (1) to make clear your general statements, (2) to amplify your meaning, (3) to impress upon hearers its significance, or (4) to offer proof of your claims. Insofar as possible, it should appeal to all of the five senses of each member of the audience.

Supporting material takes many forms. Some of them follow.

1. *Illustration.* In its larger sense, "illustration" means any form of support from statistics to visual aids. In its narrower sense, as used here, it means a *story*, such as those for which Lincoln became famous. Russell Conwell in his popular "Acres of Diamonds" speech used illustrations almost exclusively as support for his main theme.[10] So financially successful was this speech that Conwell was able to use the proceeds to found Temple University in Philadelphia. Today Temple's outgoing mail is stamped, "Founded on Acres of Diamonds." The opening story about the finding of diamonds was succeeded by several more stories supporting the main theme of the speaker. The *fable* as used in Aesop and the *parables* of Jesus are other forms of the illustration.

2. *Specific Instance.* Shortened illustrations or examples are useful to indicate that the case cited is not an isolated one. To illustrate the generalization, "Foreign musicians have been financially successful in touring the United States," you might relate the story of the triumphal tour of Jenny Lind, the "Swedish Nightingale." Then to supplement it you resort to such *specific instances* as: "Harry Lauder, the Scottish singer and entertainer, found American audiences so generous that he made several 'farewell tours.' Paderewski, Polish patriot and pianist, toured coast to coast many times, usually playing to capacity audiences. Caruso, the great Italian tenor, earned great wealth here as he became as familiar with the American scene as with his native Italy. Of more recent fame are the Beatles, England's gift to modern Western culture, who returned home after their tours here carrying large bags of teenagers' allowance money."

3. *Example.* References to a specific place, person, thing, name, happening, or scene may be classed as examples. Give us a "for instance" your listener pleads, and you cite an actual occurrence. The *example* may range from the general, and least effective, such as ". . . for example, the automobile has complicated our social life," to the *detailed example*. In the latter we give more information, saying: ". . . for example, the automobile takes us quickly from city to city as we strew the interstate highways with beer cans, wastepaper, and dead bodies. Juvenile delinquency is encouraged as we park our cars, leaving keys conveniently in the ignition. Crime is facilitated as bank robbers jump into a high-powered auto, quickly eluding their pursuers."

---

10. Agnes Rush Burr. *Russell H. Conwell and His Work* (Philadelphia: The John C. Winston Co., 1926), pp. 405–438.

Usually the *detailed example* will be needed to make your exact meaning clear. But if the audience is familiar with the subject matter, you may be able to use an undetailed example, such as: "Take a major league ball park, Pittsburgh's Three-Rivers Stadium, for example. . . ."

Real examples are generally preferable because they have the ring of truth. Sometimes a *hypothetical example* is needed—that is, when talking about how people will be expected to live on the moon or when you want to have a listener fancy himself as a participant in some unfamiliar situation. Such an example frequently begins with "if" or "imagine."

4. *Comparison and Contrast.* Usually called *analogy,* the device *comparison and contrast* is particularly effective in explaining something new in terms of what is already known. In explaining the mysteries of an auto engine to a group of women, a speaker said: "The carburetor is a device for mixing air and gasoline. It works something like a perfume atomizer." Some analogies are *literal,* as "A zebra is like a jackass, except that to visualize him you have to imagine the jackass wearing a striped prison suit." Others are *figurative.* In them you choose things from different realms, as Lincoln's apt one: "Moving an army across country," he said, "is much like carrying a shovelful of fleas across a barn floor. You never know what you're going to end up with at the other end of your trip."

5. *Statistics.* For those who are statistically minded the use of figures in this form is unexcelled in conveying your meaning. For oral use they need to be greatly simplified, carefully explained, or amplified with a visual presentation. They are particularly valuable in offering proof of a statement or to summarize. In using them, cite your sources to increase credibility, explain how the figures were arrived at, and whenever possible use round numbers because they are more readily grasped and easier to remember. Information alone may be meaningless to the listener until explained. For example, the number *382436* remain meaningless data until translated to *38–24–36.*

6. *Testimony.* The use of *testimony* of eyewitness or other authority lends credibility and authenticity to what you say. Testimony will be valuable in ratio to the respect which listeners have for its source. Identify the sources you cite, carefully explaining why the testimony is reliable. The use of exact *quotations* is advisable if the language merits it or if believability will be enhanced by reading the author's own words. Quotations of more than two or three lines have dubious value, often because the quote was not written to be read or because the speaker reads ineptly.

7. *Definition.* Many words which are familiar to the speaker who talks as a professional or specialist will be unfamiliar to his lay listeners. "Bloom" and "ingot," so well known to the steel manufacturer, are only words to the housewife until defined for her. Scientific or other appropriate terms should be used, but to be meaningful they will need translation. Some of the forms of definition include *explication, classification, synonym, antonym, negation,* and *example.*

8. *Repetition and Restatement.* Teachers of English composition warn us not to be redundant, and they are right. However, redundancy in some forms is a virtue in speech. If a listener doesn't hear or sense what we say the first time, he may get it the second or third time. Repetition of a main theme may emphasize it to the point where listeners memorize it. A summary statement at the end of each main point will enable your hearers to keep your

outline in mind. *Restatement* of your main arguments in the conclusion will serve to drive them home effectively. *Repetition* of the salient parts of an illustration can make it do double duty as you capitalize upon the audience's initial enthusiasm for it. Franklin D. Roosevelt used the device effectively as he derided three Republican congressmen by repeating their names, "Martin, Barton, and Fish," each time to the delight of his Democratic audience.

9. *Audiovisual Aids.* The use of sight and sound to amplify or illustrate your meaning helps to assure attention and understanding. How to use these forms of support is covered in Chapters 4 and 5.

To make your use of support effective you should be sure that it deals directly with the generalizations you design it to amplify. No matter how great the temptation to tell the good story you have just heard, resist using it unless it illustrates one of your assertions. Support must be geared to audience interest and understanding. An analogy made with an unfamiliar subject confuses the listeners. Support must be varied because too many of one form may become monotonous. Besides, not everyone is equally impressed with testimony or with statistics or with any other single form.

Words

Mark Twain once remarked that the difference between the right word and the almost right word is like the difference between lightning and the lightning bug. Some words, although they seem to be synonymous, can be used to express a precise meaning which their counterparts cannot. The wife of a dictionary maker caught her husband kissing the maid. "I'm surprised," the wife fumed. "No, dear," her husband coolly replied: "We're *surprised.* You're *amazed.*" In another incident a man was helping a woman editor with her coat. Noting her full figure, he remarked: "You're getting portly." "No, George," she answered. "You're portly. I'm buxom." In each case the pith of the rebuke was based upon the precise meaning of the words used.

Listeners appreciate the use of specific terms such as "five miles" in contrast to "a long walk" or "My wife and mother liked my speech" instead of "Many people. . . ." Meaning becomes clearer when you say "$50,000" instead of "a lot of money" or "twelve-room dwelling" instead of "a big house." By use of much specific terminology the listener becomes aware that he is hearing information which he can better understand.

All thoughts appear as words. A "mind reader" who had arrived in the United States with no knowledge of English was asked how he managed to get along while learning the language. "It was easy," he confessed. "I could always read the minds of the people I was with." Those who were

awed by his remark forgot that his statement was patently false since the
people he spoke of were using English in their thoughts.

Ample evidence is available to show that able people have large
vocabularies. Increase in one's acquaintanceship with words multiplies
his ability to express thoughts and to communicate successfully with
others. The listeners' understanding depends in large part upon the speaker's ability to select the words which will make his message intelligible.

Important as words are, we must remember that they have scant
value in themselves. They are but coded symbols for what we intend to
communicate. Someone has aptly said that they are but marks upon a
paper or sounds in the air until they have been sensed and reacted to by
those with whom we are trying to communicate. In short, meaning is not
in our words but in the mind of the listener. The word *cancer,* for example,
has a far different meaning for a person after he has won a bout with a
carcinoma than it had before his illness.

By our use of words we reveal our honesty or its lack. The woman
who reports to her husband that she has "put a little dent in one fender
of the car" is revealing something about her character when she notifies
her insurance that "the car is almost a total wreck." We resort to *name
calling*—"Communist," "hippie," and "demagogue" being current fa-
vorites.

In *card stacking* we are careful to use only what is favorable to our
own cause. For instance, when the salesman who has boasted of all of the
merits of his product is asked for its weaknesses, he answers: "I don't
know any." Card stackers do not deliberately lie. They merely omit the
facts which are unfavorable to their own causes.

Exaggeration is a favorite form of verbal dishonesty. In business,
"guarantee" is emphasized, but all to frequently the customer learns that
the faults which it covers are minimal. "Everybody says so . . ." can be
more accurately translated as "He and I have said so." Sidney Harris,
syndicated columnist for the Chicago *Daily Tribune,* writes an occasional
piece subtitled "Antics with Semantics." A typical statement in it may be:
"I drink occasionally. You overindulge. He's a drunk."

Use *simple* words to make meaning clear. Some speakers mistakenly
believe that they are demeaning themselves when they forsake the complicated jargon of their profession. They forget that great masters of the
English sentence, such as Winston Churchill, spoke so that even the un-
lettered could understand. One of Franklin D. Roosevelt's speech writers
suggested this line: "We are endeavoring to construct a more inclusive
society," and FDR in no way demeaned himself nor "talked down" to the
people when he revised the line to read: "We are going to make a country
in which no one is left out." Alexander Pope punctured pomposity when
he wrote:

> Such labored nothings in so learn'd a style
> Amaze the unlearned and make the learned smile.

Gobbledegook and *federalese* are terms applied to the pomposities of some who write or speak for the federal government. Learned men in business and professions are equally guilty. A most frequent cause of pomposity in speaking is the reliance on a manuscript which has been prepared in a written style, full of words which the speaker would be less likely to use in his ordinary attempts at oral communication.

Conclusion

Speeches come into being when a speaker has something to say and a compulsion to say it. They grow out of deep-seated beliefs and a conviction on the part of the speaker which he wishes to develop in others.

As you choose your subject, consider whether it is appropriate for *yourself,* your *audience,* and the *occasion.* Each of these criteria must be fully met if the speech is to serve the purpose intended for it. Purposes for speaking vary. Those most common are to *inform, to instruct, to stimulate, to entertain, to convince* or *persuade.* Your purpose in speaking will help determine the choice of materials to include in the speech.

For any speech you must have a great abundance of information, each item carefully selected and analyzed to suit your needs and those of your audience. Information may be acquired from your own *experience,* by *observation,* by *interviewing* those in a position to know what you don't, and from *reading.*

In reading, beware of relying too much on such "popular" sources as light magazines and books. Check sources against each other and decide which information is reliable and which author's biases are most honest. To avoid wasting time in discovering speech material, become familiar with the many types of indexes available in libraries.

For all research use a system of note-taking, preferably on 4-by-6–inch slips which permit ready filing and rapid rearrangement in outline making.

Establish a *specific purpose* and a *subject sentence* before starting to *outline* a speech. Make haste slowly at this stage of synthesis so as to have good standards by which to measure all speech materials. Careful planning can assure a more understandable speech, and the outline can serve as a useful tool both in assembling your information and as a guide while speaking.

Select a *title* and *introduction* that will arouse listener interest and direct it to your main idea. Prepare a *conclusion* that will help drive home the points which you want your listener to retain.

Because listener comprehension will depend largely upon the *support* used to amplify your general ideas, select it carefully for both quantity and quality. Listeners will expect much specific information which is accurate and adapted to their needs and interests.

Your vocabulary should be made up of words familiar to the listener, yet at the same time capable of expressing your ideas cogently and appealingly. Strive for simple, forceful language which is free of jargon and pomposity.

In the entire task of composing the speech, keep in mind that nothing of real significance in speech making transpires until your words are acted upon in the minds of your hearers.

FOR DISCUSSION

1. What is the difference between having an interest in a subject and having a deep concern for what it represents?
2. How may a speaker determine whether or not a speech subject is suitable for himself? for his audience? for the occasion?
3. Why is the experience of even a very young speaker of significance in his work of composing a speech?
4. What preparation should one make before undertaking to observe something which is unfamiliar to him?
5. To provide background for any speaking which he may do, what reading should the speaker do on a regular basis?
6. What hazards are there in relying upon such periodicals as *Reader's Digest, Look, Time,* and others, as primary sources of information?
7. How may information from professional journals be adapted for use in speeches before laymen?
8. How may the interlibrary loan service be used to secure hard-to-get information?
9. What criteria ought to be used in judging the quality of a system of note taking?
10. What are some of the reasons why one should have much more information about a subject than he intends to use in his speech?
11. Why, even when you are speaking about your specialty, is the preparation of a speech so time-consuming?
12. What are the essentials for a good outline?
13. Of what practical use is an outline in speech composition?
14. What criteria should be used in selecting support to be used in a speech?
15. How does a speaker select a vocabulary that is suitable for a specific audience?

PROBLEMS AND EXERCISES

1. Make list of possible speech subjects on social, economic, or other matters about which you have deep-seated feelings.
2. Make a similar list of technical or business subjects on which you feel qualified to speak.
3. For each of the subjects chosen in numbers 1 and 2 write the name of an organization before whose members you would choose to speak.
4. Choose one of the audiences listed in number 3 before whom you hope to be able to speak soon and write a careful description of its makeup after analyzing it for speech purposes.
5. Arrange for an interview with a specialist on one of the topics on which you expect to speak. Write suitable questions to ask him.
6. Select a building or other structure which you have frequently *seen*. Write a description of it. Next, *observe* the same structure for at least one hour, trying to see it as an artist, an architect, a builder, a prospective buyer, or a tenant might see it. Write a supplement to the original description.
7. Spend an hour in a library examining the indexes and other reference books which might be of value to you in preparing speeches.
8. Examine several copies of the *New York Times, Los Angeles Times, Washington Post,* or other top-quality newspaper. Compare it with your hometown or other newspapers as to scope and coverage of news, editorial policy, features, and so on.
9. Select three or more periodicals which you do not customarily read and try to determine how reliable they might be as sources for you to use.
10. Read several speeches from *Vital Speeches of the Day* or other sources. Study the structure of each, noting especially the use of introductions, conclusions, and forms of support.
11. Study the sample speeches in the Appendix. Write the Specific Purpose and Subject Sentence of each. Estimate the probable effect of the Introduction and Conclusion of each. Identify the kinds of support each speaker used.

BIBLIOGRAPHY

Books

Applbaum, Ronald L., and Anatol, Karl W. E. *Strategies for Persuasive Communication.* Columbus, Ohio: Charles E. Merrill Publishing Company.

Blankenship, Jane. *A Sense of Style: An Introduction to Style for the Public Speaker.* Belmont, Cal.: Dickenson Pub. Co., Inc., 1968.

Bradley, Bert. *Speech Performance.* Dubuque, Ia.: Wm. C. Brown Company Publishers, 1967, chap. 1.

BRIGANCE, WILLIAM NORWOOD. *Speech: Its Techniques and Disciplines in a Free Society.* 2d ed. N. Y.: Appleton-Century-Crofts, 1961, chaps. 9–13. For a philosophical approach to public speaking see chaps. 1–4.

BLACK, JOHN W., and MOORE, WILBUR E. *Speech, Code, Meaning, and Communication.* N. Y.: McGraw-Hill Book Company, 1955, pp. 5–10.

DAY, J. EDWARD. *Humor in Public Speaking.* Englewood Cliffs, N. J.: Parker Publishing Company, 1965.

FRYE, NORTHROP. Anatomy of Persuasion. N. Y.: Atheneum Publishers, 1968.

HOLTZMAN, PAUL D. *The Psychology of Speaker's Audiences.* Glenview, Ill.: Scott, Foresman and Company, 1970.

HUSEMAN, RICHARD C.; LOGUE, CAL M.; and FRESHLEY, DWIGHT L. *Readings in Interpersonal and Organizational Communication.* Boston: Holbrook Press, Inc., 1969, pt. 3 and pp. 431–53.

LARSON, CHARLES U. *Persuasion: Reception and Responsibility.* Belmont, Cal.: Wadsworth Publishing Company, 1973.

LaRUSSO, DOMINIC. *Basic Skills of Oral Communication.* Dubuque, Ia.: Wm. C. Brown Company Publishers, 1967, chap. 4.

MARSH, PATRICK O. *Persuasive Speaking: Theory, Models, Practice.* N. Y.: Harper & Row, Publishers, 1967, chap. 4–9.

MARSTON, EVERETT C.; THOMPSON, LORING M.; and ZACHER, FRANK. *Business Communication.* N. Y.: The Macmillan Company, 1949, chaps. 22–29.

MILLS, GLENN E. *Message Preparation: Analysis and Structure.* Indianapolis: The Bobbs-Merrill Co., Inc., 1966.

MITCHELL, EWAN. *The Business Man's Guide to Speech Making and to the Laws and Conduct of Meetings.* London: Business Books, Ltd., 1968.

MOHRMAN, G. P. *Composition and Style in the Writing of Speeches.* Dubuque, Ia.: Wm. C. Brown Company Publishers, 1970.

NEWMAN, ROBERT P., and NEWMAN, DALE R. *Evidence.* Boston: Houghton Mifflin Company, 1969.

NIZER, LOUIS. *Thinking on Your Feet.* Garden City, N. Y.: Garden City Publishing Co., 1944.

O'HAYRE, JOHN. *Gobbledegook Has Gotta Go.* Washington, D.C.: Bureau of Land Management, United States Department of Interior, United States Government Printing Office, 1966.

OLIVER, ROBERT T. *The Psychology of Persuasive Speech.* 2d ed. N. Y.: Longmans, Green and Co., 1957, chaps. 15, 16, 18, 19, 20.

OLIVER, ROBERT T.; ZELKO, HAROLD P.; and HOLTZMAN, PAUL D. *Communicative Speaking and Listening.* 4th ed. N. Y.: Holt, Rinehart and Winston, Inc., 1968, chaps. 3–8.

PARSON, DON W., and LINKUGEL, WIL A. *The Ethics of Controversy.* Lawrence: Department of Speech and Drama, University of Kansas, 1965, p. 135.

REIN, IRVING J. *The Relevant Rhetoric.* N. Y.: The Free Press, 1969.

STRUNK, WILLIAM, JR., and WHITE, E. B. *The Elements of Style.* N. Y.: The Macmillan Company, 1959.

WALTER, OTIS M., and SCOTT, ROBERT L. *Thinking and Speaking.* 3d ed. N. Y.: The Macmillan Company, 1973, chaps. 2–4.

WEAVER, CARL H., and STRAUSBAUGH, WARREN L. *Fundamentals of Speech Communication.* N. Y.: American Book Company, 1964, chaps. 4–6, 12.

WILCOX, ROGER P. *Oral Reporting in Business and Industry.* Englewood Cliffs, N. J.: Prentice-Hall, Inc., 1967.

WILSON, JOHN F., and ARNOLD, CARROLL C. *Public Speaking as a Liberal Art.* 3d ed. Boston: Allyn & Bacon, Inc., 1974.

WISEMAN, GORDON, and BARKER, LARRY. *Speech: Interpersonal Communication.* San Francisco: Chandler Publishing Company, 1967, chaps. 4–6, 8.

Periodicals

"Audio-Visual Training Is Ready to Blossom." *Air Conditioning, Heating* and *Refrigeration News,* 131 (January 14, 1974):19.

BROCKREIDE, WAYNE E. "Rhetoric and Public Address." *Quarterly Journal of Speech* 52 (April 1966):198.

BUCHANAN, P. C. "How Can We Gain Their Commitment?" *Personnel,* January 1965, pp. 21–26.

CALLAGHAN, J. CALVIN. "How Long Should a Sermon Be?" *Today's Speech* 12 (February 1964): 10–11.

"Clarity with Words." *Distribution Age* 64 (April 1965):14.

CLARK, BLAKE. "Is Your Vocabulary Good Enough?" *Reader's Digest*, February 1973, pp. 37–42.

COUSINS, NORMAN. "Education and the Clarifying Experience." *Perspectives on Education*, Teachers College, Columbia University, 2 (Winter 1969):1–5.

DYER, G. W. "Semantics of Success." *Personnel Administration*, March 1965, pp. 39–40.

FEINBERG, M. "Gentle Art of Effective Persuasion." *Dun's Review and Modern Industry* 86 (December 1965'):41–47.

FINEGELD, THOMAS E. "The Ability to Select Words to Convey Intended Meaning." *Quarterly Journal of Speech* 52 (October 1966): chap. 6.

"The First Viewpoint You Hear May Be the Biggest Persuader." *Science Digest*, February 1958, pp. 13, 14.

FRANK, JEROME D. "The Face of the Enemy." *Psychology Today*, November 1968, pp. 24–29.

HARRINGTON, ELBERT W. "A Modern Approach to Invention." *Quarterly Journal of Speech* 48 (December 1962):373.

HAZEL, HARRY C. "Harry Truman: Practical Persuader." *Today's Speech* 22 (Spring 1974):25–31.

HESS, S. W. "Communicating with Physicians." *Journal of Advertising Research* 14 (February 1974):13–18.

HILTS, PHILYS J. "David Brinkley's Journal." *The Washington Post/Potomac*, January 27, 1974.

JEFFREY, R. C. "Ethics in Public Discourse." *Vital Speeches of the Day* 40 (December 1973): 113–16.

KERR, HARRY P. "Using Opinion and Evidence." *Quarterly Journal of Speech* 16 (January 1967):19.

LYNCH, D. "Confessions of a Speechwriter: Why So Many Business Speeches Sound Lifeless and Artificial." *Dun's Review and Modern Industry* 86 (November 1965):42–43.

McGLON, CHARLES A. "How I Prepare My Sermons: A Symposium." *Quarterly Journal of Speech* 40 (February 1954):54–55.

MARINE, DONALD R. "An Investigation of Intra-Speaker Reliability." *Quarterly Journal of Speech* 14 (March 1965):128.

MAYER, MARTIN. "The Brilliance of Spiro Agnew." *Esquire*, May 1970, pp. 117–19, 207, 208.

MILLER, GERALD R., and HEWGILL, MURRAY A. "The Effect of Variation in Nonfluency on Audience Rating of Source Credibility." *Quarterly Journal of Speech* 50 (February 1964):36.

NEWMAN, JOHN B., and HOROWITZ, MILTON W. "Writing and Speaking." *College Composition and Communication* 16 (October 1965):160–64.

NICHOLS, ALLAN C. "Audience Ratings of the Naturalness of Spoken and Written Sentences." *Quarterly Journal of Speech* 32 (June 1966):156.

OLIVER, ROBERT T. "Ethics and Efficiency in Persuasion." *The Southern Speech Journal* 26 (Fall 1960):10–15.

OLSON, DONALD O. "Confusion in Arrangement." *Quarterly Journal of Speech* 13 (September 1964):216.

"Persuasion—Soft Soap or Hard Sell." *Iron Age* 204 (April 17, 1969):30.

REID, PAUL E. "Psychiatry and Persuasion: Professional Twins." *Ohio Speech Journal* 2 (1963): 129–36.

SCHMIDT, RALPH N. "Offering the Invocation." *Today's Speech* 11 (November 1963):16.

SCOTT-ATKINSON, DAVID. "Some Clear-Cut Rules on Speech Making." Reprinted from *Marketing*, November 26, 1973, in *The Toastmaster* 40 (May 1974):26–29.

SHAW, C. "How to Give Oral Instructions." *Office* 60 (December 1964):71–75.

STEVENSON, JOHN W. "A Man Speaking to Men." *Humanities in the South* (newsletter of the Southern Humanities Conference) 39 (Spring 1974).

SUNDSTROM, H. W. "Speech Writing—PR's Silent Service." *Public Relations Journal* 30 (March 1974):48–49.

"System and Order." *Royal Bank of Canada Newsletter* 52 (May 1971).

WILCOX, ROGER. "Characteristics and Organization of the Oral Technical Report." *General Motors Engineering Journal*, June 1959, pp. 1–12.

WILLIAMSON, M. A. "Watch Your Language." *Research Development*, June 1966, pp. 41–42.

ZELKO, HAROLD P. "What's Wrong with Public Speaking?" Reprinted from *Public Relations Journal*, January 1970, in *The Toastmaster* 38 (June 1972):6.

ZELLY, E. S. "How to Say a Few Words." *Nation's Business* 64 (July 1966):80–83.

Films

"The Anatomy of a Presentation." Part 1, thirty minutes; Part 2, five minutes.
"Imagination at Work." Twenty-one minutes.
"Pattern for Instruction." Twenty-one minutes.

All films can be obtained from Roundtable Films, Inc., 113 North San Vicente Boulevard, Beverly Hills, Cal. 90211.

Let us have a reason for beginning,
and let our end be within due limits.
For a speech that is wearisome
only stirs up anger.

St. Ambrose

Reading a Manuscript

A young minister, eager to have helpful criticism of his preaching, asked an elderly Scot what he thought of the sermon.

"Well, laddie," the canny Scot observed, "In the fairst place ye r-r-read the sairmon. In the second place ye r-r-read it vairy bodly, in the thaird place it was no' worth r-r-reading."

Here in a nutshell we have the most frequently raised objections to speeches which are read. The act of reading so often leaves out most contact with the listeners. The reader concentrates on reading, not on communicating his ideas. He has eyes solely for his manuscript and ignores feedback from his audience.

The speaker *reads*—as contrasted with speaking—aloud it may be true, and audibly, but with concern only for reading and not for interpreting or for whether he is communicating. Concentrating as he does on his notes, he unconsciously reads at a monotonous rate and without expression. Occasionally a hasty glance is directed at the ceiling. Pauses are neglected because of the urge to utter the next words in view on the page. Words are misspoken as "indicted" becomes "indicated" and "marital" is spoken as "martial," such errors are an indication that the speaker's mind is on reading words rather than on *communicating* ideas to his listeners. Impatiently he makes corrections as he hurries on, rarely pausing to consider whether or not his corrections have been understood. Facial

Reading a speech from a manuscript may make direct contact between speaker and listener more difficult. This man seems overly concerned with his manuscript.

expression remains immobile, and gestures are confined to jerks of the chin or virbrating elbows. The hands are locked in a firm grip on the lectern[1] with only an occasional lifted finger to reveal an inner urge to use the hands to illustrate or emphasize. As pages are turned, auditors begin counting them, trying to estimate how soon their ordeal may end. All of the elements of bad speaking tend to be exemplified by the inept reader.

Speak Only to Communicate

Such speakers seem to believe that some virtue lies in articulating words. They forget that words are but sounds in the air until they are caught by the ear of the listener and decoded into messages. The speaker who reads without attempting to get feedback from his audience by keeping in direct visual and vocal contact with its members cannot hope for good comprehension by them. Researchers have concluded that reading a speech is often thirty percent to forty percent less effective than giving an extemporaneous or even an impromptu speech. The veteran owner of

---

1. Reading desk—as distinguished from *podium,* a dais, platform, or rostrum.

a prominent lecture bureau used to advise his speakers: "You can't speak through a paper screen." The speaker who reads should remind himself that his primary aim is to keep in constant communication with each listener if he has any hope of making his speech serve whatever purpose he intended.

The able speaker uses a manuscript only for the purpose of refreshing his memory. As in conversation or in impromptu and extemporaneous speaking, his prime attention is centered on the listeners. During manuscript preparation, the words to be spoken are put on the page in such a way as to be instantly recognizable, and in rehearsal the speaker becomes familiar enough with his speech so that in a single glance he may identify a phrase, a sentence, or even a whole paragraph.

If a speaker prepares himself and his speech competently, his performance before an audience will be a great contrast to that of the all-too-frequent readers of speeches. As he stands, he confidently speaks his opening lines with no reference to his manuscript. He had already assured himself of what was in his opening paragraphs before standing to speak. Because the introduction of a speech is of supreme significance, he uses all of his physical and mental powers to make it effective. He stands erect, expressing confidence in his manner; his hands are held loosely at his sides, ready for instant use in gesturing should the impulse to do so reach him. His eyes are on his audience, and his voice carries his message to them clearly and distinctly. During a slight pause after his sentences of introduction, his eyes fall to his manuscript, remaining just long enough to *read* the next few phrases. Eyes again on his audience, he *speaks* what he has just read. Throughout the speech he continues to alternately read and speak. Because he has written in an oral style, ease in speaking is more noticeable, and the listener finds that comprehension is proportionately easier. The speaker's time spent in silent reading, in a ratio of about ten percent reading to ninety percent speaking, gives the listener time to relax, to comprehend what has just been said, and to prepare himself to continue listening. For the speaker, the pauses are a means of emphasizing and making more intelligible the thoughts which he is attempting to communicate. Because he is concentrating on the act of communication, his mind is on what he is saying; and because he maintains good visual contact with his audience, he is able to notice their feedback and to respond accordingly.

Since his hands are free, his gestures appear natural as he effectively supplements or illustrates what he is saying. With weight well balanced on both feet, rather than leaning on table or lectern, he can use his body with equal effectiveness in interpreting his meaning. Should his speaking time grow short, he does not speed up his reading rate. Instead, he mentally edits his copy and omits such parts of his speech as necessity decrees, proceeding at a normal pace to his planned conclusion.

At all times during his speech such a speaker remains in control of himself, his copy, and close visual and vocal contact with his audience. Because of this close contact, he is in a position to notice and interpret the response of the audience, and he is able to adapt to it much the same as if he were speaking extemporaneously.[2]

Use Oral Style

The man who writes his manuscript usually takes the first step toward poor speaking as he uses a written style instead of an oral style. If he hires a ghost writer, he usually elects a journalist or other person skilled in the craft of writing, rather than one skilled in speaking. Charles James Fox, the English seventeenth-century orator, insisted that "a speech is not an essay standing on its hind legs." Matter written for silent reading can seldom be spoken easily or effectively.

More illustrations are needed in a speech than most essayists use. The listener must understand instantly as he hears the speech, while the reader of an essay may take time to think. He can supply his own illustrations, he can reread sentences to discover any hidden nuances, and he can even turn to a dictionary or other reference book to discover meanings of words or references which may be unfamiliar to him.

The listener has none of these advantages. If he pauses to think, the next few sentences of the speech slip past without his hearing them. An unfamiliar word or phrase is identified through its context or missed completely. The misunderstood statement remains fixed and indelible. The leisure of the reader is nonexistent for the listener. His rate of comprehension is fixed by the speed and skill of the speaker. As he listens he identifies what he hears, taking in the meaning as he hears it with none of the reader's leisure for cogitation.

The speaker who intends to read his speech verbatim must keep his listener's identify and needs in mind as he writes. Spoken style is more easily comprehended as one listens to it. A written style is more difficult when read orally. The truism holds for most listeners, for paying strict attention to a speaker is difficult even for skilled and interested listeners. With this in mind as he writes, the speaker will anticipate the need for

---

2. Review Chapters 4 and 5. To overcome the handicap of needing to read his manuscrpit, the speaker must take extra pains to *communicate* his views directly—using full powers of his voice and maintaining eye contact with each listener.

illustrations, for interpretation of statistics, for identification of authors quoted, and for paraphrasing of complicated quotes. He will continually ask himself if what he is writing can be easily comprehended by the listener for whom it is intended.

Because a listener's ability to give undivided attention is measured in seconds, a speech writer will be alert to insert interest-provoking items in his speech, even more frequently in the manuscript to be read than in the extemporaneous speech—references to familiar names or places, citations from local authors, use of material appealing to one's interest in competition, and to anything of vital importance to one's hearers, such as health, family, or pocketbook. Such references will effectively offset a listender's tendency to go wool-gathering when his interest in what is being said tends to wane.

Read Interestingly

When the manuscript is finished and read competently, it should sound as interesting and be as comprehensive as the best of extemporaneous or impromptu speaking. Its style should be that of the most interesting conversationalist, captivating and challenging. One way to try to achieve such a style is to dictate from notes rather than to rely on pencil or typewriter to record one's thoughts. Speaking to a stenographer or even into the microphone of a tape recorder serves to encourage a directness in style that laborious writing cannot achieve. This is particularly true if the speaker does not try to envision before him those persons with whom he is trying to communicate. As he dictates, he must try to imagine how they will respond and to compose his speech accordingly.

Once the first draft of the manuscript is written, revision is usually necessary to make certain that both content and writing style are suitable for *oral* presentation. Clichés must be stricken and sentences sometimes shortened by changing commas to periods. References to "the writer" or "the speaker" should be changed to "I," and any instances of passive voice changed to the more vigorous active voice. All such tongue twisters as "bulk milk tank trucks" should be paraphrased lest they trip an unwary tongue during delivery. Occasionally, sentences must be broken into fragments, often with exclamation points to remind the speaker of needed emphasis. Key sentences are set apart as separate paragraphs. Additional explanatory remarks are inserted where needed, and transitional summaries used at the ends of all main points. Such contractions as "I've" for "I have" or appropriate slang phrases may be needed to help the listener understand or to feel that the speaker is conversing with him.

In all of the revising, what will appeal to the listener should be a major criterion in deciding what to write. For it is the listener—not the speaker—for whom the speech is intended. Successful speaking can best be measured by whether it has had its intended effect on the audience, so keep each member of the audience in mind while working on the speech.

While preparing a manuscript, test portions of it—either by listening to your own recording or by having some trusted colleague listen—both for accuracy and clarity of factual data and for interest appeal of the material. Beware of seeking opinions from too many people. The late Clarence Randall, former president of Inland Steel Corporation, warned speakers of such a practice, saying that speeches submitted to one's colleagues for review would come back with nothing but clichés left, with all that made the speeches interesting and valuable blue-pencilled.

Some companies have a speech editorial committee. The only legitimate function of such a committee is to test a speech for accuracy of statement and as to whether it conforms to company policy. Any tampering with the author's style, his attempts at humor, or his point of view is not properly within such a committee's purview. To usurp such authority has the effect of reducing all speeches made by company officials to the same common denominator, of stultifying creativity, and of elevating committee members to the post of company spokesmen. Such a system might easily relegate a potentially able speaker to a mere reader of someone else's manuscript.

Special Reading Copy

Once composition has been finished and revisions are at an end, a special reading copy can be prepared. Nonrustling paper of a good weight should be used. Thirty-pound mimeograph paper is ideal. It rattles very little when handled, and 8½-by-11–inch sheets of that weight have sufficient body to permit easy handling, especially if no lectern is available while the speech is being given. Wide margins ought to be left on all four sides with body of the copy just wide enough to permit reading of an entire line at one glance. Each line should contain only enough words to be spoken between pauses, even though your typist tells you that the margins will be uneven.

Even if there's extra room at the bottom of a page, insist that the typist stop at the end of the paragraph or a phrase or sentence requiring a pause. The pause needed then will give time to find the place on the next page. An extra help is to type at the bottom of the page the first line to appear at the top of the next. A typewriter with three-eighth–inch type is desirable, for even with bifocals the speaker will be able to see his

copy from some little distance without seeming to be concentrating on it.[3]
Be sure the typewriter ribbon is the darkest possible, the keys clean, and
for extra visibility place a sheet of carbon paper, wrong side to, against
the back of each sheet of paper. Black ink on the reverse side can help
make the typing stand out more clearly against the white paper.

Avoid all use of binders, notebooks, staples, or other means of fasten-
ing pages together. Use of the manuscript should be so unobtrusive that
listeners are scarcely aware that you have one. Keep pages flat and un-
folded. A manila folder or envelope will do to carry them in, and if they
are prominently numbered at the top of each page, they can easily be put
in numerical order if accidentally disarranged.

Once the final draft is typed, rehearse from it and mark it where
necessary with a nylon- or felt-tipped pen. Words or phrases needing
special emphasis can be underlined. Vertical lines or slashes can indicate
the need for extra pauses. Marginal direction, such as "Slow down," "Look
at audience," or "Show slides here," can be useful. The use of one chap's
reminder to himself, "Argument weak here. Yell like hell," is questionable.
The principal aim in manuscript preparation is to permit maximum
visibility in order to achieve the desirable end of looking at the audience
ninety percent of the time as you are speaking and at the paper but ten
percent in order to read what comes next.

Rehearsal Necessary

Almost as much time is needed for rehearsal as for writing the
speech. Properly done, it can enable the speaker to communicate with
his audience as directly as if he were giving an extemporaneous speech.
Practice looking at the copy, reading the lines silently, then at the audience as the words are spoken. During a suitable pause, look at the page
for the next thought, read it, then speak it to the listeners. Here the value
of extra care in making the copy legible becomes evident. If properly
prepared, reading can be done at a glance while the speaker focuses his
attention on the listeners. To test one's skill during rehearsal have someone listen while you speak. Occasionally insert some impromptu remarks.
If your critic cannot determine which parts are being read and which are
impromptu, you are probably ready to *speak* your manuscript speech.

If a lectern is to be used, test it first to see if there is plenty of room
for two sheets of 8½-by-11–inch paper to lie side by side. If so, good, for

---

3. Compare type used for David L. Lawrence's speech in Appendix. (This type
has been reduced by one-third.)

MR SPEAKER   MR PRESIDENT   MEMBERS OF THE CONGRESS

I SPEAK TONIGHT FOR THE DIGNITY OF MAN

                            AND THE DESTINY OF DEMOCRACY.

I URGE EVERY MEMBER OF BOTH PARTIES

                AMERICANS OF ALL RELIGIONS   AND OF ALL COLORS

FROM EVERY SECTION OF THE COUNTRY   TO JOIN ME IN THAT CAUSE.

AT TIMES   HISTORY AND FATE MEET AT A SINGLE TIME

                                    IN A SINGLE PLACE.

TO SHAPE A TURNING POINT IN MAN'S UNENDING SEARCH FOR FREEDOM.

SO IT WAS AT LEXINGTON AND CONCORD

        SO IT WAS A CENTURY AGO AT APPOMATOX

            SO IT WAS LAST WEEK IN SELMA ALABAMA.

THERE LONG-SUFFERING MEN AND WOMEN PEACEFULLY PROTESTED

                THE DENIAL OF THEIR RIGHTS AS AMERICANS.

MANY WERE BRUTALLY ASSAULTED

    ONE GOOD MAN - A MAN OF GOD - WAS KILLED.

THERE IS NO CAUSE FOR PRIDE IN WHAT HAS HAPPENED AT SELMA.

THERE IS NO CAUSE FOR SELF-SATISFACTION IN THE LONG DENIAL

    OF RIGHTS OF MILLIONS OF AMERICANS.

BUT THERE IS CAUSE FOR HOPE   AND FOR FAITH IN OUR DEMOCRACY

    IN WHAT IS HAPPENING HERE TONIGHT.

Sample of speech typed for ease in reading while speaking.

then you won't have to turn pages and so distract the listeners. Instead, put page one to the left, the rest of the pile to the right, *sliding* page two and each succeeding one to the left as you finish reading it. Unless you betray the secret by faulty eye contact, the audience need never know when you shift from one page to the next.

Before time to speak, be sure that the lectern is at the right height for you. If it is too low, learn how to elevate it. Some lecterns have hydraulic lifts; others may be set by inserting wooden pegs into holes to attain the proper level. Sometimes propping up the lectern with books may be necessary if it is not otherwise adjustable. When a nonadjustable lectern is too high, find something to stand on, even at the risk of being accused of speaking from a soapbox.

If no lectern is available, use a sheet of 8½-by-11–inch lightweight cardboard as a backing for the entire manuscript. As each page is read, it can be unobtrusively slipped to the bottom of the pile, a movement less noticeable than dropping it to desk or table.

There are several advantages in being able to read a speech without benefit of a lectern. You will be completely visible to the audience, hence they will be able to see all of your gestures and bodily action. You will find yourself unhampered by the lectern when you must move. You may approach the audience as closely as you wish, and as you hold the manuscript by one edge in either hand, your thumb can conveniently serve as a place marker, serving as a guide each time as you look at the page to read. Being able to lift the manuscript instead of lowering your head will also help you maintain better eye contact with the audience.

When you are sure that you are completely ready with a speech that has been prepared with extra care and are certain that it is one which is worth speaking, you can approach your task with confidence. From the moment you stand to face your listeners, you can concentrate on them, using all of your skills to hold their attention and to cause them to respond as you desire them to. From the introduction to the peroration you can *speak* with your listeners as if you were giving an impromptu speech but with all of the advantages of a skillfully constructed manuscript. Seek to achieve two-way communication constantly with each listener as you speak. Strive for the highest accolade: "He spoke straight from the shoulder and seldom looked at his notes."

Check the public-address system. Is the microphone conveniently located? If you must move about to show slides or other exhibits is a lavaliere microphone available? Is the volume control properly set, and is a well-qualified attendant near to keep it so? How adequate is the reading light? Is it adjusted so as not to shine in your listeners' eyes? Is there a clock conveniently located, or a place to put your own watch for easy visibility? Your speaking time may be limited and you will need to know if a part of your speech must be omitted.

Let the Listeners See

How visible will you be to your audience as you speak? Glare from a picture window behind you, if speaking during the daytime, may make you almost invisible, especially to those with light-sensitive eyes. Should some chairs be moved so that their occupants will be more strategically placed? Will you have footroom near the lectern? Some speakers' platforms are crudely built and have openings into which an unwary speaker might fall. Some, especially at luncheons or dinners, are crowded with guests, permitting only limited space.

Are you using visual aids? If so, how visible are they to the audience? Test them from the back of the room. If you are slightly nearsighted and yet can distinguish your aids readily, they are adequate for your audience. If you are using a projector, be sure to have extra bulbs and know where the fuse box is located. Check beforehand with your projectionist to be certain he understands his assignment and the signals to be used. Has someone been assigned the duty of handling light switches on signal? The author once saw a speech interrupted by an eager volunteer projector operator who said: "Now that you've seen the speaker's film I want you to see the one that I made on my trip last year."

Do you have a means of keeping charts or models out of sight until you are ready to use them? If not, they can be a source of distraction instead of aid. Charts can be covered with plain paper and models draped with cloth until you are ready to show them.

Have you posted a trusted friend in the back of the room to let you know whether or not you can be heard? Agree on a set of signals that will let you know when to increase volume. If people cannot hear you, you may as well not be speaking.

Are you to speak out-of-doors? Sudden gusts of wind may play havoc with your notes. Perhaps the answer will be the use of large rubber bands to fasten them to the lectern. The precaution will prevent the notes from being scattered among the band members as happened once to those of a high school commencement speaker. Although the band members scrambled chivalrously to pick up the cards, the speaker grew hopelessly lost. He had too many cards, they were not numbered, so in his confusion he abandoned his speech and launched into the speech which he had given at the same school the previous June. Will you have to compete with traffic noises—auto, train, or airplane? If so, how will you adapt your speaking so that you may be heard? How will you compensate if the weather is warm and humid and the mosquitoes troublesome, both to you and the audience?

Maybe all of these petty details seem picayunish and unnecessary. Perhaps they are, but genius is sometimes defined as the capacity for taking infinite care. Being prepared for all contingencies and knowing how to cope with all aspects of speaking help to distinguish the difference between the successful professional speaker and the diffident amateur. If the success of your speech is important to you, paying attention to all details is a small price to pay for winning your audience.

Business and professional people have many chances to read. As secretaries of organizations, they must read minutes and correspondence. Treasurers give financial reports. At conferences and conventions custom decrees the reading of "papers." Corporation executives often are expected to read written reports exactly as written. Those who rise high enough in rank find that policy speeches must be written and then read verbatim.

Full benefits often are not gained from the opportunity to speak. The speaker, tied to his manuscript, forgets that he must maintain close contact with his listeners, always in direct visual and vocal contact with them if he is to communicate his message effectively.

Conclusion

The speaker with a manuscript before him reads only because he cannot remember what he wants to say. Since his purpose is to communicate, *reading* is incidental to *speaking*. Only the speaker should be aware of the act of silent reading, the audience being concerned only with the *spoken* message.

To make the message more readily understood it must be written in oral style, as distinguished from the essay. Sentences should be shorter, technical words must be translated, and more illustrative material will make instant comprehension easier.

Special attention must be given to the preparation of a manuscript to facilitate silent reading during the speaker's pauses. Large type, few words to a line, short paragraphs, and underlining for emphasis can enable the reader to seem to be speaking extemporaneously.

Once the manuscript is ready, much rehearsal is needed to enable the speaker to appear to be speaking without reading. Complete familiarity with the manuscript's contents will allow him to concentrate on his listeners and their understanding.

The speaker has the responsibility to see that all audiovisual aids can be used to accomplish what is expected of them. He must test all equipment in advance to make certain that it works correctly and that the

audience can see and hear what he expects them to. He must keep re-
minding himself that he is to speak for the purpose of communicating
a message.

FOR DISCUSSION

1. Under what circumstances may reading a speech from manuscript
   be necessary? Is lack of preparation time a valid excuse? Why?
2. What are the advantages for the speaker? What are the disadvantages?
3. What are the advantages for the listener? What are the disadvantages?
4. What precautions must the speaker take in writing his speech to be
   sure that his listener will be interested and able to comprehend the
   meaning of the speech?
5. What advantage is there in giving the illusion that a speech is *not*
   being read?
6. What techniques may be used in preparing a manuscript to make it
   easier to read?
7. If the listeners have arrived expecting to hear an important speech,
   why is it necessary for the speaker to take infinite pains in composition
   and delivery?
8. How can a speaker maintain eye contact with his audience and use
   gestures while reading his speech?
9. How can a speaker improvise if no lectern has been provided?
10. What hazards for the speaker exist if he tries to read from a conven-
    tionally typed manuscript?
11. What are the advantages and disadvantages of using a chalkboard
    as a visual aid?
12. What audio aids might be useful?
13. What precautions should be taken if one is planning to use live models,
    for example, dogs, rats, babies, adults?
14. What is the speaker's ultimate aim in giving a speech from manu-
    script?
15. How may multiple copies of a speech be used if the speaker needs to
    move about the platform during a presentation?

PROBLEMS AND EXERCISES

1. Choose a short speech which someone else has written and read it
   "cold" into the microphone of a tape recorder. Deliver it as though to
   a real audience.
   Next, study the speech with great care, retype it in good form for
   reading purposes, rehearse it several times, then record it again. Compare both tapes to note any differences.

2. Attend a convention or other meeting where speakers customarily read papers. Observe and make notes on (1) what one or more speakers did which was helpful to the listener and (2) what they did which was distracting to watch or to listen to.

3. Have someone make a motion picture or video tape recording of you reading one of your short speeches. Afterward watch yourself on the screen, taking notes on aspects of your speaking which might be improved.

4. Study the manuscripts of several speeches and several essays. What differences do you note in their language? in structure and use of forms of support? What changes, if any, would you recommend in the speeches?

5. Prepare a speech to be given extemporaneously. When preparation is finished, tape-record it, using few, if any, notes. Then, have the speech typed. As you read the manuscript, what differences do you note between it and your usual written style?

6. Write out a set of instructions for a typist to follow in preparing a speech for you to read. How will you motivate the typist to violate most of the customs normally followed in spacing, paragraphing, and sentence structure?

7. Prepare and deliver a speech in which you read parts and give other parts extemporaneously. Test your success in reading by having qualified observers note which parts were extemporaneous. If they are unable to detect differences, what inferences may you draw about your delivery?

8. Write the descriptions and specifications for what you consider to be an ideal lectern for you to use in reading speeches.

9. To improve your ability in interpretation of the spoken word, practice reading poetry aloud to your family and friends or stories to children.

10. Attend a meeting where some speeches are read and some are given extemporaneously. Estimate their respective effectiveness. Attempt to ascribe reasons for any differences.

11. Make a list of all of the occasions when people of your business or profession may be expected to read a written statement.

BIBLIOGRAPHY

Books

BRIGANCE, WILLIAM NORWOOD. *Speech: Its Techniques and Disciplines in a Free Society.* 2d ed. N. Y.: Appleton-Century-Crofts, 1961, pp. 273–74.

BRYANT, DONALD C., and WALLACE, KARL R. *Fundamentals of Public Speaking.* N. Y.: Appleton-Century-Crofts, 1960, pp. 237–43.

Hunsinger, Paul. *Communicative Interpretation*. Dubuque, Ia.: Wm. C. Brown Company Publishers, 1967.

Lantz, J. Edward. *Reading the Bible Aloud*. N. Y.: The Macmillan Company, 1959.

Marston, Everett C.; Thompson, Loring M.; and Zacher, Frank. *Business Communication*. N. Y.: The Macmillan Company, 1949, pp. 452–54.

Oliver, Robert T.; Zelko, Harold P.; and Holtzman, Paul D. *Communicative Speaking and Listening*. 4th ed. N. Y.: Holt, Rinehart and Winston, Inc., 1968, pp. 310–15.

Walter, Otis M., and Scott, Robert L. *Thinking and Speaking*. 3d ed. New York: The Macmillan Company, 1973, pp. 131–33.

Wilcox, Roger P. *Oral Reporting in Business and Industry*. Englewood Cliffs, N. J.: Prentice-Hall, Inc., 1967, pp. 295–98.

Periodicals

Brown, Davis S. "The Speaker Will Answer Questions." *Adult Leadership* 15 (June 1966):39.

Dance, Frank E. X. "Go to the Lectern." *Today's Speech* 9 (February 1960):20.

Dudley, E. Samuel. "Warfare at the Waldorf." *Today's Speech* 11 (November 1963):2–3.

Goldner, P. B. "Speaking of Speakers." *Sales Management* 92 (March 20, 1954):153–55.

Haaksenson, R. "How to Handle Questions and Answers." *Sales Management* 96 (March 1966):151.

Hildebrandt, Herbert W., and Stevens, Walter W. "Manuscript and Extemporaneous Delivery in Communicating Information." *Today's Speech* 11 (November 1963):369.

Jenkins, R. L. "Conference Communication." *Advanced Management Journal*, April 1965, pp. 88–89.

Lynch, D. "Confessions of a Speechwriter: Why So Many Business Speeches Sound Lifeless and Artificial." *Dun's Review and Modern Industry* 86 (November 1965):42–43.

"Managers Are Made." *Royal Bank of Canada Newsletter* 54 (June 1973).

Miller, H. "Letter to a Business Spokesman." *Management Review* 52 (November 1963):55–59.

Palzer, Edward. "Visual Materials with a Point." *Today's Speech* 10 (April 1962):15–16.

Randall, Clarence B. "Speak Up!" *Today's Speech* 10 (November 1962):1–3.

Schmidt, Ralph N. "Speaking a Written Speech." *Today's Speech* 11 (February 1963):4–5.

It is the province of knowledge to
speak and it is the privilege of
wisdom to listen.

Oliver Wendell Holmes
The Poet at the Breakfast Table

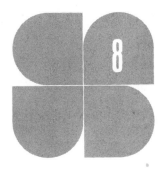

Listening

To listen is to act, to be alert to what is heard, to strain one's ears to catch the oral sounds made by a speaker and to let the mind dwell upon their meanings. To listen effectively you must concentrate your attention, becoming oblivious of all that is peripheral to that which you are attending. To speak well is tiring, to listen well is equally so. George Bernard Shaw's ability to concentrate as a play listener is accurately described as being of an intensity equal to that displayed by the actors before him as they spoke their lines. Active listening requires complete absorption of the mind and body. Louis Nizer in his book, *My Life in Court,*[1] reports that following a day of listening in court he would find himself wet with perspiration induced by the intense effort exerted.

No woolgathering can be permitted by the person who intends to concentrate on what he hears. Our attention span is measured in seconds, so constant and conscious effort is required to prevent the mind from wandering. While the speaker may be doing little to foster our attention, we listeners permit distractions. "Where shall I eat dinner tonight?" or "That light hurts my eyes." or "What makes him think I'll believe that?" or "I have better evidence to prove my side than he has." All such thoughts

---

1. Louis Nizer, *My Life In Court* (New York: Doubleday & Company, Inc., 1961), pp. 297–98.

prevent our concentration on what is being said. Rigid self-discipline is required to offset all such types of distraction. If the listening is to be purposeful and efficient, the listener must learn to use all of his abilities to overcome both outside and internal distractions.

General of the Army George C. Marshall, famous for the Marshall Plan which provided aid for war-torn Europe after World War II, was famous for his ability to listen. Staff members were instructed to walk into his office without saluting and to take a seat in front of his desk. At his signal, they would begin their briefing.

General Marshall listened intently, then questioned the speaker, usually ending with "What is *your* recommendation?" He listened aggressively and with absolute attention, sitting militarily erect, eyes riveted on speaker and arms folded.

His mastery of a press conference was amazing. In Algiers in 1942 after the Allied landings in North Africa, he once faced sixty correspondents. Announcing that each would be allowed one question, he listened to sixty questions. When the last reporter had spoken, Marshall paused briefly to think. Then, for forty minutes he spoke in answer relating all in an integrated whole and faced each questioner as he gave the answer to the question asked by him. True or not, the anecdote illustrated how perfect concentration might be used profitably in listening.

What Is Listening?

Hearing and listening are two different types of activity. Hearing is primarily a physical activity. Sound impinges upon the eardrum and sets a complicated apparatus into action. Listening is primarily a mental activity which begins as soon as the sense of hearing is actuated. Listening is a reaction to whatever stimulates our sense of hearing. We hear a signal, then convert it to a message, relate it to our past experience, and say that we comprehend it through our ability to listen.

In listening we tend first to *separate* from all other signals the sounds, ideas, or facts to which we want to pay attention, *distinguish* or give meaning to the signals being heard. Parents who can sleep through thunderstorms wake quickly at the first cry of a baby. A physician in a hospital may not notice the paging of a score of his colleagues but reacts instantly when his own name is called. Once we have separated and distinguished the signals, we proceed to *integrate* them with our past experience. At this stage we begin to *understand* what the signals mean. To enhance their meaning for us we add items which we feel the sender of the message may have omitted. For example, if he says "horse" we recall the kind of horse we know best, or if he names two people who have had broken legs, we add one or two others about whom we know. With this comes a period of *self-reflexiveness* when we start to discover how we are being affected by what we hear. At this stage we may decide whether to accept or withstand what the signals have revealed to us. We may even decide to build a strong defense against them. Having learned how to listen and having practiced until we are competent at all stages, we have a means of self-protection regardless of what any speaker may say to us. Because of the daily increase in opportunities for oral communication, we should learn all that we can about the art of listening and practice it daily. The principles of effective listening are not difficult, but they must be learned well if we are to use them to protect ourselves from the daily barrage of oral signals which beset our ears.

LISTENING AS SELF-PROTECTION   The alternative to learning to listen well is to rely on our reflexes, as most animals do—a clearly incompetent method, except in the face of danger, such as being in the path of a runaway truck. Then we'd best let our reflexes take over when the signal of danger is heard.

Competency in listening can serve us well against the almost constant barrage of persuasive appeals to which man is subject. We can resist the blandishments of the huckster who implores us to use his brand of cigarette, the demagogue who advocates hatred or violence, or the jingoist who would have us go to war on the slightest of fancied insults to our nation.

Not only can we use competency in listening to help us resist undesirable attempts at persuasion, but we can use it to make more perfect the interaction which occurs in face-to-face communication, such as conversation or interviews. By listening well we can comprehend better what we hear and inspire our partner to greater effort in speaking with us as he notes that what he says is being heard and understood. In the field of industrial relations, for example, or in certain branches of medicine, patient, competent listening proves rewarding, both in getting more information and also in the therapeutic effect which active listening may have upon the speaker who is encouraged to talk about his troubles.

To use our listening ability to the best advantage for ourselves, we learn to pay strict attention to what a speaker is saying to us, rather than waiting impatiently for our own turn to speak. We use a permissive, understanding attitude, ignoring everything about the speaker, such as his status in the organization he represents or his authority over us. Constantly, as he speaks, we ask ourselves what his words mean, what are the sources of his information, and "Are there any omissions which we ought to know about?"

Until we begin to *listen,* the words which a speaker uses are nothing but sounds in the air, harmless as the touch of a butterfly's wing. Only as we listen do they have the power to galvanize us into action, to induce hatred or goodwill.

Frequency of Use of Listening

Judging by *frequency of use,* listening is our most important tool of communication. Various studies show that we read much more than we write, that speaking takes far more of our waking time than reading and writing, but that we listen for almost as many hours of each day as we spend on the other three. Most researchers agree that about forty-five percent of the communications time of business and professional groups, taken as a cross section, is spent in listening. Time spent by specific groups varies—students, fifty-seven percent; dietitians, sixty-three percent; nurses, forty-two percent; and business executives, forty percent. The amount of time used in each of the communicative skills will vary with individuals, depending greatly upon their habits and occupations.

Despite the endless hours which we spend in listening, our nation's schools and teachers have been reluctant to give instruction in the art. A probable reason is that too few of us understand the phenomenon of listening well enough to teach it as a skill, and that still fewer people know that good listening techniques can be taught. The consensus long seems to have been that listening ability depended solely upon hearing acuity and intelligence. Our slowness in discovering that listening skills can be successfully taught seems odd when for centuries men have depended greatly upon oral communication in most fields of endeavor.

Faults in Listening

Rejecting a speaker's message as uninteresting before trying to analyze its significance is a frequent deterrent to good listening. It ranks with the practice of the person who makes a wry face and says, "I don't like olives," at the same time admitting that he has never tasted one.

To condemn a speaker's message because we don't like his appearance, his gestures, or his voice prevents us from getting any benefit from his message. The same effect results if we are critical of his grammar, vocabulary, or accent. Such a practice is similar to refusing to accept a birthday gift because we object to the way it is wrapped.

Watch the listener who is ready with his objections before a point is completed. He is so sure of what the speaker intends to say that he sees no need of exercising patience until the message ends. Lack of comprehension results, a common barrier to successful listening.

Searching for only the facts or other details which one wants to hear or to which one objects prevents a listener from getting the speaker's entire message. We miss the qualifying statements, the transitions, or the warnings about a need for interpretation. Consequently, we fail to realize that what the speaker says and what we hear may be in gross disagreement.

Most of us can listen to speeded-up versions of speech to rates as high as 400 or more words per minute. Most speakers' talks average about 125–130 words per minute. The variance in rate of hearing and rate of speaking gives us much time to assimilate what is said. To use that time for nonrelated activities, such as reviewing notes on earlier parts of the speech or glancing at a newspaper, wastes valuable time which ought to be devoted to getting the speaker's meaning.

Permitting such distractions as traffic noises, audience restlessness, inaudibility of the speaker, or excessive heat or bad air in the room is a strong deterrent to good listening. The audience has an equal responsibility with the speaker to see that such limitations are not permitted.

Anyone who has taught a year or more is familiar with the listener who seems to be eagerly catching every word that is spoken, when in reality he is asleep with his eyes open. Seeming to pay attention while consciously daydreaming effectively insulates one's mind from the message intended for him.

Westinghouse Nuclear Energy Division

Note the attentive expression on the face of each listener. What may we infer about the message being received? Does an attentive attitude prove that communication is successfully taking place?

"I'll go to hear him because I'm expected to, but I won't listen to him or agree with his ideas" marks the flaw in thinking which prevents some of us from learning what the opposition has to say. Biases and prejudices make listening more difficult when someone who holds an opposite view talks with us.

Skipping anything which seems difficult to understand not only causes the listener to miss an important part of the message but also helps to make permanent the bad habit of not trying to comprehend what seems outside of our range of learning.

Experimenters have learned that sometimes taking notes can deter us from understanding what is being said. Time spent in writing causes us to lose a few words, and the habit of writing everything down prevents us from forming stronger memory patterns.

Forming Good Listening Habits

An easy way to give advice here would be simply to say to avoid all of the bad practices listed in the previous section.

"What's in it for me?" sounds like a selfish question. It is, but quite desirable for the person who wants to be able to utilize his sense of hearing to the utmost. Listen to each message intended for you in order to seek what values you can glean from it for yourself. Form the habit of searching in it for means which may contribute to your own betterment. Look at each

Westinghouse Nuclear Energy Division

How does one's facial expression serve to help improve a telephone conversation? What precautions need to be taken to improve one's listening skills?

message for what is intended for you. Train yourself to adapt each item that your hear for your own benefit.

Good speakers state central ideas and develop them by means of supporting materials. Conversely, good listeners develop the ability to locate and identify which of the speaker's ideas are central to his purpose. Listeners note the language which serves as transition to main ideas and the added emphasis that the speaker gives to what he deems important in his message. Form the habit of summarizing each oral message after you hear it. If possible, query the speaker to learn if you got the message in the form which he intended. Knowing that you intend to prepare a summary afterward will tend to help you listen more intently.

A person who reads only comic books or popular magazines seldom develops an ability to read more difficult writing. Similarly, the listener who is content to limit his television viewing to sports programs or situation comedies is helpless when faced with a news roundup by a corps of crack reporters or a discussion-type show whose panel is composed of scholars. To seek the latter kind of program or other similar listening situations tends to strengthen listening skills, just as the reading of weighty material helps to develop superior reading ability. Colleges which are criticized for "spoon-feeding" their students may be guilty of not introducing their students to lecturers who give "mind-stretching" materials to their classes.

"What shall I do while waiting for the speaker's next thought?" is a legitimate question. The answer is to utilize the time by an attempt to summarize what he has already said and relate it to what he is now saying. If he is giving points in an apparent series, keep repeating the earlier ones so as to be less apt to forget them. Try to anticipate what he will say next as a test of whether you can follow his logic. Note the form of support which he uses for each point, selectively remembering the stronger items for greater ease in reconstructing his message later. Avoid all tendencies to let your mind wander while waiting for each succeeding point.

Good listening requires the formation of a habitual approach to the oral messages of others. It is a skill which needs to be learned and can be improved with careful instruction and practice.

Learning to Listen

All of the research results which have been published show that listening skills can be learned and that proper instruction can help even the poorest listeners to improve. Realistically, and most frequently, listening is taught in conjunction with speaking.

At conventions of the Conference on College Composition and Com-

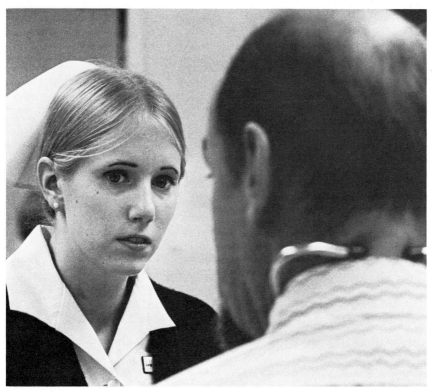

The Western Pennsylvania Hospital

The listener here is responding to a signal not given by the speaker. Under such circumstance what might a speaker do to regain the listener's attention?

munication, of the Speech Communications Association and of its off-shoot, the National Society for the Study of Communication, more attention is being given to the consideration of problems in listening. Few of the new textbooks in speech or communication now neglect to include a chapter, or at least several pages, on the topic. A few companies have already taken positive steps to help their managers become more proficient in the art. Journals of both business and professional organizations carry occasional articles to stress the importance of listening and to offer suggestions for improvement.

As yet the study of listening and how to improve it is in its infancy, most of the research regarding it having been done during the past twenty-five years. The results seem to indicate that listening is best taught with the companion skill of speaking. In earlier chapters we have stressed the speaker-listener relationship, including the circular response which must be maintained between speaker and listener if communication is to take place. Linguistic and organizational skills seem to be those elements of listening (and of speech) which can be most effectively taught. Instructors can do much toward making students aware of the importance of listening and to give plenty of opportunity for practicing the skill.

One approach to teaching improved listening habits is by the use of lectures which direct attention to what the art involves and to offer stimulation for wanting to improve. Group study with plenty of opportunity to practice gives the dual advantage of working with one's associates and also getting critical advice from them.

To coordinate listening instruction with speech teaching necessitates making listening assignments in conjunction with all speaking assignments. By this method students learn that there is more to a speech class than worrying about their own speeches while classmates perform. Instead, they learn to discover the gist of what others say, test it for accuracy and logic, and determine what values there may be for them in what they hear.

In the laboratory method of instruction, quiet listening rooms or cubicles are used. Each is equipped with suitable materials on tapes or discs with tape recorders or record players which each listener uses himself. The video tape recorder is now in common use and gives the listener the added advantage of being able to watch as well as listen. By working at his own rate, the student is able to concentrate on his practice in listening, selecting recordings which match his abilities, choosing ever-increasingly difficult ones as his skills develop. He can also work without the distracting influence of others in the class and without need for waiting his turn to use equipment and repeat as often as he chooses the recordings which he wants to hear.

Critical Listening

To listen critically is to discriminate rather than to accept gullibly whatever is said. To listen critically is to place yourself among those who get most from what is said. You hear all of the message, and by critically listening, put yourself into the position of being able to retain it more successfully. You complete more fully the circular response which is so necessary in the act of communication.

Among the questions which the critical listener should form the habit of asking are these: (1) What do you mean when you use the words you do? (2) What is your motivation or purpose? (3) What items have you omitted? (4) Why should I believe what you are saying? (5) What makes your statements significant?

MEANING   Beware the speaker who relies on *glittering generalities, slogans,* or *abstract terms.* We have already learned that true meaning exists in people—not in their words. Demogogues are notorious in hiding their true purposes. They hide behind such generalizations as *our country's honor, for the sake of the children, our national heritage,* or *for the good of the service.* Slogans such as "Time for a change," "Honest government for honest citizens," or "Buy American" are so ambiguous as to have scores of possible interpretations. An honest speaker must translate them, and a critical listener should demand that his meaning be explained if the speaker fails to do so. *Democracy* is a noble word, just as are such other terms as *Americanism, justice,* and *mother love.* And yet all are so abstract as to enable their users to mean something quite different from what the listener expects. Demand that the speaker be explicit, to supply you with names, places, dates, or statistical evidence in order that you may be able to understand his motives as well as his ideas.

PROPAGANDA   Study the methods of the propagandist. You will find that many who use propaganda to suit their needs are completely honest in their motives and seek only the welfare of mankind. However, there are others whose methods must be carefully watched. You will discover that *name calling* is a favored device. The meaning of *Communist* has degenerated until it is now used principally as an epithet by those who want to discredit those whose beliefs they oppose. Other such terms are *chiseler, square, pseudointellectual, outsider,* and *hippie.* People who use such terms often discredit the very democratic system which they claim to be upholding.

TRANSFER   *Transfer* is a device for making what is proposed appear respectable, to indicate that the new proposal is in the favored category of the listener's current beliefs. Such respected sources as the university, the Sunday School, the federal Constitution, the home, and the flag are used with noticeable success. The critical listener needs to ask to have explained the connection between what he already believes and what the speaker is asking him to support.

TESTIMONIALS   *Testimonials* are used to get us to buy everything from autos and belts to soup and perfume. Polly Starlet, who could hardly be expected to know the difference between a four-barreled carburetor and a stick shift, speaks glibly about the qualities of her favorite auto, and the unknowing car buyer is impressed. Listeners should be quick to ask the question: "How does she know?" or "How reliable is her statement?"

PLAIN FOLKS   *Plain folks* is the device the politician uses when he appears in miner's clothing to impress people with his humble background. Assuming a local dialect is another form of this technique. Its purpose is to help persuade the listener that the speaker can be trusted because he is just like the listener.

CARD STACKING   *Card stacking* is building upon half-truths. By it the speaker carefully chooses only the evidence favorable to his point of view, carefully omitting any that might be in opposition. The method is a particularly harmful and insidious one, often difficult for the slightly informed listener to detect.

BANDWAGON   The *bandwagon* appeal is based upon the desire of many people to do what others are doing. The technique employed is to give the impression that the listener will feel completely left out if he fails to accept the speaker's views or follow the action which he recommends. For the listener who doesn't like to be "different," the appeal is a strong one. To withstand it he needs to double-check all of the facts which he hears.

BLACK OR WHITE   "There's your side, my side, and the right side" is a saying that indicates a two-valued situation (dichotomy) doesn't always exist. "The wrong way, the right way, and the army way" is another statement which indicates that a multivalued orientation exists for most situations.

Between the *black* of one point of view and the *white* of the other lies a broad *gray* area which many speakers choose to overlook. "Hawks" and "doves" are familiar terms in describing supporters or opponents of war, yet a few minutes of conversation with each of several hawks and doves will reveal that they have a wide range of opinions. The general semanticist deplores the black-white style of thinking because it involves the error of *allness.* Such statements as these are potentially untrue: *"All* people who want the House Un-American Activities Committee abolished are Communists." *"Everybody* supports my politics." *"All* Southern Democrats favor segregation of the races." "Politicians cannot be trusted."

Beware of the speaker who can see but two points of view—his which he knows to be faultless and yours which he believes to be totally wrong. You must lead him to explore with you the gray area between the two extremes.

SCAPEGOAT   The most horrible example in modern times of a speaker's deluding people into blaming a *scapegoat* for their misfortunes is that of Adolf Hitler. Repeatedly he named the Jews as guilty of all that caused the Germans' losses or discomforts. Because they believed him, a slaughter of six million Jews resulted. Yet the circumstances of Germany's ills were brought about by many causes such as their defeat in World War I and a subsequent worldwide depression. Most of the causes could not honestly be blamed on the Jews any more than on any other group.

People who blame the weatherman if rain spoils a picnic or those who blame their wife or husband because they overslept are looking for a *scapegoat*. In listening to such a speaker, examine carefully any cause-effect relationship which he may use in order to remove blame from himself. Recently "national security" has been much used in Washington as an excuse for not giving out requested information.

Improving Critical Listening

As a means of learning to be a critical listener you should develop the habit of being a *healthy doubter*. To doubt everything you hear would soon lead you to the psychoanalyst's couch. To believe everything you hear would keep you constantly in trouble because you would be trying to agree with every point of view presented to you. Learn to take on faith only that which you have tested to the limits of your critical ability.

Some of the tests available are these:

1. Is the evidence cited recent or is it out of date? What a U.S. president has to say about Communism today may be quite different from what he said in 1950 when circumstances were different.
2. Is the evidence presented taken from a reliable source? A report from the Department of the Interior on how many people used our national parks last year will doubtless be more authoritative than one issued by a travel bureau.
3. Is the source prejudiced? Is it to the advantage of the speaker to have us believe him? Is the source in a position to profit greatly if we believe him? Testimony given by five men who were protesting the cancellation of the Penn Central Railroad passenger service between Pittsburgh and Sharon, Pennsylvania, was easily discredited. The railroad's attorney simply asked: "Was traffic heavy on Route 19 when you drove here today?" Of course the witnesses had to admit that like most other former train passengers they now travel by other means.

By applying these and similar tests to what you hear you will have a much better defense against those who use speech primarily to gain their own selfish ends at the expense of their listeners.

Using One's Knowledge in Listening Critically

A personnel director went to his company president with a proposal for reorganizing the personnel department. He reported later: "I knew that there were two areas of weakness in my proposal. The president's first two questions were about those two flaws. The old boy had done as much homework as I had." Reading, observing, and discussing a subject will enable you to listen more profitably and objectively to a speaker's views.

By being informed in advance, you will be better able to judge the quality of the speaker's sources, whether his ideas are his own or copied from someone else, whether he has analyzed what he is trying to speak about or whether he is merely quoting or echoing the opinions of someone else.

By keeping yourself well informed on many subjects, you will find that your own knowledge can be an effective standard by which you can measure what you hear from others. And by being able to ask intelligent questions, you will warn the speaker not to take liberties with the truth.

Responsible Listeners

Equally responsible with the speaker for successful communication, the listener helps to determine the course of a free society's actions. The same statement can be made with equal certainty about an industry or a

Westinghouse Nuclear Energy Division

How would you interpret the reaction of these "listeners"?

profession. Responsible speaking and listening are the component parts of wise decision making. As we listen, we need to search as diligently for the truth in what we are being told as the speaker searches for it while preparing himself to speak. If we have learned not to trust him, we must be even more diligent in our attempts to discriminate between fact and fancy, between truth and falsehood.

In our democratic society, each citizen must accept responsibility for not only what we say ourselves but for what others say also. Demagogues arise when people stop listening critically. Totalitarian governments are formed when the citizenry fail to demand that truth be spoken. The 1968 invasion of Czechoslovakia by Soviet Russia came about largely because the Soviet government dared not permit the Czechoslovakian government freedom of communication. Business managers who refuse to listen to subordinates or customers deny themselves much useful knowledge and advice.

Protecting the Right to Listen

The federal Constitution's First Amendment forbids Congress to make any law which will abridge our freedom of speech. Obviously our freedom to listen is included. Militants of the sixties consistently interfered with the rights of others by using force to prevent speakers from addressing scheduled meetings. Misguided patriots have used similar means to prevent speakers whose views they disapprove to speak on college campuses. Because our government is run by "jawbone," it is imperative that each of us be completely free to listen to whomever we choose. Only by the freest of discussion methods can we hope to settle questions of public policy wisely. Truth in collision with error can be strengthened. People who hear all points of view have a better basis for discovering what is truth.

Listen to All Sides of Controversial Questions

To man who chooses to be the "devil's advocate" in a discussion does so in an attempt to be sure that no points of view are overlooked. The debater who wants to find flaws in his affirmative case studies diligently everything he can find on the negative side. The engineer who proposes a new structure anticipates all possible objections, listening carefully to each. Success in selling, a famous salesman asserts, begins when the salesman listens to his customer's "no" and discovers what his objections are.

We laugh when we read about the infamous Judge Bean, The Law West of the Pecos, who, when the attorney for the defense wanted to speak, replied: "My mind is made up, don't confuse me with facts." Yet some people would have us believe that we should listen to but one side just as Judge Bean did. Pity the hapless people who must rely on our judgment in such cases.

Levels of Listening

Not everyone listens or can listen with equal skill. People with the greatest amount of skill can intelligently listen at many levels. The following listening levels are arranged in ascending order:

1. *Listening for entertainment or escape.* Much of television programming, including situation comedies and "stand-up" entertainers, is geared to this level. Humorous lectures and funny stories call for a low level of listening. Soap operas or horse operas give us a chance to escape from humdrum duties without exercizing our minds.
2. *Listening for inspiration or for appreciation.* Church sermons are usually designed to inspire us to lead a better life. We listen to sales managers' pep talks and to the speeches of politicians who represent our party. In all such cases we don't expect to learn much that is new, but we do hope to have our faith renewed and our spirit uplifted.
3. *Listening for information and ideas.* At this slightly higher level we find the need to exercise more effort, to pay stricter attention, and to

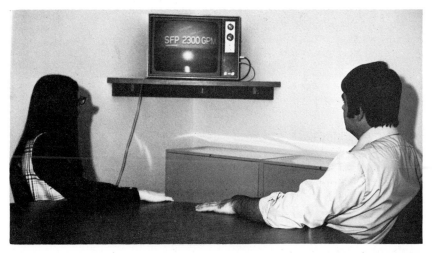

Westinghouse Nuclear Energy Division

Skill in listening becomes of increasing significance as people tend to rely more upon the broadcast media than upon newspapers.

double-check what we hear. When someone gives us road directions we try to understand them so as not to make any wrong turns. The lawyer listens carefully to his client's statements in order to be more certain of the facts in the case. The physician knows that listening to his patient talk may guide him in prescribing treatment. For such listening more effort is required and the brain kept active.

4. *Listening for appraisal and evaluation.* Greatest ability in critical listening is needed at this level. To be effective we have to open our closed minds and sometimes listen to unpopular or unwelcome ideas. Because such listening is difficult, too many of us avoid it. We like to have our old opinions confirmed, rather than listening with the possibility of forming new ones. Critical listening is difficult and takes much practice in order to become highly skilled.

Listening for entertainment or for escape requires only a minimum of skill, and people who limit their listening to that level are generally no more than semiliterate. As one develops his ability to listen for inspiration or appreciation, he rises slightly in ability, but he achieves most when he is able to absorb new information and novel ideas and to appraise and evaluate what he hears.

How to Listen

Since objective listening requires effort, one must prepare himself for his task.

1. *Get ready.* Stand or sit where you can hear easily. If necessary, shut doors to keep out noise or ask the speaker to go with you to a quieter place. If you are in your office, don't let the telephone or staff members interrupt. Focus your whole attention on what the speaker is saying, maintaining eye contact with him.

   Free your mind of bias and prejudice, resolving to hear what is being said no matter how much you may disagree. Keep emotions under control. Becoming angry is as bad as having a hearing aid break while you are listening. Decide to encourage the speaker to continue regardless of what he is saying. It will doubtless make him feel better and you may learn much that is valuable to you.

2. *Begin with the first word and listen continuously.* What is said in the first sentence may be of great importance but is often overlooked. Beware of thinking that skipping a few minutes now and then won't matter. What is said in a conference while you take a phone call might be the most important single item of the day.

3. *Listening for the central idea* of what is being said. To listen only for

facts or illustrations may be interesting, but afterward you may wonder why they were spoken. If you can repeat the central idea at the end of the listening period, you'll then be able to interpret the meaning of the details.

4. *Relate subordinate ideas to the central idea.* By this means you'll be able to restructure what you've heard and be able to recall it with more understanding.

5. *Be a responsible listener,* one who cooperates with the speaker and helps complete the circular response. Keep alert, continue to pay attention, let the speaker have the benefit of your feedback.

6. *Pay more attention to what is being said than to the way in which it is spoken or how the speaker looks.* Facts and ideas are more important than grammar, gesture, or garb of the speaker.

Conclusion

Effective listening is an activity equal in importance with speaking and requires much effort. To listen requires that we go beyond the physical activity of hearing and engage all of the resources of the mind so as to interpret what is heard.

By active listening we can protect ourselves from the almost constant barrage of signals which reach us daily. We can put up a defense against the blandishments of those who would have us follow their patterns or buy their products. We can also separate from all that we hear the messages which are important and those which we need for our guidance.

Some forty-five percent of our communications time is spent in listening. Because the time of any business or professional person is valuable, he or she must learn to listen with the greatest skill possible. Schools and teachers have been reluctant to teach listening, one reason being that its study is a recent addition to school subjects and relatively few people know how to teach the skill.

Faults in listening include rejecting a message because it seems to be uninteresting or because something about the speaker's appearance repels us. We often impatiently stop listening before the message is finished or pick out only details, overlooking main ideas. Because we can listen faster than most people can speak, we tend to daydream instead of focusing continuously on what we hear.

To form good listening habits we need to look for the values which are important for us. We look for the central idea in each message and try to understand the materials used in support of it. Exercising listening skills is as important as any other form of exercise if we are to grow in listening ability. Learning to listen well can be accomplished in classes by means of lectures, by preparing speaking-listening assignments, and by the use of recorded materials for practice purposes.

To *listen critically* serves to discover the errors in fact or logic of the speaker or to uncover some of the practices of the propagandist. A phase of critical listening is healthy doubt, a device which protects us from being too gullible. We learn that not everything can be separated into black and white, right and wrong, that usually there is a huge gray area between. By asking questions about the reliability of the speaker's information and of his ability to observe, we may learn how much to rely on what he has to say.

A listener has equal responsibility with the speaker for completing the act of communication. Each of us must listen critically and evaluatively because our government, business, and all other activities are based on talk.

Levels of listening include *listening for entertainment or escape,* a level which requires but little ability; *listening for inspiration; listening to get information;* and the most difficult of all—*listening for appraisal and evaluation.*

To listen well: (1) Get ready—physically and mentally, (2) Begin with the first word spoken and listen continuously, (3) Listen for the central idea, (4) Relate subordinate ideas to the main idea, (5) Be a responsible listener—alert and attentive, and (6) Pay more attention to what is being said than to the way it is being spoken.

Much of our success in business and the professions depends on the skill of listening. It is an art which we can learn and which requires strong mental ability.

FOR DISCUSSION

1. Is there a difference between *hearing* and *listening*? Explain.
2. What are the characteristic actions of the mind and body of a person who is listening intently to a speaker?
3. Why do we prefer to watch the person to whom we are listening?
4. What is your attitude toward permitting people to listen to speakers with whose opinions you strongly disagree? Why?
5. Do you believe that students should not be allowed to listen to Communists or anarchists? Does the age of the student make a difference?
6. How can we protect ourselves from dangerous ideas which speakers expound?
7. What effect on you does the status or reputation of a man have as you hear him speak? Should it have any effect? Why or why not?

8. How does freedom of discussion serve to protect our liberties?
9. What is the effect on their clients, patients, or associates when business and professional people do not listen responsibly?
10. When should we respond favorably to emotional appeals? When not?
11. How can learning to speak effectively serve to improve our listening ability?

PROBLEMS AND EXERCISES

1. Visit a speech and hearing clinic or an audiologist and have your hearing tested. Discuss with the clinician how to protect your sense of hearing.
2. Have someone read a 500–700-word article from a popular magazine. Take no notes during the reading. Write a 100–150-word summary of the article, including the main idea, or ideas, and the most important support.
3. Immediately after a speech broadcast by the president or other public figure, write a 300–400-word report of what he said. Check with several newspaper accounts afterward to compare what you have written with the reports of others.
4. Listen to several short speeches by your classmates. Write for each speech the probable specific purpose, subject sentence, and a brief outline. Check with each speaker to learn how accurately you listened.
5. Record a radio or television newscast, but avoid making any written notes. After the newscast make a list of each of the news items covered with as many of the details as you can remember. Listen to the recording and see how accurate your written notes are.
6. For a week keep a log of your working day. Estimate the percentage of the time which you usually spend in *listening*.
7. Attend a lecture or listen to a broadcast on a subject which you know little about. Strive to listen intently and get as much information as possible. Continue to repeat this exercise and observe whether your ability to comprehend increases.
8. Write a list of what you believe to be your greatest barrier in listening.
9. Read John Stuart Mills' essay *On Liberty* and write a report on what he believed about freedom of speech.

BIBLIOGRAPHY

Books

ADDEO, EDMOND G., and BURGER, ROBERT E. *EgoSpeak: Why No One Listens to You.* Radnor, Pa.: Chilton Book Company, 1973.

AUER, J. JEFFREY. *The Rhetoric of Our Times.* N. Y.: Appleton-Century-Crofts, 1969.

BARBARA, DOMINICK A. *The Art of Listening.* Springfield, Ill.: Charles C Thomas, Publisher, 1958.

———. *Your Speech Reveals Your Personality.* Springfield, Ill.: Charles C Thomas, Publisher, 1959.

BARKER, LARRY L. *Listening Behavior.* Englewood Cliffs, N. J.: Prentice-Hall, Inc., 1971.

BORMANN, ERNEST G.; HOWELL, WILLIAM S.; NICHOLS, RALPH G.; and SHAPIRO, GEORGE L. *Inter-Personal Communication in the Modern Organization.* Englewood Cliffs, N. J.: Prentice-Hall, Inc., 1969, chaps. 9-12.

BRIGANCE, WILLIAM NORWOOD. *Speech: Its Techniques and Disciplines in a Free Society.* 2d ed. N. Y.: Appleton-Century-Crofts, 1961, chap. 5.

DUKER, SAM. *Listening Bibliography.* 2d ed. Metuchen, N. J.: Scarecrow Press, Inc., 1968.

———. *Listening: Readings.* Metuchen, N. J.: Scarecrow Press, Inc., 1968.

EISENSON, JON; AUER, J. JEFFERY; and IRWIN, JOHN V. *The Psychology of Communication.* N. Y.: Appleton-Century-Crofts, 1963, chap. 15.

ERWAY, ELLA. *Listening: A Programmed Approach.* N. Y.: McGraw-Hill Book Company, Inc., 1969.

HUSEMAN, RICHARD C.; LOGUE, CAL M.; and FRESHLEY, DWIGHT L. *Readings in Interpersonal and Organizational Communication.* Boston: Holbrook Press, Inc., 1969, pt. 7.

JENSEN, J. VERNON. *Perspectives on Oral Communication.* Boston: Holbrook Press, Inc., 1970, chap. 5.

LARUSSO, DOMINIC. *Basic Skills of Oral Communication.* Dubuque, Ia.: Wm. C. Brown Company Publishers, 1967, chap. 7.

LEE, IRVING J. *How to Talk with People.* N. Y.: Harper and Brothers, Publishers, 1952, chaps. 2, 8.

LUNDSTEEN, SARA W. *Listening: Its Impact on Reading and Other Language Arts.* Urbana, Ill.: National Council of Teachers of English, 1971.

NICHOLS, RALPH G., and STEVENS, LEONARD A. *Are You Listening?* N. Y.: McGraw-Hill Book Company, 1957.

ROBINSON, KARL F., and BECKER, ALBERT B. *Effective Speech for the Teacher.* N. Y.: McGraw-Hill Book Company, 1970, chap. 4.

WEAVER, CARL H. *Human Listening Process and Behavior.* Indianapolis: The Bobbs-Merrill Co., Inc., 1972.

WISEMAN, GORDON, and BARKER, LARRY. *Speech: Interpersonal Communication.* San Francisco: Chandler Publishing Company, 1967, chap. 11.

WHYTE, WILLIAM H., JR. *Is Anybody Listening?* N. Y.: Simon & Schuster, Inc., 1952.

ZELKO, HAROLD P., and O'BRIEN, HAROLD J. *Management-Employee Communication in Action.* Cleveland: Howard Allen Inc., 1957, pp. 151–62.

Periodicals

ABBATIELLO, AURELIUS A., and BIDSTRUP, ROBERT T. "Listening and Understanding." *Personnel Journal,* August 1969, pp. 593–96.

AYARS, WILLIAM B. "Listen Your Way to Profits." *Personnel Journal* 47 (July 1968):505.

BARBARA, DOMINICK A. "Listening with a Modest Ear." *Today's Speech* 60 (February 1961):1–3.

BLACK, J. W. "Aural Reception of Sentences of Different Lengths." *Quarterly Journal of Speech* 47 (February 1961):51.

BROADBENT, D. E. "Failures of Attention in Selective Listening." *Journal of Experimental Psychology* 44 (1952):428–33.

BROWN, CHARLES T., and KELLER, PAUL W. "A Modest Proposal for Listening Training." *Quarterly Journal of Speech* 48 (December 1962):395.

BROWN, CHARLES T. "Introductory Study of Breathing as an Index of Listening." *Speech Monographs* 29 (June 1962):79.

BROWN, JAMES I. "The Objective of Listening Ability." *Journal of Communication* 1 (1951):44–48.

CARTIER, FRANCIS A. "Listenability and Human Interest." *Speech Monographs* 22 (1955):53–57.

CATHEY, P. J. "Learn about Egospeak: Why No One Listens to You." *Iron Age* 212 (November 1, 1973):37–38.

ERNEST, CAROLE H. "Listening Comprehension as a Function of Type of Material and Rate of Presentation." *Speech Monographs* 35 (June 1968).

GILLISPIE, MYRTLE EDDINS, and BLACK, JOHN W. "A Self-Administered Technique in Auditory Training." *The Speech Teacher* 34 (March 1967):98.

HALL, EDWARD. "Listening Behavior: Some Cultural Differences." *Phi Delta Kappan* 50 (March 1969).

HARMS, D. S. "Listener Judgment of Status Cues." *Quarterly Journal of Speech* 47 (April 1961): 164.

HARPER, H. G. "Management Is Not Listening to Its Employees" (how to establish internal communication climate). *Public Relations Journal*, August 1966, pp 16–17.

HEILMAN, ARTHUR. "Critical Listening and the Educational Process." *Education* 72 (1952):481–87.

IRVIN, CHARLES E. "Motivation in Listening Training." *Journal of Communication* 4 (1954):42–44.

KELLY, CHARLES M. "Mental Ability and Personality Factors in Listening." *The Quarterly Journal of Speech* 49 (April 1963):152–56.

LIEB, BARBARA. "How to Be Influenced Discriminatingly." *Today's Speech* 8 (April 1960):24–26.

MONAGHAN, R. R., and MONAGHAN, J. G. "Symbolic Interaction: Analysis of Listening." *Journal of Communication* 18 (June 1968):127–30.

NICHOLS, RALPH G. "Do We Know How to Listen? Practical Helps in a Modern Age." *The Speech Teacher* 10 (March 1961):118–24.

ROGERS, CARL. "Communication: Its Blocking and Its Facilitation." *Northwestern University Information* 20 (April 21, 1952):8–15.

STEPHENSON, HOWARD. "How to Win by Listening." *Trained Men* 48 (1968):2–8.

WAGNER, GUY. "Teaching Listening." *Education* 88 (November–December 1967):183–88. Valuable bibliography.

WEAVER, CARL H. "Don't Look It Up—Listen!" *Speach Teacher* 6 (September 1957):240–46.

WEISMANTEL, GUY E. "Management by Listening." *The Toastmaster* 34 (August 1973):14–17, and 34 (September 1973). (Reprinted from *Chemical Engineering*, July 28, 1969, and August 25, 1969.)

Listening Tests

Brown-Carlson Listening Comprehension Test. World Book Company, 313 Park Hill Avenue, Yonkers, N. Y. 10705.

Clyde W. Dow Listening Comprehension Test. For the test and full instructions see *The Speech Teacher* 4 (November 1955):239–46.

Tape

NICHOLS, RALPH G. *Complete Course in Listening: Practice and Readings in Listening Skills.* N. Y.: Dunn and Bradstreet, 1971. License fee, Leader's Manual, and six casette tapes, $3.00; Conference Workbook, $4.40.

Films

"The Engineering of Agreement." Twenty-one minutes.

"Listening." Fourteen minutes, color.

"Meeting in Progress." Forty-three minutes.

All films can be obtained from Roundtable Films, Inc., 113 North San Vicente Boulevard, Beverly Hills, Cal. 90211.

A man's power to connect his
thought with its proper symbol, and
so to utter it, depends upon the
simplicity of his character—that is,
upon his love for truth and his
desire to communicate it without
loss.

Emerson

Interviewing: Conversation with a Purpose

Success in interviewing depends upon the effective interaction of interviewer and interviewee. An interview is frequently defined as planned conversation. More accurately, it might be termed two people engaging in *conversation with a purpose*. As the usual two participants interact, they seek to get or to give information pertaining to a common goal. Occasionally a studied attempt is made by the respondent to conceal his thoughts or to withhold information. The interviewer may unconsciously reveal his prejudices or preconceived ideas by showing his feelings, by supplying answers, or by drawing unwarranted inferences or conclusions. To become a skillful interviewer much study and experience is needed. Similar study is needed if the interviewee is to best present himself.

Self-Interest

As each party to an interview participates, we may be sure that self-interest is a dominating feature. It is a central determiner of the course of thought and of subsequent speaking. The interviewer finds himself under the necessity of formulating his questions so that they will coincide with the interests of his respondent. Linked with this he must establish a community of purpose—the truth which he is seeking must also be the goal of the interviewee. Unlike the person who asks questions, he may not feel the responsibility for being objective, and yet he must be led to understand that an interviewer is concerned with the respondent's interests as well as with his own. Without a successful integration of interests there can seldom be a successful interview. For example, a middle-aged banker, on recruiting college seniors, made the mistake of allowing his own interest in his bank's retirement program to dominate his interviews. Few of the seniors were interested in talking about retirement before they were hired for their first job.

Not only the respondent is subject to the limitation of self-interest. The interviewer finds himself equally subject to his own prejudices, to his own personal likes and dislikes, just as the banker was. These are reflected in the types of questions he asks and in the interpretation which he makes of the answers received. Sometimes he hears only what supports his own preconceived notions, or he has a tendency to record only what harmonizes with his own thoughts. Counterindications or data unfavorable to his own desires may not be noticed. And yet, if the interview is to have any real value, an objective attitude is imperative. In listening to what the respondent may say and in recording it, the interviewer must be as impersonal and as accurate as a tape recorder.

In preparing himself to become an interviewer, a person must first identify his own dominating predilections, opinions, and prejudices, then analyze each to learn how to keep it under control and to avoid letting it intrude upon any interview. In his own self-interest he will learn self-control—a matter not of showing approval or amazement regardless of what the responses to his questions reveal, but of recording exactly what he hears and observes and keeping the data being collected free of any inferences or interpretations which might tend to distort the respondent's meanings. A skilled interviewer must learn early that he himself can be the prime source of errors and misunderstandings which may be generated during an interview. Self-interest demands that he discipline himself rigorously to remove from his own personality all conditions which might serve to contaminate any of his feelings. A person to be interviewed needs to remember his own self-interest before and during the interview.

For successful interviewing the respondent's wants or interests must be known; he and the interviewer must pool their efforts in order to obtain the truth by honest investigation. To do this they engage in frank discussion and exchange of ideas. Hopefully, both will feel satisfaction with the results of the interchange.

Objectives of Interviewing

Interviewing as a technique has become indispensable as a tool of business and the professions. Business managers use it endlessly as they search for new employees or probe for information for those already on the payroll. Physicians interview their patients, and lawyers search with their clients for all data pertinent to the case before them. Educators interview students or search for data needed in their research. Social scientists find the interview technique invaluable in most aspects of their work. Students use interviews in gathering data for speeches and dissertations. As skills improve, additional uses are discovered for the method.

The development of objectives for interviewing can be as fruitful as the ingenuity of the interviewer dictates. As his ability to be creative permits and his insight and experience grow, the interviewer can develop more specific objectives for each succeeding interview. Through the reading of professional literature and in the constructing of theories derived from study, observation, and experience he can develop an ability to determine what kinds of information to seek and how to go about getting it.

Customarily, the objectives of the interviewer can be classified under three main headings: to influence or to motivate people (including therapeutic use), to teach, and to collect data—both objective and subjective. Under the first of these the interviewer, such as a sales manager with a higher quota for the new year, may be attempting to win the cooperation of the sales force. A physician may be trying to teach a patient how to formulate new habits of living essential to maintenance of health. A public health officer may spend days interviewing citizens of a community in gathering data essential to determining the severity of an air pollution problem. Each of these professional people's interviews illustrates one of the types of interview objectives.

In seeking information, the interviewer learns to look for subjective information, such as opinions or interpretations and attitudes, as well as objective data regarding conditions or events. He not only asks the interviewee what he knows but also how he feels about some topics. Attitudes and emotions can be as revealing as a recital of factual evidence. Having a respondent express feelings about any given matter may reveal as much information about himself of value to the interviewer as any factual data spoken by him. Experienced interviewers have discovered that respondents' feelings and attitudes can be discovered as accurately by skillful interviewing as by secret ballots. To overlook the search for subjective information is to limit the value of an interview.

Training for the Interviewer

Interviewing is more than sitting down to ask a list of questions, whether or not they have been written in advance. As in any form of face-to-face communication, a considerable amount of learning and training is required. One form of practice recommended is that carried out in a group where all members are attempting to develop skills. Lecturing on a limited scale has its place in such a group, but its members will learn best by observation, practice, by critical review offered by instructor and classmates, and by continuing practical experience. John Dewey's dictum that we learn to do by doing applies here. By capitalizing on his own successes and mistakes and by those of his fellows, he progresses more rapidly than if more conventional methods were to be used.

Proficiency in interviewing can be learned. A knowledge of psychology and of the elements of interpersonal communication are essential. Because interviewing is an art rather than a science, the proficient interviewer should realize that he must be creative, that he dare not restrict himself by rules and maxims. Above all he is required to school himself to be objective, to recognize and to keep under control his biases and preconceptions in order that he may more successfully obtain the data he is seeking. And the interviewee must learn to be equally unbiased and objective if he is to appraise successfully what is occuring during the interview.

ENVIRONMENT   Responsibility for providing a suitable site for an interview falls upon the shoulders of the interviewer. A highly successful woman supervisor of a university cafeteria avoided using her office for corrective interviews. Instead, she invited the employee to take a walk with her on the campus or have coffee at a neighboring restaurant. The informality afforded more freedom of expression to both.

A prime requirement for success is adequate privacy with freedom from interruptions which would be hurtful to the rapport being established between the persons involved in the interview.

Every interview is different because each participant brings to it his own background, his own experience, his personally developed ideas, and an individualistic behavior pattern. For these reasons each interview is a unique happening and cannot be precisely reproduced. Each participant's unconscious attitudes, his conscious attitudes, his perceptual and cognitive processes, and his sensory observation of the environment are constantly interacting, each modifying and changing the other. No interview can be an independent, isolated event. Each is a part of a complex social environment and may be but one phase of an ongoing chain of events. The participants' perception of themselves is largely unconscious, thus they may be unaware of many of the factors which are influencing them. The interviewer, in assessing the environment, does well to keep these phenomena uppermost in his mind.

Interpersonal Communication

To succeed in conducting an interview, an understanding of the complexities of interpersonal communication is necessary.[1] Listening to spoken words or observing visual signals made by the respondent is not enough. Such psychological variables as human perception, motivational factors, and the social or cultural context in which the informational exchange takes place must be considered. Noise in a busy office or factory can block the communicative process, but psychological factors can be even stronger deterrents. Each participant must rely heavily on evidences of feedback and develop a sensitivity to the cues given by his respondent. Only by this care can he effectively test the success he is having in the transmittal and reception of information.

Obviously the same factors must be of concern to the interviewee. He has much, or more, at stake as has his questioner, and needs to strive as hard as the other to aid in the communicative process.

MOTIVATION   Motivation of the interviewee is largely a responsibility of the interviewer. The latter must be led to believe that he may feel safe in saying what he chooses without fear of criticism and that he is being understood. Being reassured will keep him from feeling the need to be on the defensive, thus leading him into a position where the topics being considered can be more fully developed.

The respondent should be led to understand that both he and the interviewer have a related interest. He should also know what the purposes of the interview are and how the information is to be used. Best of all as a means of motivation would be the assurance that gathering of such information as he possesses would lead to changes which he considers to be desirable.

The means so far described tend to be *extrinsic* motivation. To motivate the interviewee *intrinsically* is to help him receive personal gratification from the communication process and the personal relationship of which it is a part. A warmhearted, friendly interviewer can do much to lead his respondent to feel that he can be interested and involved to the point where he is eager to be helpful. Some of the characteristics of an interview which leads to intrinsic motivation include warmth and responsiveness on the part of the interviewer, an air of permissiveness in allowing the respondent to express his feelings, and complete freedom from any signs of pressure or coercion. The interviewer must remember

---

1. A review of Chapter 3 may be helpful at this point.

that all human behavior is motivated toward one or more goals, and that to help a respondent see that frank answers will lead him nearer to a desired goal can add greatly to the interview's success.

Nor should a respondent overlook the need to wield influence on the interviewer. He is also receptive to the ordinary means of motivation. While the respondent may consider himself inferior to the interviewer, especially if the latter is his employer or prospective employer, or otherwise in a position of power, the respondent still possesses his own human qualities. These give him an equality of opportunity to act and react during the interview. If he has prepared himself adequately, he may communicate as an equal without appearing to be brash or cocky. Elimination of some of the demeaning marks of servility may even be welcomed by the interviewer.

Each of us tends to consider first in interpersonal communications our own self-protection. As a consequence, we have developed ways and habits of reacting to each other that are not intended to ease the process. We are inclined to use them as protective devices to avoid making unfavorable revelations about ourselves. Women, for example, notoriously hesitate to reveal their age. None of us wants to appear ridiculous or unintelligent. Conversely, we want to appear intelligent or brave or in possession of other virtues which we consider desirable. Because we tend to be both rational and emotional, the interviewer should know well how to motivate his respondents both extrinsically and intrinsically.

PSYCHOLOGICAL BARRIERS   Strongest of the barriers of successful interviewing is the built-in *bias* of the interviewer. Perhaps equally strong is that of the respondent. Some of the causes for bias, such as prejudice, can be eliminated by a conscientious person. Others, such as those which stem from one's position, authority, or economic status, are more difficult to overcome, since they can hardly be hidden from respondents. Each participant comes to the interview with a set of characteristics formed by his group memberships, his educational background, his social environment, and his family inheritance. All of these are potential sources of bias. Even well-trained, conscientious interviewers are prone to reveal their prejudices as they make their reports. For example, the personnel director who is prejudiced against women workers in his plant will tend to minimize, albeit unconsciously, the skills of potential female employees. Stress on secretarial skills may seem completely logical to the male interviewer but infuriating to the would-be female executive. Conversely, as women perceive his prejudice, they may, as a means of self-protection, give inaccurate information.

The *role* which either one of the participants sees for himself in an interview may possibly be a barrier. Almost surely a hindrance is the role which he imagines others expect him to play.

Memory failure can result not only in the loss of information, such as the person who cannot remember the name of a person or place, but also in distortion when numbers are increased or lessened. Psychologists tell us that we tend to remember in a selective fashion, our emotions largely determining what we retain. Our psychological inability to remember gives rise to the old saying that any little scrap of paper is better evidence than the most honest man's memory.

Language, which is quite static and relatively inflexible, may be a barrier because we try to use it to describe reality, the sources of sensory stimulation, which is highly dynamic and ever-changing.

Sometimes respondents resort to *defense mechanisms,* often as a result of feeling adversely criticized. By *withdrawal* they become increasingly remote and reluctant to express themselves. Hostile and overbearing manners show aggression. Assigning and believing plausible "reasons for what is done" is called *rationalization.* One *projects* by assigning to others in his psychological field characteristics which are his own. By *repression* unsatisfied needs are "forgotten." All such forms of defense mechanisms are strong psychological barriers to success in an interview.

According to Kurt Lewin's *field theory,*[2] people have reasons for all of the things they do, and when we are able to understand their motivations and to see the situation as it appears to them, their behavior becomes intelligible to us. Any given behavior of an individual, Lewin believes, is the resultant of a myriad of forces which often exert pressures in many different directions and which interact or conflict with each other. The resultant pattern of all such forces constitutes the *psychological field* of the individual. Hence, his behavior at any given moment becomes understandable in terms of the characteristics of that field.

To recognize that psychological barriers to freedom of expression exist, either in the interviewer or the respondent or both, is the first step toward effective elimination of them. Allowing for them is needful if the purposeful conversation of the interviewer is to realize its goals. In the interview process, each participant is trying to a greater or lesser degree to influence the other, and each actively accepts or rejects the attempts. Whatever arises from this interaction is the end product of the interview.

---

2. Kurt Lewin, *Field Theory in Social Science* (New York: Harper and Brothers, 1951).

The Interviewer and the Interview

With all of the faults which the interview may have, it remains as the best tool in business and the professions to accomplish the purposes for which it is intended. There seems to be no practical alternative for it, and most critics are agreed that the technique succeeds when the interviewer knows well how to use it. Trained, knowledgeable interviewers are effective, negative critics usually concentrating on unskilled practitioners rather than the technique itself. One example is the misguided supervisor who merely converses, often doing most of the talking, learning too late that he has not obtained the desired data.

RELIABILITY   Faults attributed to the tendency of the respondent to avoid giving information or to falsify it more often can be traced to a lack of understanding between the participants. Sources of unreliability, of course, include the interviewee who may be ineffectual as a subject, but more often they lie in the interviewer who cannot formulate his own problem nor articulate it. He may neglect vital steps of preparation such as forgetting to collect background information, not suiting his questions to his purpose, nor arranging his topics for conversation in sequential order, or not wording key questions with sufficient precision. Overlooking any of these can result in gathering insufficient or even unreliable data.

QUALIFICATIONS OF AN INTERVIEWER   Being a well-adjusted person with sound mental health and an objective view of his own biases and idiosyncrasies is essential for the interviewer. His ability to accept himself as he is must precede his attempts to deal with others in a way which will lead them to interact cooperatively. He has a need to understand the stature of his role and to develop a kit bag of suitable leads and responses, each of them capable of ready adaptation to each new circumstance. Pat phrases soon grow to sound trite or stilted and need constant refreshment.

RAPPORT   To have *rapport* means that persons are in harmony with each other, that a good frame for understanding exists. The relationship is free of restraint, a warm emotional climate exists, and both are better able to function as mature, responsible persons.

Some of the ways to establish rapport include accepting each other as persons of goodwill and in possession of a cooperative attitude; helping each other by friendly gestures and comments to release pent-up emotions or feelings; by humor or conversational byplay to reduce tension; the use of open-ended questions which allow the respondent to answer in his own manner or permitting silence to prevail when he obviously needs time to think; and by admitting mistakes when appropriate or by offering to compromise when agreement seems to be coming nearer.

Working to establish and maintain rapport is a responsibility of the interviewer and is a necessity in gaining good results from the interview.

EMPATHY   *Empathy* is the human emotion which leads us to side with the underdog or to rise in the stadium and cheer when our star fullback makes a ninety-yard run to score a touchdown. By having empathy, the interviewer can imagine himself in the other person's situation, enabling him to appreciate deeply the feelings and outlook of the respondent, and yet do so in an intellectual, detached way. Because emotional stress weakens the ability to think rationally, one must be on his guard against showing *sympathy,* a quite different kind of emotion which leads one to become involved in the lives of others.

BACKGROUND CHARACTERISTICS AND SKILLS   What sort of person the interviewer is, the race he belongs to, or the level of education attained are all of greatest importance in establishing a suitable atmosphere for the interview. From that point on, knowing, understanding, and being able to employ the appropriate technical skills become of greater importance. Where the background characteristics can be exceedingly broad, the range of skills needed is relatively small. Hence, people of varied types can learn to become good interviewers. The degree to which they are able to develop the skills of interpersonal communication will be a stronger determinant for success in interviewing than their background characteristics.

PREPARATION FOR THE INTERVIEW   In previous chapters the need for careful *preparation* in all speaking situations was stressed. The interview requires time and energy spent in preparation lest the "purposeful conversation" give way to "idle talk." Just as a poorly prepared talk can be boring, repetitious, and ineffectual, so may an interview fail miserably. Knowing what the general purpose is gives one a good start, not in the interview, but in knowing what areas to concentrate on during the time of study or note-making.

To give sequence and structure to the course of the interview follow the general purpose with a carefully developed list of specific objectives. Try to put them in the order which will appeal to the respondent and yet be of greatest help to the interviewer as he probes for the data required.

For each objective write one or more appropriate key questions designed to help accomplish the objective. In the beginning of your experience as an interviewer, a few supplemental questions will need to be added to each key question. All questions should be capable of being reworded to suit the climate of the interview and the interests of the respondent.

Once objectives and questions have been formulated, begin to plan an introductory statement. As a minimum, it should explain the purpose of the interview and give some indication to the interviewee of how the questions to be covered may contribute to his own interests and goals. Plan to make clear to him what uses are to be made of the data which he is expected to contribute. Of great importance is the explanation of precisely what is expected of him in his answers.

Adequate time and effort spent in preparation for an interview can help one use his time with the respondent to better advantage, making the interview more productive.

INTERVIEWER'S RESPONSIBILITY To assume full *responsibility* for the outcome of the interview, the interviewer first must have enough self-insight to be aware of his own needs, motives, and attitudes. Without this he may not realize how frequently he injects his own views into the conversation instead of searching for those of the respondent. His initial duty in the interview is to stimulate the appropriate attempts at answering his questions. Coincidentally, he must observe all of the cues which the respondent reveals as he speaks—or falls silent. During the entire interview the questioner must continue to observe, at the same time preparing himself to describe accurately, evaluate objectively, and report conscientiously what has taken place.

As a participant-observer, the interviewer must busy himself with asking questions, phrasing each one in language appropriate to the moment or supplementing in a reworded form any that are not understood. *Listening* intently and sensitively will not only help him in hearing what is said but will also serve as a stimulus to the interviewee. Being an active listener tends to make more valuable the product of the interaction which takes place between the participants.[3]

In short, the primary responsibility of the interviewer is to establish a favorable climate for the interchange, to help the respondent understand what his role is and how he may best fulfill it, to maximize the elements leading to effective communication, to reduce or eliminate any barriers which might impede the progress of the interaction, and to direct

---

3. A review of Chapter 8 is advisable.

or steer the conversation in such a way that the interview may best accomplish the purpose for which it was intended.

INDIRECT APPROACHES For some subjects an *indirect approach* may be necessary because of possible embarrassment of the respondent. For example, if he has served a prison sentence he may not want to talk about it, and questions having to do with his feelings about our penal system may be more productive than a blunt "Why were you sent to prison?" type. Any ego-threatening approach may result in unproductive responses. In all such cases, an oblique approach may be the preferable alternative up to the limits of available time.

QUESTIONS The prime characteristics of any *questions* are (1) that they convey to the respondent the ideas which have been developed in the specific objectives for the interview (2) that they be designed to bring responses which can be recorded and analyzed and at the same time help to motivate the interviewee to give the needed information, as "Suppose you were in a situation which . . ." can help make one's meaning clearer.

The respondent needs to be as ready with questions appropriate to the interviewer as does the questioner. That is one way in which he may keep from being constantly on the defensive or to be ready when he is asked the usual "Have you any questions?"

While sharing a common language is a prerequisite to success in interviewing, it cannot be considered a guarantee of success. Other elements may intervene.

SUMMARIZING RESPONSES To *summarize* or *restate* what the respondent says can be a useful device in helping him to know that the interviewer is trying to understand him. The technique also permits the respondent to make any necessary corrections or amendments. Care is needed in its use lest an air of disbelief or incredulity is created. The interviewer uses the summry to enhance the favorite relationship between the participants. He must show no concern with the social, moral, or political views being expressed, nor even seem to be expressing agreement or disagreement with any of the interviewee's sentiments. "Nonevaluative" describes the interviewer's attempts at summarizing; his chief aim is to be certain that he understands what he is hearing. To evaluate information as he hears it would be to set up a needless barrier and so prevent his collecting the data being offered to him.

A summary by the interviewee of what the interviewer has said may have equal value for both persons. It can help the questioner by showing him how what he has done has been interpreted, and can serve to inform him of whatever may need to be repeated or enlarged upon. If the interviewee shows that he has any misconceptions, they can be corrected.

RECORDING INFORMATION   Data which are not quickly *recorded* are soon lost, only the spectacular or unusual impressing itself upon one's memory. For some purposes a form can be devised on which numbers, checks, or tally marks may be sufficient for the purpose of later recall. Writing answers in some detail can be useful, even more so if the interviewer can write shorthand. For some purposes a tape recorder is almost a necessity. Depending upon the circumstances, the services of a stenographer may be employed. In all such cases the device must be used unobtrusively so as not to be a distraction. *Caution:* No attempt to deceive the interviewee should be used. It might be discovered—to the embarrassment of the interviewer and result lack of success in achieving the objectives of the interview.

Conclusion

An interview is a purposeful conversation between two people—a respondent who possesses a valued opinion or data believed to be useful and an interviewer who wants the opinion or data. His task is to get information, handling it as objectively as his biases will permit. Whatever one of the participants in an interview does has an effect, profitable or unprofitable, on the other. This is evidence of the fact that each interview is an interactional process.

For successful interviewing, the interviewer must establish both general and specific objectives, then develop a plan for achieving them in the interview. Before the interview he attempts to provide an environment which will insure privacy and suitable comfort for the participants. He must know in advance his own prejudices and biases, keeping them from contaminating what he is to hear in the interview. By helping to develop a pleasant association with the respondent, he attempts to earn the latter's confidence and respect.

During the first few minutes of the interchange, the interviewer not only tries to set the interviewee at ease but also lets him know definitely and specifically what information is expected of him and what use is to be made of it. The interviewer listens attentively, then summarizes or restates what he hears, both to be sure that he has understood and also to give his respondent a chance to correct or add to what he has said. The interviewer maintains control of the conversation, using questions to direct it, and yet allowing necessary latitude through the use of open-end questions for the interviewee to develop any thoughts for which closed questions may prove inadequate.

Keep a careful record of data collected so that reports will actually show what was heard. Even the best of interviewers tend to interpret opinions and factual information according to their own frame of reference. The interview can be as successful as the knowledge and skills of the interviewer permit it to be.

FOR DISCUSSION

1. In what ways is an interview like ordinary conversation? How different?
2. What are the differences in aim among several types of interviews?
3. Why is preparation needed for each? What kind of preparation is essential?
4. Why is the ability to *listen* intently essential in an interview? the ability to translate *nonverbal* cues?
5. Of what value, if any, to an interviewer is the lawyer's ability at cross-questioning?
6. How can an interview be kept on the point at issue and yet still permit the interviewee sufficient latitude in answering questions?
7. How can one maintain suitable physical surroundings for a successful interview, including adequate privacy?
8. How can an interviewer follow a planned set of questions without being too formal, making his approach and aims too evident, or cutting off responses too abruptly?
9. Under what circumstances during an interview might an interviewee take over the responsibilities of an interviewer? How might he prepare himself to be able to do so?
10. How can responses during an interview be recorded (in writing or on tape) without inhibiting responses?
11. How can one who conducts many similar interviews, for example, an employment manager, avoid becoming perfunctory or asking trite questions or developing a set pattern not applicable to all circumstances?
12. What responsibilities has the interviewee for keeping up his part of the interview?

PROBLEMS AND EXERCISES

1. Whether or not you want a job, answer a newspaper advertisement asking candidates to apply in person. Make suitable preparation for the interview, apply for the job, and write a critique of your own and the interviewer's techniques.

2. To get information for an assignment arrange an interview with a local specialist on the subject. Plan carefully for it, including background information on your subject and a list of questions to be asked and biographical data on the interviewee.

3. Get permission to be a spectator of an interview conducted by an experienced interviewer. Note the methods used and write a critique of them.

4. When corporation interviewers come to your campus seeking new employees, arrange to be interviewed by two or more of them. Write a report comparing their techniques.

5. Visit an experienced newspaper reporter. Learn from him the techniques of interviewing which he uses in getting a story.

6. Arrange to do some role-playing before a small audience of classmates or others interested in learning about methods of interviewing. Take turns with others in being interviewer and interviewee.

   a. Take the role of a disgruntled employee who wants to resign and who goes to his boss to do so.

   b. Reverse the roles and become the executive who believes that the employee should be kept if possible.

   c. Take the role of a boss who must say no to a person who approaches him with what seems to the employee a legitimate request.

   d. Reverse the role, removing the "no" answer as a qualification.

   e. Play the role of a physician who must tell a patient that he has a fatal disease.

   f. Role-play a lawyer examining the witness to an auto accident.

7. Interview someone who has recently resigned his job to discover why and to learn all you can about the personnel practices of the employer whom he left.

8. Notify the local newspaper of an important speech which you are to make and ask to have a reporter interview you.

9. Choose a person with whose views on one or more subjects you strongly disagree. Record an interview with that person, write a report on what information you secured, then examine both tape and report to see whether or not you revealed your biases.

10. Do the same with a person with whose views you strongly agree.

BIBLIOGRAPHY

Books

BASSET, GLENN A. *Practical Interviewing: A Handbook for Managers.* N. Y.: American Management Associations, Inc., 1965.

BELLOWS, ROGER M., and ESTAP, M. FRANCES. *Employment Psychology: The Interview.* N. Y.: Rinehart & Co., Inc., 1954.

BENJAMIN, ALFRED. *The Helping Interview.* Boston: Houghton Mifflin Company, 1969.

BERMASK, LORETTA, and MORDAN, MARY I. *Interviewing in Nursing.* N. Y.: The Macmillan Company, 1964.

BINGHAM, WALTER VAN DYKE, and MOORE, BRUCE VICTOR. *How to Interview.* rev. ed. N. Y.: Harper and Brothers, 1959.

BLACK, JAMES M. *How to Get Results from Interviewing.* N. Y.: McGraw-Hill Book Company, 1970.

BLUM, MILTON L., and NAYLOR, JAMES C. *Industrial Psychology: Its Theoretical and Social Foundations.* N. Y.: Harper & Row, Publishers, 1968.

CAMPBELL, JAMES H., and HELPER, HAL W. *Dimensions in Communication Readings.* Belmont, Cal.: Wadsworth Publishing Co., Inc., 1965, pp. 36–55.

CARIN, ARTHUR A., and SUND, ROBERT B. *Developing Questioning Techniques.* Columbus, Ohio: Charles E. Merrill Publishing Company, 1971.

COFFIN, ROYCE A. *The Negotiator: A Manual for Winners.* N. Y.: AMACOM, a division of American Management Associations, Inc., 1973.

CONNELL, CHARLES F., and KAHN, ROBERT L. "Interviewing." In *Handbook of Social Psychology,* II. 2d ed. Reading, Mass.: Addison-Wesley Publishing Co., Inc., 1968, pp. 526–99.

DRAKE, FRANCIS. *Manual for Employment Interviewing.* N. Y.: American Management Associations, Inc., research report no. 9, 1946.

FEAR, RICHARD A. *The Evaluation Interview.* N. Y.: McGraw-Hill Book Company, 1973.

FENLASON, ANNE F.; FERGUSON, GRACE BEALS; and ABRAHAMSON, ARTHUR C. *Essentials in Interviewing.* Rev. ed. N. Y.: Harper & Row, Publishers, 1962.

GARRETT, ANNETTA. *Interviewing: Its Principles and Methods.* N. Y.: Family Service Association of America, 1942.

GORDEN, RAYMOND L. *Interviewing: Strategy, Techniques, and Tactics.* Homewood, Ill.: Dorsey Press, 1969.

GOYER, ROBERT S.; REDDING, W. CHARLES; and RICKEY, JOHN T. *Interviewing Principles and Techniques: A Project Text.* Dubuque, Ia.: Wm. C. Brown Company Publishers, 1968.

HUNKINS, FRANCIS P. *Questioning Strategies and Techniques.* Boston: Allyn & Bacon, Inc., 1972, chap. 3.

HUSEMAN, RICHARD C.; LOGUE, CAL M.; and FRESHLEY, DWIGHT L. *Readings in Interpersonal and Organizational Communication.* Boston: Holbrook Press, Inc., 1969, pt. 4.

Interviewers Manual. Ann Arbor: University of Michigan, Institute for Social Research, 1966.

JOHNSON, WENDELL. "The Fateful Process of Mr. A. Talking to Mr. B." In *Business and Industrial Communication: A Source Book,* ed. W. Charles Redding and Geroge A. Sanborn. N. Y.: Harper & Row, Publishers, 1964, pp. 125–39.

KAHN, R. L., and CONNELL, C. F. *The Dynamics of Interviewing.* N. Y.: John Wiley & Sons, Inc., 1960.

LEE, IRVING J. *How To Talk with People.* N. Y.: Harper and Brothers, Publishers, 1952.

LEVINSON, HARRY. *The Great Jackass Fallacy.* Boston: Harvard Business School, Division of Research, 1973.

LOPEZ, FELIX M., JR. *Personnel Interviewing.* N. Y.: McGraw-Hill Book Company, 1965.

MAIER, NORMAN R. F. *The Appraisal Interview.* N. Y.: John Wiley & Sons, Inc., 1963.

MANDELL, MILTON M. *Employment Interviewing.* Washington, D.C.: U. S. Civil Service Commission, 1956.

MARSTON, EVERETT C.; THOMPSON, LORING M.; and ZACHER, FRANK. *Business Communication.* N. Y.: The Macmillan Company, 1949, chap. 31.

MERTON, K.; FISKE, M.; and KENDALL, P. *The Focused Interview.* N. Y.: Bureau of Applied Social Research, Columbia University, 1952.

OLIVER, ROBERT T.; ZELKO, HAROLD P.; and HOLTZMAN, PAUL D. *Communicative Speaking and Listening.* 4th ed. N. Y.: Holt, Rinehart and Winston, Inc., 1968, pp. 308–10.

PAYNE, STANLEY L. *The Art of Asking Questions.* Princeton: Princeton University Press, 1951.

ROSENFELD, H., and ROSENFELD, LAWRENCE. *Human Interaction in the Small Group Setting.* Columbus, Ohio: Charles E. Merrill Publishing Company, 1973.

SCHUBERT, MARGARET. *Interviewing in Social Work Practice.* N. Y.: Council on Social Work Education, 1971.

SMALLHEISER, IRWIN. *Techniques of Interviewing.* Davenport, Ia.: Personnel Associates, Inc., 1963.

STEWART, CHARLES J., and CASH, WILLIAM B. *Interviewing: Principles and Practices*. Dubuque, Ia.: Wm. C. Brown Company Publishers, 1974.

WEINLAND, JAMES D., and GROSS, MARGARET V. *Personnel Interviewing*. N. Y.: The Ronald Press Company, 1952.

WISEMAN, GORDON, and BARKER, LARRY. *Speech: Interpersonal Communication*. San Francisco: Chandler Publishing Company, 1967, pp. 227–31.

YOUNG, RICHARD. *Recruiting and Hiring Minority Employees*. N. Y.: American Management Associations, Inc., 1969.

ZELKO, HAROLD P., and O'BRIEN, HAROLD J. *Management-Employee Communication in Action*. Cleveland: Howard Allen Inc., 1957, chap. 5, pp. 151–62.

Periodicals

BALINSKY, BENJAMIN, and DISPENZIERI, ANGELO. "An Evaluation of the Lecture and Role Playing Methods in the Development of Interviewing Skills." *The Personnel and Guidance Journal* 39 (1961):583–85.

BARRON, MARGARET. "Role Practice in Interview Training." *Sociatry* 1 (June 1947).

BAVELAS, ALEX. "Role Playing and Management Training." *Sociatry* 1 (June 1947).

BROWN, CHARLES T. "Introductory Study of Breathing as an Index of Listening." *Speech Monographs* 29 (June 1962):79.

BUCKHEIMER, A. "The Development of Ideas About Empathy." *Journal of Counseling Psychology* 10 (1963):61–70.

COONEY, MICHAEL J. "There are Two Sides to the Interview." *Personnel Journal* 46 (April 1967): 238.

DOHRENWEND, BARBARA S. "Some Effects of Open and Closed Questions on Respondents' Answers." *Human Organization* 24 (1965):175–84.

DYMOND, R. F. "A Scale for the Measurement of Empathic Ability." *Journal of Counseling Psychology* 13 (1949):127–33.

ENGLESMAN, R. G., JR. "Unscrambling Nonverbal Signals." *Best's Review* (Life Edition) 74 (April 1974):304.

ERLICHMAN, J. S., and RIESMAN, D. "Age and Authority in the Interview." *Public Opinion Quarterly* 25 (Spring 1961):39–56.

HATFIELD, ROBIN B. "Interview Training." *Personnel Journal* 46 (September 1967):514.

HOLLSTEIN, RAYMOND. "Appraisal Reviews: Communication Not Confrontation." *Trained Men* 50 (1970):21–25.

HOROWITZ, R. "How to Sell Yourself: Or, Why It Doesn't Pay to Hold Hands at an Employment Interview." *Senior Scholastic* 104 (April 18, 1974):6–7.

KATZ, D. "Do Interviewers Bias Poll Results?" *Public Opinion Quarterly* 6 (1942):248–68.

KILWEIN, JOHN H. "A New Look at the Exit Interview." *Personnel Journal* 45 (June 1966):371.

KIRK, E. B. "Appraisal Participation in Performance Interviews." *Personnel Journal* 44 (January 1965):22–25.

KNIGHT, GORDON F. "Skills for the Sometime Interviewer." *Personnel Journal* 45 (May 1966):276.

LEVINSON, HARRY. "Management by Whose Objectives?" *Harvard Business Review* 48 (July-August 1970):125–34.

LEVIT, GRACE, and JENNINGS, HELEN HALL. "Learning Through Role Playing." *Adult Leadership* 2 (October 1953).

LINDZEY, G. "A Note on Interview Bias." *Journal of Applied Psychology* 35 (1951):182–84.

MAIER, N. R. F.; HOFFMAN, L. R.; and LANBOLZ, L. N. "Human Relations Training as Manifested in an Interview Situation." *Personnel Psychology* 13 (1960):11–30.

MAIER, N. R. F. "Sensitivity to Attempts at Deception in an Interview Deception." *Personnel Psychology* 19 (Spring 1966):55–66.

MAYER, N. A. "Non-directive Employment Interviewing." *Personnel* 24 (1948):377–96.

NICHOLS, RALPH G. "Do We Know How to Listen? Practical Helps in a Modern Age." *Speech Teacher* 10 (March 1961):118.

NOLAND, ROBERT L. "Reflections Before the Interview." *Personnel Journal* 45 (October 1966):541.

ORDINI, LOUIS A. "Why Interview?" *Personnel Journal* 47 (June 1968):430.

ORTH, RAYMOND A. "Selecting New Employees." *The Credit Union Executive* 4 (Fall 1965):5–8.

PAYNE, STANLEY L. "Interviewer Memory Faults." *Public Opinion Quarterly* 13:684–85.

POGREBIN, L. C. "Job Interview Can Be a Trap." *Ladies Home Journal,* July 1972, p. 56.

PORTER, L. H. "The Development and Evaluation of a Measure of Counselling Interview Procedures." *Educational and Psychological Measurement* 3 (1963):105–26.

ROBINSON, F. P. "The Unit in Interviewing Analysis." *Educational and Psychological Measurement* 9 (1949):700–716.

SAYRE, N. "Manhattan Job-Hunting." *New Statesman* 69 (April 23, 1965):633.

SHERWOOD, HUGH C. "How to Interview Businessmen." *Writer's Digest* 48 (June 1968):53–55, 93–96.

STAGNER, ROSS. "The Gullibility of Personnel Managers." *Personnel Psychology* 11 (Autumn 1958):3.

UHRBROCK, RICHARD S. "The Personnel Interview." *Personnel Psychology* 1 (1948):273–302.

VROOM, VICTOR H. "Projection, Negation, and the Self Concept." *Human Relations* 12 (1959): 335–44.

WAGNER, R. "The Employment Interview: A Critical Summary." *Personnel Psychology* 2 (1949): 17–46.

WEALE, W. BRUCE, and TERRELL, ODIES. "Are Recruiters Listening?" *Personnel Journal* 45 (April 1966):216.

WEIS, D. J., and DAWES, R. V. "An Objective Validation of Factual Interview Data." *Journal of Applied Psychology* 44 (1960):381–85.

Films

"The Correct Way of Correcting." Twenty-four minutes, color.

"The Counsel Interview." To help subordinates handle problems. Fifteen minutes, color.

"The Discipline Interview." Sixteen minutes.

"The Engineering of Agreement." Twenty-one minutes.

"I'd Rather Not Say." To teach how to overcome forces which block getting needed information. Thirty minutes, color.

"Judging People." Twenty-three minutes, black and white.

"The Making of a Decision." Thirty-two minutes.

"Time to Think." To be efficient and to progress, a manager must allow himself time for planning. Twenty minutes, color.

"You're Coming Along Fine." To stress the need for honest and accurate appraisal of employees. Thirty-six minutes.

All films can be obtained from Roundtable Films, Inc., 113 North San Vicente Boulevard, Beverly Hills, Cal. 90211.

Executives hold conferences at all levels in an organization; scientists work in teams; educators serve on committees; church workers hold conferences; parents serve on action groups; teachers educate by the use of participation methods; psychologists and psychiatrists practice group therapy; and teenagers hold meetings. Everyone at some time or other finds himself working on some kind of project.

Norman R. F. Maier

Speaking
in Groups

Since the beginning of civilization men and women have been congregating in small groups to talk over matters of common interest. To *dialogue* is the modern fad term. Surprisingly, for an enterprise of such antiquity, results are often not in keeping with the amount of time and brain power expended in the activity.

In business, "meetings" occupy a disproportionate amount of management time. Every professional organization holds conventions, conferences, workshops, and myriads of variously termed meetings. They range from highly structured events to informal get-togethers where participants air their views or release their tensions.

As we learn more about group dynamics and concern ourselves more with individual rights and responsibilities, we discover the need for more reliance on group decisions and less on edicts issued by a top leader. Hence, the need for developing our skills in speaking in groups.

Successful group deliberation requires that participants contribute to the best of their ability in order to reach a common goal. Groups tend to fail when individual aims are set above those of the group. For example, a discussion among realtors could hardly hope to reach its best decision regarding a tract of land if one of the group had been negotiating secretly with a view to purchasing it. In such a situation, a *hidden agenda* is polluting the discussion. Delegates to a convention may be hampered in

171

group decisions if they have been instructed in advance of how they must vote. Riesman terms such people as "other-directed," hence unable probably to evaluate evidence introduced or to join in a decision contrary to instructions, regardless of what their reasoning may show to be a wiser path to follow.

Communicate, Criticize, Cooperate

Able and successful group discussion requires that all participants *communicate,* each contributing to the group the *knowledge* which he holds pertinent to the topic under discussion and indicating the tentative conclusions which he reaches while deliberating. Any withheld shred of knowledge might well change group results if shared. Any failure to state an opinion may cause the group to overlook a possible tack worthy of consideration. *Criticism* of purported facts and stated ideas is necessary for the purpose of testing what is spoken. As long as scientists accepted the dictum "The atom is the smallest particle of indivisible matter," the atomic age was pushed further into the future. But when one or more bright young scientists asked "Is it true?" we were well on our way to learning how to use atomic power. Criticism (questioning) is not for the purpose of showing up the ignorant nor the chuckleheaded, but rather to make sure that data being used by the group are accurate and the conclusions drawn the result of accurate and clear thinking.

Any group to succeed must have members who are dedicated to the idea of *cooperation.* The motto of Dumas' *Three Musketeers,* "One for all, and all for one," is an appropriate one for every discussion group. Of course differences will exist, but they need not lead to disputes or quarrels. Strong feelings will be expressed but they need not lead to refusing to listen to unpopular ideas nor reluctance in examining facts which show up the falsity of someone's pet ideas. Cooperation includes mutual helpfulness, listening as avidly as one speaks, sharing time with the slow of tongue, and the encouragement of the shy, retiring group member. It means helping the leader to lead, rather than to leave him to his own devices.

Reflective Thinking Needed

In contrast to debate, argumentation, or persuasion, all requiring the use of *intentional* thinking, group discussants need to rely upon *reflective* thought. In debate, a participant says: "I know. . . . ," "You must agree. . . . ," "The facts prove. . . ." The persuader has already determined a viewpoint or course of action and seeks to gain the support of his listeners.

Intensity of concentration is revealed by each of the three participants at the table.

Discussion, properly a precursor of debate, is a means of seeking a point of view, a set of facts, a policy, or a solution to a problem. The discussant says: "I believe this statement is true. What do you think?" or "Can you find flaws in my reasoning?" or "Have we the necessary facts to warrant our proposed conclusion?"

Both reflective and intentional thinking require the use of much evidence, sound reasoning, and the threshing out of divergent opinions. The major difference lies in the attitude of the thinker. The reflective thinker says: "I believe that I know, but I want help in examining my belief." The intentional thinker says: "I know and I can prove it." Each method of thought has its place, but in discussion only reflective thought can lead to successful group discoveries or conclusions.

What Is a Group?

A discussion group is a number of people with a common purpose who have assembled to talk over a matter. Ten people waiting for a bus is not a group even though they have a common purpose. Such people are usually notably silent while waiting. Yet they might easily become a group should word reach them that their bus had had an accident and would not arrive. Their common purpose would then change to what alternative means of transportation might be found, and most of those present would contribute their views to the ensuing conversation.

Groups range in size from the obvious minimum of two up to the maximum number which can reasonably be expected to participate readily without being inhibited by an unwieldy size. Generally fifteen to twenty

With these participants at the table either a symposium *or a* panel *discussion is taking place.*

should be considered the maximum that can be expected to cogitate together with profit. Adding to the number affects adversely those who have speech fright, and when time is limited a larger number prevents all present from participating.

Large groups can be separated into smaller ones to encourage and permit participation. Two techniques useful for this purpose are "Phillips 66" and "buzz sessions." The former was named for its inventor who allowed six people to talk for six minutes, then to report to the parent body. The Buzz session was so named because of the sound generated by several small groups all participating at once in the same room. After the smaller groups have had a brief time to talk together about the same subject, the leader calls the members together and asks one person from each group to report their findings. In this way, group consensus can generally be found quickly and effectively.

Group Aims

The aims which groups have are as varied as the groups themselves. Some meet for *social* purposes, their aim being to get acquainted, or to plan a social event, or to entertain themselves.

To *learn* may be the purpose of a Great Books study club or of a group of students who are preparing for an examination. A group interested in ecology may meet to try to discover what local, state, or federal laws may be used to suit their purposes. In each such instance, the group is attempting to get information.

The success of such groups as Alcoholics Anonymous and Weight Watchers depends upon *group therapy*. The theory behind each is that one person by himself cannot be as successful in accomplishing his aim as he might be if he had like-minded people to help. The *gripe* session is closely related, for in such cases the individual relieves his feelings by talking in the presence of sympathetic listeners.

Giving of information is the aim of a group that discusses a question in the presence of an audience gathered to learn from the discussion.

One of the most common purposes of groups is to *solve problems*. As in each group situation, success in pooling of information depends upon how well informed members of the group are. Planning and study by each member are obligatory if suitable solutions to problems are to be solved.

Steps in Problem Solving

Problems arise when there is a felt need. Discovering what the problem is is the first step in discovering a solution. For example, if one's auto stalls, and the gas tank is found to be empty, resolution of the problem is easy. A temptation when a problem arises is to immediately start looking for a solution. Much wasted effort is caused by following false leads before discovering the group's interpretation of the problem. A thorough discussion of what the problem is (*definition*) can often reduce the total time needed, for if the problem is clearly defined by the group, the solution may be self-evident, just as in the case of the stalled auto.

Step two in problem solving is to learn the *history* and *background* of the problem. Historians tell us that those who won't study history must repeat it. That is the reason why learning how the problem arose and all that has a bearing upon it is necessary so that we may avoid repeating the same mistakes that others may have made. For example, recently several cases of equine encephalitis were diagnosed in New England. Because the disease attacks humans as well as horses, and is carried by mosquitoes, quick action was necessary. Since mass spraying with conventional insecticides has become nonproductive, new strains of mosquitoes having become poison-resistant, a different mode of attack was necessary. Much time and expense might have been wasted had the recent history of mosquito control in the United States and abroad not been studied. Ultimately a new nontoxic product, Flit MLO, was discovered. Sprayed on mosquito-

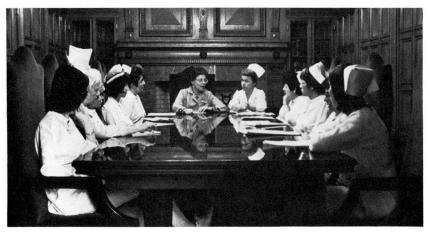

The Western Pennsylvania Hospital

A typical discussion group. The meeting may be a learning session with an instructor or a problem-solving group depending primarily upon the expressed purpose.

breeding water sources, it effectively smothers the mosquito larva, yet has no adverse effect on other animal life. And since its effect is mechanical, new mosquito defenses will hardly be developed against it.

The third step in problem solving is to develop *criteria* or *standards of measurement* for suggested solutions. Without first setting such criteria, the owners of a steel mill installed a sonic device to control a severe smoke emission. The resultant noise proved to be equal to smoke as a pollutant, and the expensive sonic device was discarded and replaced by an electrostatic smoke controller. In addition to such standard criteria as cost, practicality, and availability, the question needs to be asked whether attempting to solve the existing problem will create other problems.

Once the group has agreed upon criteria, the fourth step is to *suggest solutions.* Each needs to be carefully measured by the criteria. The group will customarily offer a far larger number of possible solutions than they would if acting independently.

Out of those suggested, one solution will probably be called the *best solution* because it will match more of the criteria than any of the others. In settling upon the *best solution,* the group reaches the fifth step in the problem solving process.

In this step, *problem solvers* sometimes seek outside help by using a device called *brainstorming.* The moderator calls a group together, quickly outlines the problem and relates what is being looked for. He then taps a bell as a signal that he is ready to accept suggestions. One or two secretaries sit with pencils poised ready to jot down all solutions offered. Speed is encouraged, and no attempt to appraise or evaluate is permitted. That will be done later by those assigned the original problem. *Hitchhiking* and *leapfrogging* are encouraged—that is, offering solutions inspired by others already suggested.

Brainstorming is often done at a luncheon table following the meal, is limited in time—often half an hour—and capitalizes upon intensity of thinking and speed of response. The wilder the ideas generated, the more apt the group is to think up new possibilities that had never been conceived of before.

When a brainstorming session was suggested as a means of finding additional room for autos in a company parking lot, those responsible for the lot objected, saying that they had studied the division of space for hours and that no more cars could be parked there. However, when a brainstorming session was held room for an additional twelve cars was found. Brainstormers are encouraged to be uninhibited, and often are not hampered in konwing what "cannot be done."

The final step in problem solving is to *make plans for putting the best solution into effect.* Superiors must be informed, public approval secured, and budgets planned for. After these plans have been made, those responsible turn from reflective to intentional thinking, for at this stage argument, debate, and persuasion may all be called into use.

Group Leaders

Some groups do well without an appointed leader, relying upon the willing cooperation of all participants to work toward a common end. Occasionally, a natural leader emerges from the group, members looking to the leader for guidance.

More commonly a *leader* or *moderator* is chosen before discussion begins. He may be self-appointed because he knows most about the subject under discussion or has the responsibility for organizing the group. Sometimes the moderator is elected by the group. Generally a *secretary*, who may or not be a group member, is appointed to keep a record of what is discussed. An audio or video tape recorder is invaluable for keeping a record of what is said. A videotape playback is invaluable in helping discussants with self-appraisal of their participation.

A group moderator needs to be well informed, alert, diplomatic, enthusiastic, fair, and particularly capable in using, and encouraging, reflective thought.

The moderator should be responsible for arranging for a suitable meeting place, providing such equipment as chalkboard or equivalent, recorders, scratch pads, pencils, ashtrays, and drinking water. Attention should be given to heating, lighting, ventilation, and seating. Although there is little evidence to support the view, groups who sit in circles where they can readily see each other seem to be more successful than when seated in rows.

Rules of Procedure

Only a few of the rules of parliamentary procedure are needed for use in discussion groups: one person speaks at a time, all have equal opportunity to speak, authority is centered in the group rather than in the leader, and votes are taken on questions of procedure only and not on questions of fact or opinion.

Such matters as time and place of meeting, whether to employ an outside consultant, and whether a meal is to be served are proper matters to be settled by vote. However, whether last year's local tax rate was seventy or seventy-five mills, or whether Brand X is superior to Brand Y, cannot be determined by vote. For regardess how votes may be cast, the facts or opinions will remain as they were.

The use of parliamentary rules can be observed informally as long as discussion is orderly and people respect each other's rights. Rules need to be enforced if one or two attempt to dominate the conversation, if the moderator becomes dictatorial, or if several people try to speak at the same time. Once order is restored, the discussion may proceed informally. The smaller the group, the less formality is required. Informality also tends to help members of the group to speak more readily.

Formulating Questions

Particularly in conference or convention programs, people often select *topics,* rather than *questions,* for discussion. The result is that the succeeding conversation lacks cohesiveness, each group member tending to veer off on his own selected tangent. A far better practice is to *formulate a question* which will serve to focus the attention of all upon the most salient points. Such questions should be written so as not to suggest conflicting answers, lest the group immediately be divided and tend to engage in intentional thinking.

"Does the use of marijuana lead to the use of other drugs?" is inappropriately worded because yes or no are immediately appropriate answers. A better form of the question would be: "What are the effects on the user of smoking marijuana?"

In the opening stage of discussion, the group needs to agree upon a common *definition of the question,* just as is needed in the first step in

A radio discussion group. The earphones may indicate an audience participation show.

solving a problem. While each individual will have his own interpretation of the question, conversation is needed to learn if all interpretations are sufficiently alike to enable the group to proceed. In the example given, "effects" will need to be defined by the leader by asking such a question as "Do we mean *harmful* or *beneficial* or *both*?" "User" and "smoking marijuana" will also need *group definitions* to avoid wasted effort in later stages of discussion.

Once all have greed upon a working definition of the question, the wording may be changed. The new structure of the question might appear this way: "What are the probable harmful effects on a teenager who regularly smokes as many as twenty joints of marijuana per week?" Development of a group definition helps to prevent deviation from the immediate topic as discussion continues. For example, if someone tries to talk about the *beneficial* effects of "grass," the moderator will properly call his attention to the wording of the question as previously agreed upon.

Discussion Before an Audience

When a group of three to seven discuss a matter before an audience, the term generally used to describe it is *panel discussion*. When but two engage in conversation, the conventional term used is *dialogue*. If in the

U.S. Steel News

At this meeting two distinct groups are participating—discussants and participants. What do you think of the arrangements of the seats? Of what importance might it be to have every participant visible to every other participant? What might make hearing difficult for the spectators?

panel each speaker gives a prepared statement, each talking in turn, the presentation is called a *symposium.*

Frequently after a panel has ended its part of the discussion, the members of the audience are invited to participate by questions or statements. Panel members respond appropriately. This part of the discussion is called a *forum.* The moderator must be alert to keep the crowd orderly and discussion pointed. Each member of the audience is allowed to speak but once until all other members have had a turn.

Conference is generally the name applied to a meeting, or series of meetings, where conferees assemble to discuss matters of common interest. They may use a variety of formats, especially if the attendance is too large for a conventional small group discussion.

Preparation for Discussion

Whatever the form used for a discussion, much preparation by participants is necessary. "Pooling of ignorance" is all to often an adverse criticism of group work. According to the Bible, an ancient sage asked: "Who is this that darkeneth counsel without knowledge?" To be effective, each participant needs an abundance of information and a clear understanding of what he and his colleagues are talking about. Experiencing, observing, experimenting, interviewing, and reading are as necessary in preparing for discussion as for any other speaking experience.

Broad knowledge of the whole subject will enable one to understand better what others are talking about and to note whether what they say has a bearing upon the main subject. To be able to criticize helpfully, one needs to be more than generally acquainted with numerous aspects of the question. Otherwise blind acceptance of whatever is said results, for the unprepared person will not have the ability to test statements made by other discussants.

For the specific areas of one's expertise, a grasp of knowledge must be so thorough as to enable the expert to inject appropriate facts or opinions into the conversation so as to help the group to progress toward its desired goal. Generalities are of questionable worth unless arrived at by a consideration of substantial data which will warrant the conclusions. The specialist's duty is to have data available to help the group to reach conclusions.

For some discussions, calling upon an outside source may be desirable. A recess may be called to enable one or more to retire to a library to collect data or to telephone a known source. Another method is to have near at hand one or more resource persons to whom the group may turn when advice or information is needed.

Preparing an Agenda

For the purpose of helping a group to get started with as little wasted time as possible, and to help them keep on the subject, an agenda is often used. Generally it is constructed by the moderator or someone in the group to whom he delegates the responsibility.

The question, rather than statement, form of agenda is desirable in order to help discussants maintain an objective attitude. The number of questions will be planned to suit the extent of the topic and the amount of time expected to be available for discussion. Questions to be written and the order they follow should be determined by the nature of the topic and the primary aim of the meeting. When feasible, a copy of the agenda should be provided well in advance in order to help members know what to prepare for.

When discussants meet, amendments may need to be made in the agenda as suggested by the research which each member has done beforehand. Every item in the agenda needs to be looked upon as suggestive rather than one which must be slavishly followed.

A tentative agenda for a discussion group might look like this:

Question: What are the effects of smoking marijuana?

Terms needing group definition:

> "effects" (Harmful or beneficial or both? On whom?)
> "smoking marijuana" (In what quantities? Under what conditions? In what locality?)

Questions to be considered:

1. What is marijuana?
2. How is it used?
3. What laws regulate its use?
4. How widespread is the habit among users here?
5. What motivates the smoker to use it?
6. What research has been done to discover the effects of its use?
7. What observations do smokers report?
8. Is there evidence to show that the use of marijuana leads to using "hard drugs"?
9. What quantity of marijuana must be smoked before effects are noticeable?
10. What has been the experience of smokers overseas where it has been used for generations?

Obviously, changes will need to be made in the agenda as discussion proceeds in order to develop the answers logically, to prevent needless repetition, and to give the group leeway to use the data which they have discovered in their research. In this, as well as in all forms of discussion, participants should try to be innovative, to discover new methods or techniques which will increase their productivity. Information in this chapter should be looked upon as descriptive of some ways of using group discussion, not as a prescription for what has to be done.

Values of the Discussion Method

Objections sometimes voiced against the use of discussion are that it is time-consuming, that arranging for suitable meeting times is difficult, that bad feelings can result when differences of opinion are expressed, that subordinates have little faith that their ideas will be listened to, and that often discussion attempts are mere pooling of ignorance.

Any one of these objections may be valid for one or more discussion groups. To accept them as an excuse for never using the method is as invalid as refusing to fly because airplanes crash. Just as with airplanes, the advantages of using the discussion method far outweigh the disadvantages.

Pooling the knowledge and ideas of a group of people during an hour of discussion can generate far more wisdom and original ideas than might be gotten from each member individually. Whenever those most concerned are invited to search for the solution to a problem the time consumed is apt to be far less than if one person makes the decision and then has to spend endless time instructing others or persuading them to accept his solution. Correcting overlooked flaws can also take much extra time.

When discussants realize that their voice is both needed and wanted, work schedules can usually be adjusted easily to permit meetings to be held. To be needed is a powerful motivating factor.

Reliance upon the reflective method of thinking leaves little room for hurt feelings, for each member of the group is attempting to question his own contributions as well as those of his colleagues. Especially in the industrial world, more and more responsibility is being given to subordinates. There is a growing trend on the part of management to seek information from the lower ranks. Once subordinates' contributions are treated with the respect they deserve, participation in discussion will be wholehearted and of much value.

Whether participants in a group are well prepared depends in large measure on how meetings are administered. Notice of a three o'clock meeting arriving at two o'clock will give little time for preparation. A week's notice with suggested agenda attached will at least permit time for study. An unprepared person is apt to be his own worst critic as he listens to the knowledgeable comments of his colleagues.

Perhaps best of all is the fact that when those most concerned with the subject under discussion have a voice in making a decision, they won't have to be persuaded afterward. By talking over the matter and reaching agreement with their peers they have already decided that the chosen solution is for them as well as for others affected by it.

Discussion is far from a perfect technique, but like most other democratic methods, it will suffice until a better system is discovered.

Conclusion

Group discussion is a device by which two or more people may consider a subject in which they have a mutual interest and move toward a common goal. For a group to be most productive, reflective thinking ought to be used, since discovery is an ultimate aim. Preconceived notions have their place, provided they are advanced for the purpose of having them observed and appraised.

Successful discussion requires that the group communicate freely, be constructively critical of their own contributions as well as those of others, and cooperate in all matters for their mutual benefit.

Groups generally select a leader who serves as a guide rather than one who makes arbitrary decisions. Both leader and members need to prepare with diligence if the group is to avoid finding itself lacking in information and also to avoid time-wasting digressions. The subject for discussion can most profitably be expressed in question form, avoiding questions with yes-no answers.

Problem-solving groups need to (1) develop a *group definition* of their problem, (2) learn its history and background, (3) formulate a set of criteria or standards for measuring suggested solutions, (4) suggest and measure solutions (at this step *brainstorming* by another group is often used to discover ideas which may not have occurred to those considering the question more formally), (5) choose the solution which best suits the criteria, and (6) plan how to get their solution put into effect.

To get ideas quickly from a large group and to permit more people to participate, the Phillips 66 plan or Buzz Session is used. Each small group appoints a spokesman to report its findings to the main body.

When an audience is involved, the *panel, dialogue,* or *symposium* method may be employed. Two or more people who supposedly are well informed carry on a discussion for the benefit of the audience. Following the initial presentation, a *forum* is held during which the audience asks questions or makes statements.

An experienced moderator usually prepares a tentative agenda for the benefit of the group. In his capacity as leader he reveals some aspects of the question which the group may want to explore but encourages revision of the agenda when the wisdom of group members senses a need for it.

Discussion by groups can be profitable when members prepare diligently and communicate freely in an open-minder manner.

FOR DISCUSSION

1. What evidence can we observe to determine whether members of a group are communicating effectively?
2. How can one offer criticism of another's statements and avoid seeming to assign blame or be faultfinding?
3. How can the use of intentional thinking deter a group from having a productive discussion?

4. What are some methods which may be used to help a group member who appears to be noncooperative?

5. How can a group deal with a member who is noncommunicative? (Think of all the reasons why he may be unwilling to speak.)

6. Under what circumstances would you expect a group to be nonproductive in solving a problem?

7. What is the meaning of *group dynamics*? How can an understanding of it lead to more successful group action?

8. How can group discussion be planned for and used so as to overcome the criticism that it is often time-consuming and a pooling of ignorance?

9. What are the salient features of a well-planned agenda?

10. How can a group discover and deal with a member who is "other-directed" or who has a "secret agenda?"

11. How does a well-trained member of a group transmit his knowledge of how to use discussion techniques profitably without alienating other group members?

12. What are the advantages claimed for the discussion method? How valid are they?

13. How should a moderator choose and instruct the members of a panel who will appear before an audience?

14. What instructions should be given to the audience and how can they be enforced?

PROBLEMS AND EXERCISES

1. Observe a series of discussion groups in action. Make note of how well (a) they develop a group definition of their subject, (b) use reflective thinking, (c) engage in communication, criticism, and cooperation, (d) show evidence of careful preparation.

2. For two days, try to engage only in reflective thinking in your ordinary activities, e.g., family discussions, leisure-time talk with subordinates, peers, and superiors at work.

3. Find an opportunity to lead a discussion group. Take full responsibility for composing a notice to be sent to each member. Suggest what preparation each might make, and write a proposed agenda with a copy for each discussant. Afterward, write a critical appraisal of why (or why not) the discussion succeeded.

4. Observe a series of conversations among family, friends, and coworkers. Note carefully how often a defensive attitude is used (intentional thinking). Consider how the use of reflective thinking might have reduced the defensiveness.

5. For the next discussion group that you are to join, make a special effort

to assemble needed information, studying it until you will not have to refer excessively to notes.

6. Observe yourself and others during a group discussion until you determine how well (or badly) each of you listens to what others are saying.

7. Choose someone with whom it is easy to start a dispute—for example, spouse, teenage child, or a political opponent. After the other person has stated a viewpoint, restate it until he agrees that yours is an accurate restatement of what he said. Then, answer his viewpoint. Insist that your opponent do the same with your statement before offering rebuttal to it. Observe to see whether or not the differences become resolved more unemotionally than usual.

8. Observe a problem-solving discussion group. How well did they follow the customary steps of problem solving? If they did not, what difficulties arose as they proceeded?

9. Choose a problem involved in your business or profession. Select a group who ordinarily would not be directly involved in its solution. Have the group brainstorm the problem.

10. For a conference of fifty or more people who are considering a specific question, arrange for a Phillips 66 or Buzz Session. Compile the reports given by the spokesman of each small group and consider whether the results were productive.

11. Classify ten recent discussions which you have heard as to (a) purpose and (b) accomplishment of purpose.

BIBLIOGRAPHY

Books

AUGER, B. Y. *How to Run Better Business Meetings.* N. Y.: AMACOM, a division of American Management Associations, Inc., 1973.

BALES, ROBERT F. "In Conference." In *Basic Readings In Interpersonal Communication,* ed. Kim Griffin and Bobby R. Patton. N. Y.: Harper & Row, Publishers, 1971, pp. 418–31.

BORMAN, ERNEST G.; HOWELL, WILLIAM S.; NICHOLS, RALPH G.; and SHAPIRO, GEORGE L. *Interpersonal Communication in the Organization.* Englewood Cliffs, N. J.: Prentice-Hall, Inc., 1969.

BRILHART, JOHN K. *Effective Group Discussion.* 2d ed. Dubuque, Ia.: Wm. C. Brown Company Publishers, 1974.

BUSCH, HENRY M. *Conference Methods in Industry.* N. Y.: Harper & Row, Publishers, 1949.

CLARK, CHARLES H. *Brainstorming.* Garden City, N. Y.: Doubleday & Company, Inc., 1958.

DAVIS, KEITH. *Human Behavior at Work.* N. Y.: McGraw-Hill Book Company, 1972.

EWBANK, HENRY L., JR. *Meeting Management.* Dubuque, Ia.: Wm. C. Brown Company Publishers, 1968.

GOLDHABER, GERALD M. *Organizational Communication.* Dubuque, Ia.: Wm. C. Brown Company Publishers, 1974.

HANEY, WILLIAM. *Communication and Organizational Behavior.* Homewood, Ill.: Richard D. Irwin, Inc., 1973.

HOWE, REVEL L. *The Miracle of Dialogue.* N. Y.: The Seabury Press, Inc., 1963.

HUSE, EDGAR, and BOWDICH, JAMES. *Behavior in Organizations.* Reading, Mass.: Addison-Wesley Publishing Co., Inc., 1973.

HUSEMAN, RICHARD C.; LOGUE, CAL M.; and FRESHLEY, DWIGHT L. *Readings in Interpersonal and Organizational Communication.* Boston: Holbrook Press, Inc., 1969.

JANDT, FRED E. *Conflict Resolution Through Communication.* N. Y.: Harper & Row, Publishers, 1973.

KEYES, KENNETH S. *How to Develop Your Thinking Ability.* N. Y.: McGraw-Hill Book Company, 1950.

NEILSEN, E. "Understanding and Managing Intergroup Conflict." In *Managing Group and Intergroup Relations,* ed. J. Lorsch and P. Lawrence. Homewood, Ill.: Dorsey Press, 1972, pp. 329–43.

PARNES, SIDNEY J., and HARDING, HAROLD F., eds. *A Source Book for Creative Thinking.* N. Y.: Charles Scribner's Sons, 1962, pt. 4.

PHILLIPS, GERALD M. *Communications and the Small Group.* 2d ed. Indianapolis: The Bobbs-Merrill Company, Inc., 1973.

REID, CLYDE. *Groups Alive—Church Alive: The Effective Use of Small Groups in the Local Church.* N. Y.: Harper & Row, Publishers, 1969.

ROSENFELD, LAWRENCE B. *Human Interaction in the Small Group Setting.* Columbus, Ohio: Charles E. Merrill Publishing Company, 1973.

RUCH, FLOYD L., and ZIMBARDO, PHILIP G. *Psychology and Life.* 8th ed. Glenview, Ill.: Scott, Foresman and Company, 1971, pp. 429–93.

SHAW, MARVIN E. *The Psychology of Small Group Behavior.* N. Y.: McGraw-Hill Book Company, 1971, pp. 270–74.

STANFORD, GENE, and STANFORD, BARBARA DODDS. *Learning Discussion Skills.* N. Y.: Citation Press, 1969.

WILLIAMS, FRANK E. *Foundations of Creative Problem-Solving.* San Jose: California State College, 1960.

ZANDER, ALVIN. *Motives and Goals in Groups.* N. Y.: Academic Press, Inc., 1971.

Periodicals

ALBANE, C. "A Conference Isn't a Meeting." *Supervisory Management* 18 (April 1973):11–16.

BLATNICK, JOHN A. "Making Cigarette Ads Tell the Truth." *Harper's,* August 1958, pp. 45–49.

CECIL, E. A., et al. "Group Composition and Choice Shift." *Academy of Management Journal* 16 (September 1973):412–22.

CRISSY, W. J., and JACKSON, D. W., JR. "Dynamics of the Purchase Interview." *Purchasing and Materials Management* 10 (February 1974):55–67.

DOBBS, R. C., and WALL, V. "Contemporary Learning Needs Participation Training." *The Clearing House,* no. 45, April 1971, 480–82.

DUNNETTE, MARVIN D. "Are Meetings Any Good for Solving Problems?" *Personnel Journal* 45 (April 1966):12–16, 19.

DYKSTAL, HENRY. "Dissolve Problems in the Right People Solution." *Credit Union Executive* 13 (Summer 1972):23–25.

ELLIOTT, J. "Learning Through Discussion." *New York Times* Educational Supplement, November 13, 1970.

FISCHEL, W. A. "Aesop's Paradox: The Classical Critiques of Democratic Decision Processes." *Journal of Political Economy* 80 (January 1972):208–12.

GOLDE, R. A. "Are Your Meetings Like This?" *Harvard Business Review* 50 (January 1972):68–77.

GREINES, L. "What Managers Think of Participative Leadership." *Harvard Business Review* 51 (March 1973):111–17.

HIGHET, GILBERT. "Man's Unconquerable Mind." *Reader's Digest,* February 1972, pp. 274–87. (From book by same title. N. Y.: Columbia University Press, 1954.)

"How to Handle Squares at Roundtable Discussions." *Sales Management* 100 (January 15, 1968): 87–91.

LEIGHTON, R. B. "Panel Discussions: Is There Any Hope?" *Physics Today* 24 (April 1971):30–34.

LEVINSON, HARRY. "Asinine Attitudes Toward Motivation." *Harvard Business Review* 51 (January 1973):70–76.

MAIER, N. R. F., and SOLEM, A. R. "The Contribution of a Discussion Leader to the Quality of

Group Thinking: The Effective Use of Minority Opinions." *Human Relations* 5 (1952):277–88.

MAYER, MILTON S. "How to Read the *Chicago Tribune*." *Harper's* April 1949, pp. 24–35.

MYERS, D., and BISHOP, G. "Discussion Effects on Radical Attitude." *Science* 169 (October 21, 1970):778–79.

OWENS, JAMES. "Problem Analysis: Guidance System for Decision Making." *Credit Union Executive* 12 (Winter 1972):17–23.

PATTULLO, G. W. "Why Staff Meetings Fall Flat." *Nation's Business* 61 (May 1973):67–68.

PRINCE, GEORGE M. "Creative Meetings Through Power Sharing." *Harvard Business Review* 50 (July 1972):47–54.

————. "How to Be a Better Meeting Chairman." *Harvard Business Review* January-February 1969 (reprint), pp. 98–108.

ROWLAND, S. JAMES, JR. "Honor Thy Father." *A.D., Presbyterian Life Edition* 3 (March 1974): 48–49.

SANDELL, R. M. "How to Create Climate for Good Discussion." *Sales Management* 97 (September 15, 1968):136.

SANDERS, N. "Eight Golden Rules for Chairing a Meeting." *Director* 26 (November 1973):280–82.

SAXON, C. "What's Going On Under the Sun." *Fortune,* October 1972, pp. 104–7.

SEDWICK, R. C. "Company Recruiters—Unpersuasive Pitchmen." *Personnel* 50 (August 1973): 63–70.

SUDMAN, S., and BRADBURN, N. M. "Effects of Time and Memory Factors on Response in Surveys." *American Statistical Association Journal* 68 (December 1973):805–15.

WONG, P., et al. "Problem Solving Through Process Management." *Management Review* 62 (November 1973):4–10.

ZAWACKI, STANLEY T. "Making Meetings Count." *Machine Design* 41 (January 23, 1969):130–32.

Films

"The Making of a Decision." Thirty-two minutes.

"Meeting in Progress." Forty-three minutes, sound and color film.

"Problem Solving: A Case Study." Twenty-two minutes, color.

"Problem Solving: Some Basic Principles." Eighteen minutes, color.

All films can be obtained from Roundtable Films Inc., 113 North San Vicente Boulevard, Beverly Hills, Cal. 90211.

The purpose of parliamentary law is to assist an assembly in carrying out its purposes. It is the code of ethics of working together—the rules of the game. Parliamentary law is concerned with the means by which beliefs and ideas are best translated into group action. It must provide orderly ways of determining the will of the majority. It must be considerate, kind, fair, and it must effect the desired aims of the assembly. It must, in other words, be democratic.

Alice Sturgis

Speaking in Meetings

"We Greeks invented democracy," a Greek acquaintance said one day, "but it remained for you Americans to show us how to make it work."

Democracy means *rule by the people.*

By a long, slow, often painful, process, we have been learning how to govern ourselves by rule rather than by force. The method which we use is called *parliamentary procedure. Parliamentary law,* which is used to regulate our activities in such varied voluntary organizations as churches, labor unions, fraternal groups, and speech associations, is a branch of our great inheritance from England, the *common law.*

Parliamentary law has its roots not only in ancient Greece and Rome, but in France, England, and Iceland. We are learning that Orientals, notably in India, were governing themselves in a democratic fashion as early as the Greeks were.

France gave us the name—*parler le mot,* "speak the word." In Old England the term meant "deep talk." These facts lend emphasis to the jocular definition of democracy as "government by jawbone."

In ancient Greece only men could participate in government; women and slaves were excluded. Ever since then, there has been a struggle by those denied a voice to gain the right to help establish a more democratic system. We see democracy becoming more truly a way of life as the vote in the United States is extended to include teenagers. Other evidences

189

are: the assertion of rights of Negroes through the Black Power and other movements; the election of women and young people to positions in various churches; and the much-maligned Women's Liberation movement. Reaction to the latter is reminiscent of the reception given to demands for woman suffrage before the Nineteenth Amendment was added to the United States Constitution giving women equal rights with men at the polls.

All of the demands for recognition of the right of self-determination have had their effect upon parliamentary rules. More and more voluntary organizations have tended to replace dictatorial officers with those who looked upon themselves as responsible to the members and who would become obedient to their wishes.

Parliamentary Handbooks

When Thomas Jefferson was elected vice-president, he became, as have all of his successors, president of the United States Senate. Without precedent to follow or established rules to resort to, he drew upon his vast store of knowledge and extensive classical library, and wrote a set of rules called *Jefferson's Manual*. It, with all of its many succeeding amendments, still forms the basis for regulating actions in the Senate and the House of Representatives.

The next parliamentary manual of note was written by Luther Cushing and published in 1844. Cushing's purpose was primarily to provide a set of rules for lawmaking bodies, especially state legislatures and city councils. Although used by many nongovernmental associations, and still being published, it has not been found to be well suited for use by most voluntary organizations.

The year 1876 is a landmark year, for it is the date when General Henry Martyn Robert's famous manual first appeared. When Robert first became an officer in the United States Army, he discovered that meetings which he attended were often disorderly and nonproductive. As a presiding officer himself, he felt at a loss as to how to conduct business properly. After a careful study of Jefferson's and Cushing's manuals, and other sources, he wrote his now-famous *Rules*. Publishers were reluctant to publish it, one telling General Robert that there was no need for another book of rules because Cushing's manual was satisfying all the needs of voluntary organizations.

Forced to publish his *Rules* at his own expense, Robert easily found a ready market. The book has been revised several times, the most notable edition being *Robert's Rules of Order Revised,* and the most comprehensive *Robert's Rules of Order Newly Revised.* For many, parliamentary

Speakers waiting their turn during a parliamentary debate. Properly, they will alternate for or against the subject under discussion.

procedure and *Robert's Rules* are synonymous. Sold by the million, it is referred to often, even by those who have no more than a nodding acquaintance with it. A majority of voluntary organizations have selected it as their parliamentary authority. Scores of authors have used *Robert's Rules* as the basis for their own simplified versions.

Robert's philosophy included the belief that whenever a matter arose that could not be reasonably settled, a new rule should be written. That is at once the strength and weakness of the book. A rule can be found for almost any contingency which arises in a meeting; the weakness is that the courts will not uphold the manufactured rules which are inconsistent with the common law.

Alice Sturgis has attempted in her writings to benefit voluntary organizations in two ways: (1) to simplify rules so that they may be readily understandable to the nonprofessional, and (2) to write only those rules which have been upheld in the courts. Mrs. Sturgis's most recent edition of her book, *Standard Code of Parliamentary Procedure,* was published in 1966.

George Demeter's book, *Manual of Parliamentary Law and Procedure,* also is written with attention paid to the common law.

The names of many additional useful and valuable handbooks may be found in the bibliography. Each is carefully planned for a specific use, and the majority make numerous references to *Robert's Rules.*

To understand parliamentary law and how to use it in participating in meetings and presiding over them, the study of a suitable manual is mandatory.

Purpose of Parliamentary Rules

Parliamentary rules have the same value in the conduct of a business meeting as have the rules in a football game or the laws which drivers followed in manipulating autos through city traffic. Contrary to the belief of many, parliamentary morasses occcur when rules are not followed. Their purpose is to expedite business, not to hamper it. When properly observed, business progresses expeditiously and successfully. Best of all, when properly conducted, the actions of a voluntary body will stand up in court.

Fundamental Principles of Parliamentary Law

Fundamental principles upon which parliamentary law is based are relatively few, but upon them rests the weight of our entire democratic system.

The principles of parliamentary democracy are:

1. All members shall have equal rights.
2. Decisions are made by majority rule.
3. The rights of the minority must be respected.
4. Each member must be kept informed of whatever business is being transacted.
5. Meetings shall be conducted with proper decorum.

Conducting Business

The device for getting business before a meeting of members is called a *main motion.* To make a motion, a member rises, says "Mr. Moderator," and when he is recognized (given permission to speak) by the chair, replies: "I move that...."

In most organizations a *"second"* is required. That means that someone else says "Second" to indicate that he is interested in the stated motion (not necessarily in favor of it). The purpose of requiring a second is to prove that at least two members want to have a matter considered. The value of requiring a second is questionable, and some groups, notably the

In parliamentary debate, a speaker addresses the chair even when answering direct questions from other debators. The device reduces the chance of private conversation breaking out.

Quaker church (Society of Friends), do not require it. In committee meetings, a second is usually not required.

The presiding officer states the motion and calls for remarks (debate). The principal rules observed during debate are that but one person may speak at a time and that no one may speak a second time until all who wish to speak have had a turn. Note that these rules follow the principle that all members have equal rights. To be fair, pro and con speeches should alternate.

If someone wishes to change some part of the *main motion,* he moves to *amend* it by (1) adding to it, (2) deleting a part, (3) striking out one part and substituting another, or (4) offering a *substitute motion.* Debate then begins on the amendment and continues until the amendment is disposed of. An amendment itself may be amended.

Here is a possible example:

> *Main motion:* I move that we change our meeting date from Mondays
> at 8 P.M. to Tuesday at 7:30 P.M.
> *Amendment:* I move to amend the motion by striking out "Tuesdays
> (First rank)   at 7:30 P.M." and inserting "Wednesday at 8 P.M."

Amendment to Amendment: I move to amend the amendment by
(Second rank)   deleting "8" and inserting "9."

Only one amendment of each rank may be under consideration at
any one time.

Although the main motion is the most important one of all three
offered in the example, it ranks lowest in order of precedence. Before the
main motion can again be debated or voted upon, all motions pertaining
to it must first be disposed of. This follows a practice similar to that of
completing the mending of an article of clothing before wearing it.

Other motions may apply to the main motion. If someone wants to
delay a motion until later in the meeting, he moves to *table* it. This motion
is sometimes mistakenly used when a person wants to kill a motion. A
motion may be *postponed to a definite time.* The mover may say: "I move
that we postpone this motion and all others applying to it until our next
meeting." *Object to consideration,* if made at the beginning of debate,
may be used in case someone wants no action taken. *Refer to a committee,*
if passed, stops debate until the committee's report is made.

I *move to vote immediately* (previous question) is a motion designed
to stop debate and bring the matter to a vote. A two-thirds vote is required
to adopt this motion. If passed, then all amendments, and ultimately the
main motion, are voted upon. For these, only a simple majority is needed.

Some moderators mistakenly believe that if someone shouts "Question" a vote must be taken immediately. The meaning of the shout is: "I
want to vote now." Perhaps all other members are wanting to debate the
motion further. Hence the shouter should be ignored.

Protection of Rights

Sometimes a member feels that he has been unfairly treated. For
example, the moderator may refuse to permit the member to make a
motion. The member has the right *to appeal* the moderator's decision.
He rises, must be recognized, and says: "I appeal the decision of the chair."
The moderator must then say: "All those in favor of upholding the
moderator's decision will vote yes. Those opposed no." If the members
vote to uphold the moderator's decision, that settles the matter. If the
members vote to uphold the member's appeal, he must then be allowed
to make the motion which he was previously not allowed to make.

Should the member not understand what business is being considered
or what a vote is to decide, he rises and says: "I rise to a *point of parliamentary inquiry.* Please explain to me what is now being done," (or other
appropriate question). *Personal privilege,* another incidental motion (one

not related to any main motion), is used when permission is being asked, such as to leave the room, ask for one's vote to be recorded, lighting to be changed, or for anything else that the member wants.

Voting

The simplest form of voting is for the moderator to say: "Without objection, the action is approved." It may be used for any routine matter, such as approving minutes, accepting a committee report out of the regular order of business, or any business to which the moderator expects no objection. Should even one person object, the moderator will take the vote by another method.

Voice vote is used by having all in favor say yes (yea, aye) those not in favor no (nay). As the moderator announces the result of the vote, any dissatisfied member may shout "Division." By doing so, he is asking that a second vote be taken by having members *raise hands* or *stand*. Votes can then easily be counted. In large meetings, tellers should be appointed in

By custom voluntary organizations often give awards to members or to others who have earned approval for their words or actions.

advance, eash assigned to a part of the group, who can quickly count the votes and report them to the moderator. For large groups, often a requirement is made that more than one person must request a division, for example, five percent of members present or 100 members.

A vote by *written ballot* is used when members wish to vote secretly, as in an election of officers. Sometimes the balloting is done by mail. In such a case, a two-envelope system should be devised so as to protect the secrecy of the ballot.

Adjournment

A *motion to adjourn* takes precedence over all other motions, therefore it can be made at almost any time during the meeting. Some organizations stipulate in their bylaws that at least the routine business must be transacted before a motion to adjourn may be made. Such a rule protects the organization by enabling it to get necessary business completed.

If an association has business uncompleted when the chosen time for adjournment arrives, it may *recess* until a stated time. The motion to recess is also privileged and takes precedence over other motions. When the association reconvenes, the meeting begins with the business under consideration at the time the recess was called.

Changing One's Mind

When an organization makes a decision, it is not necessarily so fixed that it cannot be changed. Passing a motion authorizing the signing of a contract, for example, cannot be reversed if the contract has been executed. During the construction of a church, church officials signed a mortgage bond promising to pay interest at the rate of nine percent. Later they regretted the action and passed a motion to reduce the percentage to seven. The lawyer for the mortgage holder quickly notified the church officials that unilateral action was unacceptable and the rate would continue to be nine percent. In other cases, previously passed motions may be reversed or otherwise altered.

A motion to *reconsider* can bring up again for debate an action previously taken. A similar motion is one to *rescind*. Passing of the latter cancels the motion with which it is concerned.

Every voluntary organization is subject to numerous limitations in the conduct of its business. No action may be taken which is contrary to local, state, or federal law. Members of the Mormon church were forced to abandon the practice of polygamy when Utah became a state because plural marriage was contrary to federal law. Numerous fraternal organizations have had to abondon the practice of barring membership to persons of a different race. No association may take action not authorized by its own constitution and bylaws. The United Mine Workers election of 1969 was overthrown by a federal court because the provisions of the UMW constitution had not been obeyed. To insure that UMW law, as well as federal law, was observed, a new election was held under supervision of the National Labor Relations Board. A final limitation on actions of a group is the parliamentary authority which has been previously selected.

Conducting a Meeting

The *presiding officer* has the main duty of conducting a meeting fairly, impartially, and efficiently. No matter how deeply he or she feels on a matter, partiality may not be shown while presiding. To engage in debate, the moderator must leave the chair, after appointing someone else to take the chair. He or she takes a seat with other members, and secures the chance to speak just as any other member does. Once the business at hand has been completed, the presiding officer resumes control.

In debate, those speaking in favor of a motion should alternate with those speaking against, the presiding officer taking suitable steps to help members present all points of view. No person may speak a second time until others have all had their turn. Parliamentary law sets no time limit for debate, hence organizations are wise if they prescribe limits for individual speeches when bylaws are written.

The *recording secretary* must keep an accurate record of all business being transacted. He prepares the minutes (written official record) of each meeting and keeps an accurate wording of all motions with any amendments, together with an accurate report of all votes taken. Authors of main motions and amendments ought to hand a written copy of each to the secretary, the copy to become the official form as stated by the moderator. If a time limit for debate is set, the secretary should notify the moderator of expired time.

All members are responsible for seeing that each member conducts himself in an orderly manner. Sometimes a *sergeant at arms* is appointed or elected, whose principal duty is to see that no member becomes disorderly and to deal with anyone who does. For extra-large meetings, security guards or local police are often employed, both to prevent trouble and to force people to be orderly.

Railroading

Domination of an organization by a minority, usually officers, in order to force action is called *railroading*. A presiding officer may railroad business by engaging in debate, recognizing only those who support his or her views, miscounting votes, or appointing committees willing to follow orders. Small cliques, often of veteran members accustomed to having their own way, may also try to exercise undue influence.

Members need to be on their guard in order to take action at the first sign of railroading. There are enough safeguards available: appeal decisions of the chair; require the moderator wishing to debate to leave the chair; insist on the election of committees; see that association employees do not abuse their position; require that the treasurer's books be frequently audited; and elect a new slate of officers at the next election.

Members who are alert to what is happening in an organization, who understand their rights and responsibilities, and who know the rules of procedure can prevent railroading or any other abuse of power by the officers or members.

Elections

Finding candidates to stand for office who are competent and energetic is often difficult. In numerous organizations a *nominating committee* is appointed or elected to conduct a search. The committee ought to be representative of the membership insofar as practicable, and large enough to have a wide acquaintance with the association membership. The committee interviews possible candidates, briefs them on what would be expected if elected, and secures permission to nominate them. Often a single slate will be selected—one candidate for each vacancy. Occasionally the committee will have instructions to name two candidates for each position to be filled. A deadline is set—usually the time when meeting notices are being prepared.

Nomination by petition means having a person's name placed in nomination by the process of having a set number of members signing a paper to indicate their choice.

Nominations from the floor are in order, unless the organization has a rule forbidding it. Sometimes a candidate nominated at the time of the election must have two or more backers, a means used to indicate that the choice was more than a spur-of-the-moment one. In any case, permission of the nominee should first be secured.

Unless a bylaw forbids it, a *sticker* or *write-in* method of nominating can be used at the time of balloting. When all other methods have failed, a minority group may at least express their dissatisfaction in this way.

Balloting

Elections are most commonly conducted by secret ballot. That method reduces the chance of any possible embarrassment for the voter as he casts his vote.

Tellers should have been appointed in advance so that they may prepare suitable ballots of a uniform size and color, together with a list of candidates, especially when a contest is likely. For large groups, instructions may also be printed on the ballot. Some groups use forms which may be counted by machine, voting to consist of poking holes at precut spots to indicate the member's choice. A portable electronic voting machine is sometimes employed if the size of the membership warrants it.

After voting is finished, tellers collect the votes by hand or by having voters put ballots in a ballot box. Ballots are first examined to see if any have been spoiled or illegally cast. These are put aside, the rest counted, and the result given to the moderator who will announce the results.

In cases where a single slate is used and there are no nominations from the floor, the moderator will ask if there are any objections. If not, he will instruct the secretary to record that the vote was unanimously in favor of the announced slate.

When voting is to be by mail, a ballot and two envelopes should be sent to each member. The larger one is addressed, preferably to a post office box number or other neutral destination, and has a designated place on it for the member's signature. The smaller envelope is unmarked and is to contain the ballot after the voter has marked it. Sealing the smaller envelope and inserting it in the larger one, he mails it in advance of an announced deadline.

At the announced time, the tellers meet at the post office, collect all ballots and carry them to where they will be counted. Signatures on the envelopes are checked against the list of eligible voters. Mailing envelopes may then be opened, and the ballot envelope put into a pile. Their secrecy being preserved, the ballots may then be opened and counted.

Constitution and Bylaws

The fundamental documents under which an organization operates are its constitution and bylaws. If incorporated, the rules will be included in the charter. Frequently, only bylaws or charter will be used, no constitution being found necessary.

Principal parts of a set of bylaws are: name of organization, its purpose, officers and their duties, elections, terms of office, method of amendment, meetings, standing committees, quorum, means of dissolution, and parliamentary authority.

Because the initial letters will generally be used as an informal means of designation, care should be taken in selecting a *name* for a new organization. Thus organizers of the Pennsylvania Speech Association chose that arrangement of the three words because they preferred PSA to SAP.

Nonprofit organizations who want to avoid the burden of unnecessary taxes are advised to consult a tax specialist before formulating their purpose statement. Both profit-making and nonprofit groups usually write a broad statement of purpose so as to make numerous amendments unnecessary as conditions change.

Officers customarily selected are *president, vice-president, secretary, and treasurer.* Often a *president-elect* is chosen a year in advance of his assuming the office of president so that he may have a year of experience and training before being inducted. If expected mail will be heavy, a *corresponding secretary* may be needed. A *sergeant at arms* is sometimes chosen. Occasionally a *chaplain* and a *historian* are named.

Following the listing of officers in the bylaws, their respective *duties* and *terms of office* are stated. An organization in New York State once had to take a case to court to decide which of two sets of officers was the legitimate one. Because the original bylaws omitted any mention of length of term of office, the judge ruled that officers served only during the meeting for which they were elected.

At least an annual meeting should be specified in the bylaws with the date flexible, such as "in March each year." A means for calling special meetings is needed. Commonly used methods are: "called by the president," or by "any two members of the executive committee," or by "any five members." As a precaution, it is well to include: "Notice of meetings shall be sent to all members sufficiently in advance to permit their attendance." If a member can prove that he or others were not notified, a meeting might prove to be illegal.

A *method of amendment* is needed. Generally a two-thirds vote is prescribed for passage of an amendment, or sometimes a simple majority, if a thirty-day notice of the proposed amendment has been given in writing. Appropriate standing committees ought to be provided for, such as financial, membership, publicity, and bylaws revision committees.

A *quorum* is the number of members present sufficient to transact business. A percentage figure is preferable, such as "ten percent of the membership."

In case an organization should build up a substantial bank account, a *means of dissolution* ought to be included. It might read: "In case of dissolution of this organization, any funds not spent shall be donated to another organization of similar purpose."

For guidance when other means fail, a *parliamentary authority* is selected. "The most recent edition of ———'s *Rules* shall be the parliamentary authority." This manner of wording will make amendment unnecessary when a new edition appears.

Corporation Rules

Contrary to the "one man–one vote" rule prevailing in most voluntary organizations, owners of a stock company have as many votes as they have shares of stock. The one-vote-per-share rule enables a few owners to control the policy of the company, even to the extent of electing themselves as directors and officers. Charters issued by the federal or state government give explicit rules for the holding of annual meetings, meeting notices, and the holding of elections. Annual meetings tend to be highly formalized and dominated by the officers and principal owners.

If the corporation is an eleemosynary one where profits are not an aim, the rules differ, for members in such groups are each entitled to a single vote. The usual rules of parliamentary procedure tend to prevail in all of their deliberations.

Parliamentarian

Because the interpretation of parliamentary rules is difficult, many voluntary organizations employ the services of a skilled and knowledgeable parliamentarian. Small groups often appoint one of their own members to help them avoid errors in observing the rules.

Associations which can afford to hire a professional parliamentarian. Generally the parliamentarian is selected by the president, the officer who will work most closely with him. The parliamentarian is not an arbitrator, but a guide, one who informs the president or other officers what rule applies to a situation where doubt exists or how to handle a troublesome matter. The presiding officer makes the decision—perhaps contrary to advice given him, for that is his prerogative. The ultimate decision will be rendered by the membership, should the moderator's decision be appealed.

Customarily the parliamentarian is given copies of the association's charter or bylaws, of minutes of previous meetings of the association and of its committees, and of any correspondence which may have a bearing on matters needing his attention.

Before a meeting, the parliamentarian meets with the officers, so that they may be briefed by him, and so that he may get answers to many matters which he needs to know about. Often expected difficulties can be minimized by early consultation.

During meetings, the parliamentarian sits beside the moderator, so as to be readily available for the giving of advice. He must remain alert to all that is transpiring, for at any time he may be queried by any officer or member who wants a point clarified. On occasion, he may be asked to moderate the meeting, a duty which is coming more into vogue.

The parliamentarian's fee will be largely determined by the amount of time expended in travel, study, and meeting participation. An extra fee will be charged for the writing of opinions, revision of bylaws, or other such duties. The amount of fees is open to negotiation, but organizations should expect the amount to be similar to that paid to lawyers or industrial consultants.

Conclusion

Parliamentary rules of procedure have arisen out of man's desire to substitute law for force and to avoid the confusion which results when anarchy is relied upon. Parliamentary law is a branch of the English common law, and has drawn upon sources in ancient Greece and Rome as well as modern developments in England and France.

Rules of procedure have been published in many manuals or handbooks including *Jefferson's Manual,* Cushing's *Rules of Proceeding and Debate in Deliberative Assemblies, Robert's Rules* and Sturgis's *Standard Code of Parliamentary Procedure.*

Any voluntary organization that wishes to govern itself effectively must know and observe parliamentary law. To obey the rules leads to easier conduct of business, the reduction of tension and disorder, and the protection of rights of members.

The presiding officer of a meeting needs to remain neutral during debate. To participate he appoints someone else to preside. He accepts main motions, amendments, and any other items of business which may be lawfully conducted. During debate he is particularly careful to see that opposing points of view are expressed.

Rules protect the rights of each member. Among them are the right to appeal a moderator's decision, parliamentary inquiry, and personal privilege. No qualified person may be denied the right to speak or vote.

Voting may be by voice, show of hands, standing, or written ballot. A mail ballot can be kept as a secret ballot through the use of a two-envelope system.

On a disputed voice vote, a member may call for a counted vote by shouting "Division" immediately after the chairman announces the result.

A motion to recess or adjourn takes precedence over all other motions unless the organization's bylaws stipulate what business may first be transacted.

To protect an organization by allowing mistakes to be corrected, motions to reconsider or rescind are available. If action under the original main motion has been taken, such as the signing of a contract, a motion to reconsider or rescind would be out of order.

Proper enforcement of rules will prevent railroading, the biased action of officers or members who force their will upon the body.

Candidates for election may be nominated from the floor, by a nominating committee, by petition, or by a "write-in" or "sticker campaign," unless bylaws prohibit one or more of these methods. A nominee's consent should be obtained in advance.

Elections are usually by secret written ballot with tellers appointed to count them. Care is needed to see that only qualified voters cast ballots.

Fundamental rules of a voluntary group are encompassed in the bylaws—or charter, if the group is incorporated. The bylaws or charter specify the general way in which business is to be conducted. When found deficient, a means of amendment may be used to change them.

Ultimate authority in any voluntary organization rests in the members acting under statutory and parliamentary law.

FOR DISCUSSION

1. What is the origin of parliamentary law?
2. By what means have changes been made in parliamentary rules since the first ones were written?
3. What led authors to write manuals for parliamentary law?
4. What do most such manuals have in common?
5. What are the basic rights of individuals which parliamentary law protects?
6. What limitations are there upon members of voluntary organizations in the conduct of business?
7. How may an individual member protect his rights in a meeting?
8. What basic principles need to be observed during the process of voting?
9. Why does a *motion for adjournment* or for a *recess* generally take precedence over other motions?
10. Since a *main motion* is so important, why is it so low in the precedence of motions?
11. By what means and under what circumstances may a group change a vote on action already taken?
12. How can *railroading* be prevented?

13. How can elections be kept honest?
14. What is the value of keeping bylaw provisions general in nature?

PROBLEMS AND EXERCISES

1. Examine several parliamentary procedure manuals and report on what they have to say about the history of parliamentary law.
2. Examine the same manuals to discover wherein they are similar and wherein different.
3. Look up several court cases involving parliamentary law and report what decision the court reached and why.
4. Study several opinions which have been written by professional parliamentarians in response to questions. Report your observations of the answers.
5. Collect the published minutes of two or more voluntary organizations to discover what they contain. Comment on how well (or badly) they have been written.
6. Attend one or more meetings of voluntary groups, observe how well rules are observed, and report what you noted.
7. Interview one or more professional parliamentarians to learn what training is required and how they conduct their work.
8. Collect copies of bylaws of two or more organizations, preferably of one which operates under simple rules and another with complicated rules. Examine and compare their bylaws.
9. Discover how the rules for industrial corporations differ from those of ordinary voluntary organizations.
10. Draw up a set of bylaws for a new organization which you know of, or propose a set of revisions for an established organization.

BIBLIOGRAPHY

Books

AUER, J. JEFFREY. *Essentials of Parliamentary Procedure.* 3d ed. N. Y.: Appleton-Century-Crofts, 1959.
Contains the essentials which are stated clearly and concisely.
BOSMAJIAN, HAIG A. *Readings in Parliamentary Procedure.* N. Y.: Harper & Row, Publishers, 1968.
A series of readings by authors and practitioners from Thomas Jefferson to modern day professors and scholars. A valuable section is devoted to court decisions related to freedom of assembly and parliamentary procedure.
CAPONE, MARGARET LYNCH. *Parliamentary Pointers.* Long Beach, Cal.: Pfanstiel Publishers, 1972.
Contains much practical advice invaluable for newly elected officers or new members of an organization. Based on *Robert's Rules.*
CRUZAN, ROSE MARIE. *Practical Parliamentary Procedure.* Bloomington, Ill.: McKnight & McKnight, 1974.

A special feature of this book is advice on forming a new club, incorporating it, and how to run a convention.

CUSHING, LUTHER S. *Cushing's Manual of Parliamentary Practice.* Rev. ed. Albert S. Boles. Philadelphia: The John C. Winston Company, 1947.
Next to *Jefferson's Manual,* Cushing's first edition was the earliest of parliamentary procedure manuals.

DAVIDSON, HENRY A. *Handbook of Parliamentary Procedure.* 2d ed. N. Y.: The Ronald Press Company, 1968.
Extensive discussion on such items as privileges, committees, how not to get pushed around, handling hecklers, and budget.

DEMETER, GEORGE. *Manual of Parliamentary Law and Procedure.* Blue bk. ed. Boston: Little, Brown and Company, 1969.
The ideas for the manual, although suitable for any deliberative body, grew out of Mr. Demeter's experience as a state legislator. He emphasizes the importance of having rules which have stood up in court trials.

DONAHUE, HAROLD W. *How to Manage Your Meeting* (with *Parliamentary Procedure* by Grant Henderson). Indianapolis: Drake Publishers, Inc., 1955.
A Canadian businessman, Donahue gives instructions in clear, terse language on how to manage the ins and outs of meetings, all the way from choosing a chairman for a public meeting to doing last-minute chores, such as writing thank you notes. Thirty-seven questions and answers are a useful adjunct to the forty-five pages on parliamentary procedure.

GRAY, JOHN W., and REA, RICHARD G. *Parliamentary Procedure: A Programed Introduction.* Rev. Chicago: Scott, Foresman and Company, 1974.
The plan of this book makes it ideal for the person who wishes to use it for self study. He may check his own learning as he progresses, such as he would with a teaching machine.

GRUMME, MARGUERITE. *Basic Principles of Parliamentary Law and Protocol.* 2d ed. Marguerite Grumme, 3830 Humphrey Street, St. Louis 63116, 1955.
A tiny pocket manual. This book is unique in that it contains a basic convention agenda and a special section on protocol, outlining correct procedures and courtesies for the meeting, the officers, and members. Mrs. Grumme has available several other booklets dealing with parliamentary procedure.

HELLMAN, HUGO. *Parliamentary Procedure.* N. Y.: The Macmillan Company, 1966.
Easy-to-read paperback with arrangement of material in lesson form.

HOOGESTRAAT, WAYNE E., and SIKKINK, DONALD E. *Modern Parliamentary Practices.* Minneapolis: Burgess Publishing Company, 1966.

JOHNSON, RICHARD B.; TRUSTMAN, BENJAMIN A.; and WADSWORTH, CHARLES Y. *Town Meeting Time.* Boston: Little, Brown and Company, 1964.

JONES, GARFIELD O. *Senior Manual for Group Leadership.* N. Y.: Appleton-Century-Crofts, 1932.
The Jones manual is particularly easy to use because a split page–center index arrangement which permits instant reference to any question of procedure.

McMONAGLE, JAMES A., and PFISTER, EMIL R. *The Membership Manual: An Encyclopedia of Parliamentary Rules Used at Business Meetings of Democratic Organizations.* N. Y.: Vantage Press, 1970.
This is the only book of its kind and is highly useful as a ready reference in helping to identify rules and parliamentary terms.

National Association of Parliamentarians. *Parliamentary Questions and Answers* II. Rev. Kansas City, Mo.: The Graphic Laboratory, 1970.
This helpful book has 1,213 questions and answers previously published in issues of *The National Parliamentarian.*

O'BRIEN, JOSEPH F. *Parliamentary Law for the Layman.* N. Y.: Harper and Brothers, Publishers, 1952.
Now regrettably out of print, O'Brien's manual's chief strength lies in its advice in how to use strategy in meetings.

OLECK, HOWARD L. *Non-Profit Organizations and Associations.* Englewood Cliffs, N. J.: Prentice-Hall, Inc., 1956.

ROBERT, GENERAL HENRY M. *Parliamentary Law.* N. Y.: Appleton-Century-Crofts, 1951.
For a serious student of parliamentary procedure this work is invaluable because of its attempt to answer 387 questions which had been posed to General Robert.

————. *Rules of Order Newly Revised.* Chicago: Scott, Foresman and Company, 1969.
Published in 1876, the Robert manual has often been copied but never surpassed. It is the most often used authority despite its sometimes ambiguous language. The newest edition is virtually a compendium of rules and explanatory notes.

————. *Parliamentary Practice.* N. Y.: Century Co., 1921.
A short book by General Robert designed to be used in the classroom for drill purposes.

SHRYOCK, RHEVA OTT. *Parliamentary Procedure Made Easy.* New London, Conn.: Arthur C. Croft Pub., 1958.
Split pages for quick reference. Based on *Bobert's Rules.*

SMEDLEY, RALPH C. *The Great Peacemaker.* Santa Ana, Cal.: Toastmaster International, 1955.
A helpful biography of Henry M. Robert.

STEVENSON, FRED G. *Pocket Primer of Parliamentary Procedure.* 5th ed. Boston: Houghton Mifflin Company, 1973.
Stevenson's manual is thumb indexed for convenience and is written in simplified language.

STRAUSS, BERT, and STRAUSS, FRANCES. *New Ways to Better Meetings.* Rev. N. Y.: The Viking Press, Inc., 1964.
A book of practical suggestions on how to keep meetings member-centered, solve problems, conduct buzz sessions, roleplay, and improve interpersonal communications.

STURGIS, ALICE F. *Sturgis' Standard Code of Parliamentary Procedure.* 2d ed. N. Y.: McGraw-Hill Book Company, 1966.
Drawing liberally upon her nationwide experience as a parliamentarian and her acquaintance with many prominent people, Mrs. Sturgis has written a valuable, practical book. Its unique feature is the basing of rules upon court decisions.

STURGIS, ALICE F. *Learning Parliamentary Procedure.* N. Y.: McGraw-Hill Book Company, 1953.
A helpful book for anyone who is attempting to learn how to apply the rules of procedure. Humorous verse by Richard Armour adds to its attractiveness.

THOMAS, MRS. HARRY H. *Simplified Parliamentary Procedure.* Washington: The Carrie Chapman Catt Memorial Fund, Inc., 1961.
A handy guide for club women to tuck into their purses or men into their shirt pockets. It is based on *Robert's Rules.*

WAGNER, JOSEPH. *Successful Leadership in Groups and Organizations.* 2d ed. San Francisco: Chandler Publishing Company, 1973.

WHITNEY, BYRL A. *Whitney's Parliamentary Procedure.* N. Y.: Van Rees Press, 1962.
Text in this book is closely keyed to a chart of motions, enabling the user to locate quickly a discussion of the type of motion under consideration.

WIKSELL, WESLEY. *How to Conduct Meetings.* N. Y.: Harper & Row, Publishers, 1966.
Instructions for people who want to become more effective members of a group; directions to chairman, vice-president, secretary, and treasurer.

Periodicals

ALBANO, C. "Conference Is Not a Meeting." *Supervisory Managament* 18 (April 1973):11–16.

ALEXANDER, W. M. "Rethinking Student Government for a Larger University." *Journal of Higher Education* 40 (January 1969): 39–45.

AMATO, P. P. "Programmed Instruction in Teaching Parliamentary Procedure." *Speech Teacher* 17 (May 1969):145–49.

AUER, J. JEFFREY. "The Role of the Chairman in Committees and Assembly." *Adult Leadership* 5 (December 1956): 185–87.

BANNON, B. A. "Authors and Editors: The Story of Robert's Rules." *Publisher's Weekly* 197 (March 16, 1970):15–16.

BLANK, BLANCHE DAVIS. "Bureaucracy or Democracy: Which Is the Enemy in Campus Confrontations?" *American Association of University Professors Bulletin* 55 (June 1969):257–58.

BULL, G. "How to Be a Thorn in the Chairman's Side." *Director* 25 (June 19, 1973):401–3.

CARTER, H. "Clubwoman's Best Friend: Rules of Order." *Saturday Evening Post,* August 19, 1961, p. 25.

"Churches 'Buy Back' Former Properties." *Presbyterian Life* 22 (February 15, 1969):30.

"Civil Courts Barred from Ruling on Doctrine." *Presbyterian Life* 22 (February 15, 1969).

DYSART, J. M. "Planning and Conducting an Effective Meeting." (abstract.) *Supervisory Management* 16 (March 1971):129–32.

FOX, E. M. "Success with the Small Meeting." *Supervisory Management* 17 (November 1972): 39–42.

GARRAHAN, M. "You Can Make Meetings Worthwhile." (abstract) *Supervisory Management* 15 (May 1970):31–34.

GIVENS, RICHARD A. "The Landrum-Griffin Act and Rules of Procedure for Union Meetings." *Labor Law Journal* 12 (June 1961).

GLICKSTEIN, IRA. "The Evolution of Parliamentary Law: From Anarchy to Robert's." *The Toastmaster* 35 (November 1969).

GOLDE, R. A. "Are Your Meetings Like This One?" *Harvard Business Review* 50 (January 1972): 68–77.

GRAY, GILES W. "Parliamentary Procedure in a Democracy: Address." *Vital Speeches* 27 (May 15, 1961):477–80.

———. "A Philosophy of Parliamentary Law." *Quarterly Journal of Speech* 27 (October 1941): 437.

———. "Points of Emphasis in Teaching Parliamentary Procedure." *The Speech Teacher* 13 (January 1964):10–15.

GROTE, R. C. "Hidden Saboteurs of Group Meetings." *Personnel* 47 (September 1970):42–48.

———. "Why Meetings Jump the Track." *Supervisory Management* 16 (January 1971):13–16.

HILL, WALTER B. "The Great American Safety Valve." *Century* 44 (July 1892):383–84.

HOLDEN, J. J., JR. "D.M. by Consensus: The Experience at Yellow Freight." *Management Review* 61 (July 1972):63–65.

"Hosting the Small Meeting." *Insurance* 74 (February 1973):39–40.

"How to Run a Meeting." *Industrial World* 166 (June 1, 1970):34–37.

KEESEY, RAY. "Don't Ask the Parliamentarian." *Today's Speech* 8 (1960):15.

LEFFLER, W. L. "Corporate Relocation: So That's What They Mean by Participative Management." *Management Review* 61 (June 1972):31–32.

MARKGRAF, BRUCE. "The Parliamentary Debate in Action." *The Speech Teacher* 22 (January 1963): 219–22.

MASON, PAUL. "The Law and Parliamentary Procedure." *Adult Leadership* 5 (December 1956): 188–90.

MORRISON, J. M. "Tired of Meetings? Try These Sure Fire Interest Arousers." *World Oil* 176 (February 15, 1973):130–32.

O'BRIEN, JOSEPH F. "Henry M. Robert as a Presiding Officer." *Quarterly Journal of Speech* 42 (April 1956):157–62.

———. "The Use and Abuse of Parliamentary Procedure." *Adult Leadership* 5 (December 1956): 178–82.

PATTULLO, G. W. "Why Staff Meetings Fall Flat." *Nation's Business* 61 (May 1973):67–68.

PHILLIPS, GERALD M. "Freedom of Speech and Majority Rule in the *Talmud.*" *Quarterly Journal of Speech* 47 (February 1961):36–40.

PRINCE, GEORGE M. "Creative Meetings Through Power Sharing." *Harvard Business Review* 50 (July 1972):47–54.

RAMSON, KENNETH C. "Sticks and Stones." *Yankee,* January 1974, pp. 64–69, 117–18.

"Shop Talk." *Quarterly Journal of Speech* 25 (December 1959):461–62.

SIGHAND, N. B. "How to Meet with Success." *Nation's Business* 59 (March 1971):76–78.

"Small Meeting: Its Role and Its Influence Today." *Insurance* 74 (January 1973):28.

STURGIS, ALICE. "Putting Parliamentary Procedure to Work." *Adult Leadership* 5 (December 1956):190–92.

"Supervisor's Guide to Managing Meetings." *Sales Management* 106 (March 15, 1971):24–26.

TACEY, WILLIAM S. "The Chair Recognizes. . . ." *Adult Leadership* 5 (December 1956):183–84.

———. "The Chairman and His Task." *Parliamentary Journal* 3 (July 1962):7–11.

———. "Tools of the Parliamentarian." *Parliamentary Journal* 7 (January 1966):3–7.

———. "Parliamentary Procedure in Church." *Parliamentary Journal* 9 (April 1968).

———. "Without Constitution or Bylaws." *Parliamentary Journal* 9 (October 1968):24–26.

———. "Chairman by Decree Ousted." *Parliamentary Journal* 10 (October 1969):20–23.

———. "Governing Ourselves Under Robert's Rules." *Pennsylvania Library Association Bulletin* 25 (September 1970):286–90, 295.

TACEY, WILLIAM S., and GENTILE, ROBERT. "From the Courthouse to the Textbook." *Parliamentary Journal* 12 (October 1971):3–13.

TACEY, WILLIAM S., and JANOCSKO, GEORGE M. "The United Mine Workers Election of 1969: A Study in the Denial of Basic Democratic Rights." *Parliamentary Journal* 13 (October 1972):44.

URIS, A. "Structured Group Thinking: Can It Solve Your Problems?" *Advanced Management Journal* 31 (April 1972):21–25.

VERSAGI, F. J. "Few Hints on Preventing Railroading." *Air Conditioning, Heating and Refrigeration News* 128 (January 8, 1973):7.

"Warning: Poor Meetings Dangerous to Company's Health." *Iron Age* 211 (April 19, 1973):25.

WEISS, A. "Member of the Committee." *Supervisory Management* 15 (July 1970):7–9.

"Who Controls Local Church Property?" *Presbyterian Life* 21 (July 15, 1968).

WOOSTER, ERNEST S. "There's a Revolution Going On." *The Toastmaster* 27 (October 1961):12.

"Your Turn to Run the Meeting." *Changing Times* 21 (July 1967):27–28.

Journals and Associations

CAPP News, ed. William S. Tacey, 1117 Cathedral of Learning, Pittsburgh, Penn. 15260. Published triennially by the Commission on American Parliamentary Procedure, an affiliate of the Speech Communication Association.

Parliamentary Journal. ed. William S. Tacey, 1117 Cathedral of Learning, Pittsburgh, Penn. Published quarterly by the American Institute of Parliamentarians. Executive secretary, Lester L. Dahms, 3½ W. Main Street, Marshalltown, Iowa 50158.

The National Parliamentarian. Published quarterly by the National Association of Parliamentarians. Mrs. Emmette Wallace, P.O. Box 8, Bryan, Texas 77801.

We should hesitate to pronounce
judgment on the conduct of such
eminent men, lest we fall into the
common error of condemning what
we do not understand.

Quintilian

And purge me from all heresies of
thought and speech and pen. That
bid me judge him otherwise than
I am judged. Amen!

Rudyard Kipling

Speeches of Business
and Professional Persons
for Study and Analysis

The study of specimen speeches can be profitable for a beginning speaker either in learning what to do or what to avoid. The accompanying speeches can be of greatest help when studying Chapter 6.

Speeches selected have been used by speakers with varied purposes and who have used varied methods of composition. Students are cautioned to analyze each carefully to see what the author did in attempting to accomplish his purpose. Each speech should be considered from the viewpoint of the social situation in which the speech was delivered.

Use of the Questions, Problems and Exercises, and Bibliography at the end of the Appendix can help make study of the sample speeches of greater value.

PUBLIC RELATIONS IN EDUCATION
by Francis C. Pray

[Mr. Pray spoke before the Pittsburgh chapter, Public Relations Society of America, on October 27, 1955. At the time he was Public Relations Counselor at the University of Pittsburgh.

This is an example of a speech in which a problem is expressed. The speaker shows in some detail the problem he faces and seems to seek help from his audience in finding a solution.

What do you think of his plan of using an extended analogy of comparing a college with a steel company? Is there any danger that some of his listeners might think the method of college administration absurd? Might his analogy be the best way to inform the audience of what a college is?

What are some of the techniques used to adapt to the needs and interests of the audience?]

I'd like to talk today about two or three things about education which create public relations problems you may not often get in industry.

And then I'd like to pose a central problem, and ask you to help me with some answers.

I work for a peculiar kind of institution, the like of which is found nowhere else in the world—the American college and university.

Just imagine that you work for a steel company that operates like the average college.

1. You charge your customer about half what the product costs you.
2. After your customers leave you go out and ask them for annual contributions—*and you get them.*
3. You take a lot of raw material and you test it as best you can but you can never analyze its component parts and tell exactly how it is likely to react in the manufacturing process.
4. After you've completed your manufactured product you can never measure exactly what you've done to it. But people come around and buy it anyway.
5. You have a very extensive research program; as much as 25 percent of your budget goes for research. You brag the most about the research which you do which has no practical objective whatsoever. Because you know that years later it may help *somebody* else *somewhere* else.
6. Your customers often tell you what they want but you decide what you're going to give them. *And they buy the product anyway.*
7. If one of your superintendents comes out and speaks in public and writes to the newspapers telling how thoroughly he disagrees with the boss, you grin and bear it. You even defend his right to do it. The American college is probably the only institution left in America—except the church —where a senior employee can come out in public against the policies of his boss, and get away with it. (If he's a professor, that is. Administrators have no tenure.) In our present inter-dependent society, colleges and universities are perhaps the last harbors of the American pioneer spirit of individual freedom and self-determinism.
8. The value your manufacturing process adds is something you can't see. You set your own standards for the kind of steel you are going to make and you believe that your conviction of what is a good process, is sufficient evidence and demonstrably free from personal bias, should prevail against the whole world, public opinion to the contrary.

Now that would be a hell of a way to run a steel company, but it's S.O.P. for a college or university. And I don't think a single one of you would want it any other way.

However, this creates some rather special public relations problems for those of us in education. It means basically that we can't blindly accept some of the easy public relations maxims we hear so much about in current writing on the subject.

Maxim No. 1. *The customer is always right.* In a college the customer is not always right. A college doesn't teach only what students want. Professors lay down a discipline of studies and say, "For this we give the bachelor's degree. This is a standard." If a governor or a senator or a wealthy benefactor asks that the degree be given for something less than full completion, a good faculty will flatly refuse to compromise. The job of the public relations man may well be to explain the action of the faculty; it is not to seek an exception in order to win a vote or a gift.

Maxim No. 2. *It is hard to change the public and easier to change yourself.* Therefore it is wise to make market surveys and find out public opinion and then agree with it.

That may work for industry when the shape or color or function of a product is concerned, but it will *not* work for the real essentials of higher education.

The job of education is to find truth, and then convince the public of that truth. And the right to seek for facts, no matter how unpopular, must be safeguarded as well.

If this sounds radical, just think back a little.

1. Quite a few people were ready to condemn Pasteur. (A market survey would have shown Pasteur that his ideas would not be acceptable and he would have tried to think up a new idea.)

2. The best minds of the day thought Galileo a dangerous subversive for suggesting that a light weight would fall just as rapidly as a heavy one. They wouldn't even watch experiments.

3. Quite a few people were all for solving the polio vaccine problem by legislation, a few months ago. You don't do scientific research by consensus of uninformed opinion.

Maxim No. 3. *People are interested first in people, then in things and lastly in ideas.* Yet it's ideas we have to work with, mostly, in higher education.

It may be that the emphasis on people and on things, as a ready-made public relations and advertising device, is a contributing factor to our great emphasis on materialism in this country. It may be this emphasis is a factor contributing to the problem I'm going to talk about. I'm sneaking up on the subject. Certainly in *education,* anyway, it would be an admission of public relations failure if we believe and lived by any such silly maxim.

I think people are interested in ideas. There seems to be a growing rebirth of interest in the great principles of Christianity and Judaism. *Those are ideas.* We aren't so much afraid of the Russian people as we are afraid of Communism, we say. And *that's an idea.* We talk a little about beauty and truth and patriotism. And *those are ideas.*

Parenthetically, we might wonder if this isn't one of our troubles in America. We public relations people, who deal in ideas, who create ideas, who sell ideas, haven't had enough faith in our fellow citizens' interest in ideas to come up with an *idea* of Americanism that will gain wide agreement.

We explain the American Way in terms of a short week, detergents, security, new cars, and TV.

We talk a lot about the idea of private enterprise but we have failed to create a dynamism on the subject in the minds of many of our fellow citizens. And in education we talk a lot about intellectual freedom, but we haven't fully explained how it must be preserved as one of the great weapons of our American democracy.

Well, in easy stages I've discussed the context in which I want to mention a central problem of public relations for our colleges and universities. It is an important problem, important to industry just as much as it is to education. So far I've been discussing it without putting a real name to it.

This central problem I want to talk about is the problem of winning support and understanding, for the basic *intellectual* functions of higher education. That sounds pompous, doesn't it? Maybe because we are afraid of it.

Oh, we've done pretty well in promoting our courses, and athletics, and student activities. We get warm and generous treatment from newspapers, radio, and TV on our science and research programs. Everybody thinks medicine is wonderful and the classrooms are crowded all across the land.

But we still haven't been successful in solving the central problem that underlies success of all our other programs and in last analysis may even be a key factor in our national security.

Let me lead into the discussion this way.

Last summer across the roads in many small towns were strung banners advertising Fourth of July jamborees. I was particularly struck by one banner which said, "Fireworks, dancing, music, *athletic* contests for all." And suddenly I wonderd why it is that it is so eminently respectable to have athletic contests for all—and why it would be almost inconceivable that we should run any mental contests for all.

Did you ever stop to think of it in just this way? I never did, before. This was the first time I think I ever realized the truly gigantic job to be done.

I looked at that sign for a long time.

I was reminded that the community spelling bee in the country school house was one of the great indoor sports in Colonial America—next to bundling, that is—but that was long before athletic leagues were founded.

Today every town has a Little League fostered by hard-working adults. But no town that I know of anywhere has given anything but lip service to the fostering of *intellectual achievement, outside the schoolroom,* as a *real community enterprise.*

Sports are made vital, challenging. How are we going to go about dramatizing the clash of minds? It goes on all around us. The youngster who has been led to believe that there is something not quite acceptable in getting good grades suddenly finds he has to make a career by using his head. What a shock that must be to him.

The man who created the phrase "C is the gentleman's grade," ought to be kept after school forever.

I'd like to ask a few pointed questions about some attitudes which are almost part of American folklore. I don't think they are healthy attitudes.

1. It's socially OK to have a quicker eye or faster legs or a higher batting average than your neighbor. But somehow we Americans, by some per-

verted kind of snobbery, have concluded that it is extremely bad taste to display a quicker mind or superior knowledge. A college graduate with a job on a production line often finds it expedient to keep his college training a secret. Why is this? Why should we be ashamed or embarrassed about intellectual attainments?

2. We are perfunctory with out scholarship prizes and generous and dramatic with trophies for athletic events. Why is this?

Did you ever put side by side a medal won by the intercollegiate debate champion and the trophy won in any track meet? Why the disparity?

3. We consider it an accepted social obligation to take care of the misfits and mentally retarded. But many citizens will rise up and call it undemocratic when we want to spend extra tax money on the gifted. Why is this?

4. Many colleges have student loan fund accounts gathering dust. Yet many a student quits college rather than borrow $200 or $500 or $1000 to stay in school. He'll take the first job he sees and sign a note at high interest to buy a car that will depreciate 70 percent in 3 years. Yet a college degree may be worth $100,000 in a life-time. Why is this?

What has happened? Why should these things be true in this country, of all countries?

It's *partly* the educator's fault.

It is very certain that we in education have not given enough thought to the necessity to explain and make dramatic

> *the process of the mind,*
> *the effort to remember,*
> *the struggle for understanding,*
> *the discipline of research, and*
> *the search for values.*

For one thing, we have got to stop talking about educational crises, about our needs, as though we were frightened to death of the future, and begin to talk about the worth of education. This is a real public relations problem.

* * *

But this is not just a problem for the educators. It's partly your fault, too, and partly your problem. We've got somehow to change our whole national attitude toward what I can only call our brain-power resources.

Last week I heard Senator Duff, 3 doors from this building, say that Russia, for instance, is training twice as many engineers as we are here in America. And you may be sure she is training biologists and physcists and agricultural experts, and men and women for every other profession needed for national supremacy. These facts are well known.

Our edge over Russia is simply this: In our country we don't just train people, we try to *educate* them. Their ability to think and reason and question is the one ingredient which we can add which Russia will omit, if she can, from training programs.

Russia can mobilize millions more bodies than we can. Our only unique natural resource, if we will develop it, is intellectual strength. Brain power, if you want to call it that, not just intelligence. We have no monoply on that. But the power of brains educated to accept or reject ideas on the basis of evidence, free to seek new knowledge down every available avenue, and motivated to use that knowledge in the service of man.

Then why this American paradox of disparaging the very thing on which we base our greatest strength?

Twenty-five percent of our gifted children never get to college. Some can't afford it and the public is not ready to step in and help them. Some aren't motivated, because we haven't placed a sufficient value on what they have to offer.

But, I said this not just a problem for the educators. Here's where you come in.

During the past few years almost a revolution has occurred in relationships between business and industry, which most of you represent, and higher education.

We have always had plenty of cooperation. Industry has sponsored research and given money on a *quid pro quo* basis for hundreds of projects.

But during the past four or five years scores of leaders in business and industry have supported this concept I'm talking about, the concept that liberal education, and a real emphasis on the intellectual processes of education, is the great hope for the future. And they are backing up their support with corporate aid to colleges and through scholarships to gifted individuals.

I'm talking about men like Ben Moreell, Gwilym Price, Frank Stanton, Harry Bullis, Keith Funston, Alfred Sloan, Frank Abrams, Robert Wilson, Irving Olds, Philip Reed—I could name others. They have all spoken publicly on this subject in recent months or been active in new programs to assist and interpret education: The Greenbrier Conference, CEAI, CFAE, etc.

Top educators and heads of foundations have joined them in their deliberations. This is cooperation on the problem at the summit.

But there has to be a lot of understanding and cooperation at the staff level also; especially, I think, at the public relations level.

We aren't going to solve the problem by perpetuating the same old disparaging attitudes toward intellectual achievement. We will solve it by helping to create a wide public understanding of what this problem is all about. We have to help change public attitudes toward intellectual achievement. We have to create a climate in which we can develop our last and greatest natural resource, the ability for free, independent, creative, and constructive thought.

This is a job education can't do alone. Business and industry, at the summit, has recognized its stake in this problem. This humble public relations person asks your ideas and assistance.

Well there, Mr. Anthony. You've now had it. There's the problem.

FEDERAL TRADE COMMISSION
by Lewis A. Engman

[Government officials, whether local, state, or national, have many opportunities to speak. Lewis A. Engman, chairman of the Federal Trade

Commission, is much in demand as a speaker. His address (untitled) before the Economic Club of Detroit, Michigan, on April 29, 1974, is a representative example of his speeches.

What might have been his reason for choosing to speak in Detroit on international antitrust policy? Why would it be an appropriate choice for Mr. Engman? What in the economic situation of the first quarter of 1974 made it an appropriate choice? Unlike many economists, the speaker used no statistics. Do you believe that to be an advantage or disadvantage? Did he successfully defend current United States antitrust laws? Was he convincing in his attempt to show our practices to be unlike those of European countries? How effectively did the chairman adapt to his audience's needs and interests?]

I needn't tell this distinguished audience how great it is for me to be back in my home State — especially at this time of year.

There are many current activities at the FTC which I presume may be of interest to some of you — such as image advertising, energy, line of business reporting, nutritional advertising, and ad substantiation. However, I understand that we will have a question and answer period when I am through, and at that point I would be happy to discuss these activities, as well as others.

For the moment, I'd like to talk about another subject — international antitrust policy. I picked that subject because it seems to me to be an area in which a little thought now might head off the necessity for making "crisis" decisions in the future.

Let me start by setting my biases out on the table. I believe in free markets and the forces of competition. Competition, like democracy, may not be perfect, but it is certainly preferable to the alternatives as I know them. Competition, in my view, is essential to the maintenance of our free economic and political institutions; and it is the best method yet devised for maximizing general welfare and living standards.

As a general proposition, anything which limits competition works to the disadvantage of the consumer. This is true domestically, and it is true internationally, where the limits to competition are familiar and take many forms.

These limits may be quotas or tariffs which protect domestic producers by limiting the quantity or increasing the price of foreign imports available to consumers.

They may be investment restrictions which — in the name of national security, payments balance or simple national pride — prevent the optimal mating of opportunity with capital.

They may be export subsidies — both low interest credits and tax incentives — which tilt the tables of comparative advantage by introducing financial considerations intended not to incarese total world trade so much as to increase the national take in a zero sum game.

Or, as we have painfully learned this past year, these limits to international competition may come in the form of *export* controls imposed to protect domestic consumers by husbanding scarce supplies or to secure concessions from foreign consumers. With world shortages looming in bauxite, natural rubber, timber and a number of other commodities, these could become more frequent. It is not impossible that the next few years could see an ill-fated trend in which basic materials are withheld from world markets in much the same way that a mercantilist Great Britain attempted to withhold labor skills and technology from international markets in the 18th Century.

Finally, there are limits to competition in the different approaches which different countries take toward the problem of market power. The fact that one country has a tough antitrust policy does not insulate its citizens from the pernicious effects of a weak — or non-existent — antitrust policy in another country. To the extent that non-competitive performance exists anywhere, the citizens of all countries are denied the full benefits of lower prices, innovation and higher quality which would otherwise come from the free competition of foreign imports. Like tariffs and quotas, non-competitive practices and conditions suspend the laws of comparative advantage. When that happens, those on whose behalf they are suspended are subsidized by everyone else — particularly by their not so favored fellow countrymen.

There are, of course, instances in which economic theology must bow to the practicalities. Perfect resource mobility and instantaneous adjustment exist only in textbooks. In the real world, we must cope with the problem of dislocation. The consumer is also a worker or an investor, and, as a voter, he demands to be protected in all of these capacities.

Similarly, national security considerations may, from time to time, require departures from the market model. Responsive democratic governments cannot always withstand pressure to intervene in such cases. If the affected interests are large enough and vocal enough, they will heard.

Anyone who doubts this need only look back over the history of the fight — now in its fifth year — to secure more liberal trade legislation from the Congress.

These hurdles and practical considerations are in the nature of our democratic system. They are our insurance against ideologues and despots. I don't question the advisability of allowing every interest its influence. I only urge that we not lose sight of the fact that for each accommodation made to an individual domestic interest — for each waiver of the laws of free competition — there is an associated cost. And that cost is borne, in the long run, by everyone. It, therefore, seems to me that trade and investment restrictions — whether on the import or the export side — should be pursued only as a last resort, only for as short a period as necessary, and only after alternative efforts to allay the social dislocations have been tried and exhausted.

There is currently a school of thought which takes issue with what I have just said. Their argument basically is that it is too costly to be a saint in a world of sinners. They look around the world at the mixed economies of some of our major trading partners and at the lenient attitude which other governments take toward aggregations of market power and they ask, "How can our industries compete in those markets when their industries have their governments as partners?" What they suggest is that the United States even up the contest by relaxing its antitrust enforcement.

There are at least two aspects of this suggestion which bother me.

The first is that I have seen very little to document specifically the assertion that the U. S. antitrust laws seriously impede the ability of U. S. firms to compete abroad.

I am not so far removed from private practice as to believe that a good lawyer not only points out to his client the pitfalls of a particular approach, but he then goes on to suggest positive alternatives. My recollection is that, generally speaking, where there was a will there was a way — and a legal way — to get the job done.

If the world has so changed that this is no longer the case, then I would like to see some specific evidence.

The other problem I have with this argument is that it seems somewhat paradoxical to me to relax our antitrust policies in order to become more competitive abroad. In any event, it may be unnecessary, since other countries have begun in recent years to adopt tougher antitrust stances.

The West German cartel office has just brought charges of price discrimination against oil companies as part of a "get tough" policy under new antitrust legislation passed last August. The Germans are also gearing up for action against their drug companies and have recently prevented one of their major appliance companies from acquiring an Italian competitor whose exports were holding down prices in the German market. The German example is not unique. The Canadian government is currently proposing major antitrust reform and there is some evidence that the European Court of Justice is taking a tougher antitrust line.

When all is said, however, I suspect that the weight of opinion among U. S. businessmen and lawyers is that the foreign antitrust rules are more easily gotten around in the pursuit of business objectives than are ours.

To those who press European competition policy on us as a model, I would make one other point.

It is true that there is a clear difference between our approach to mergers and acquisitions and theirs.

In the United States, we have a generalized statute. Enforcement is on an ad hoc basis as business combinations are held up to the statute and proceedings initiated where the two are found incongruent. In Europe, for the most part, they employ a clearance system in which prospective transactions are reviewed in advance for anticompetitive implications and either approved or disapproved.

Their system has intriguing advantages. It offers the businessman the benefit of certainty, and it requires a much faster turn around in reviewing cases. It may be that there are some aspects of the European system with which we should experiment.

But it has disadvantages, too. The European system implies much closer relationship between the private and public sectors. The private sector may gain a certain amount of freedom from the invisible hand of competition, but it becomes subject to another hand — the hand of the government planner. And that hand generally turns out to have more than one thumb.

I would ask those of you who think you would prefer the foreign systems to reflect on what they would mean not only for your freedom but for your efficiency. Any of you who have had the experience of getting into bed with the bureaucracy before are aware of that special form of government-industry symbiosis — in a sense, the reverse of synergism — in which two and two can be made to equal three.

As I reflect upon the role of competition policy and international antitrust, I am struck not only by the shifts in foreign approaches to antitrust, but also by the kaleidoscopic quality of changes in the way business operates on a global scale.

Corporate managers no longer treat domestic markets as if they were independent and discrete. Modern approaches to multi-plant investment coordination are part of the business setting in an increasing number of industries. With the aid of computers, multinational corporations are practicing the gospel of comparative advantage with a vengeance.

We don't know the full implications of these developments. Is the multinational company the answer to the free trader's dreams? Has it succeeded in hurdling barriers and impediments to trade and finally unlocked the door of comparative advantages?

If so, what are the costs? Most of those barriers have always been supported by domestic, social and political concerns. Have these companies then discovered ways to frustrate these social and political objectives? Or have they simply demonstrated that free markets can be reconciled with these social and political objectives? If so, the path for further progress seems sunny.

The question I cautiously raise is whether multinational investment may not be the long awaited cure for the malady of protectionism — or at least a major part of that cure.

But international investment also has its dark side. We see evidence of market dominance, practiced on a world-wide scale. We also see evidence of increasing concentration, and we wonder whether the economists who warn us of the anti-consumer effects of concentration in domestic economies can help us understand the effects on consumers on a world-wide scale.

And while we wonder about these things, we wonder also whether United States antitrust is up to the task. "International antitrust" to the informed practitioner has meant little more for the last thirty-plus years than a parade of jurisdictional nightmares, horror stories about cartel arrangements to divide world markets, technology licensing restrictions, and merger law enforcement.

In sum, the problems we face in our economy are not, for the most part, problems which give way to a light heart and a glib tongue. In fact, we do ourselves a disservice if we act as though they are.

An economy as complex as ours is like a gigantic machine with thousands and thousands of moving parts linked together with wheels and gears and belts. You change one part and it is going to affect all the others. That is not to say that you shouldn't change anything, just that you should not do so until you have examined its complexities and thoroughly mapped its consequences.

We learned this in trying to solve the energy and environmental problems on a piecemeal basis in an atmosphere of crisis when we discovered that their solutions related to one another like opposite ends of a seesaw.

When our economy is examined in the international context, the complexities become even greater. I would suggest that the answer to our international antitrust enigmas lies neither with protectionist chauvinists who favor increased United States self-help against foreign competition nor with doctrinaire purists to whom principle is everything and practicality nothing.

My hypothesis is that answers lie not with the theologians in either camp, but rather with those who are determined to continue to ask tough questions and who — hopefully — can look far enough ahead to enable us to avoid more rounds of ad hoc "government by crisis."

ENERGY STATEMENT
by Clifford H. Goodall

[Mr. Goodall is an example of an ever-increasing number of interested citizens who seek an opportunity to testify before representatives of government (local, state, and national) agencies. Statements must be kept to a minimum length, usually are written so that copies may be filed for later reference, and must be unusually persuasive if they are to make an impact on those conducting the hearing.

How effective might Mr. Goodall's two introductory paragraphs have been in establishing his stature as an authority on his subject? What might have been his purpose in speaking of the energy crisis as a *positive* event? Would you use a similar, or different, approach in a similar situation? In the final section, do you believe that his suggestion of a "partnership" with the federal government was good strategy?

Is the philosophy expressed in the conclusion consistent with that generally acceptable in the United States?]

My name is Clifford H. Goodall and I am the staff attorney and executive director of the Natural Resources Council of Maine. The NRC is Maine's major private environmental organization. We have approximately 3,500 individual members and 99 affiliate organizations which are listed on the back of the first page of this statement. In total, we represent about 12,000 Maine residents.

Recently *Business Week* said that environmentalists have "as much political muscle in the Pine Tree State as oilmen display in Texas." This testimony does not represent a formal position that has been adopted by Maine environmentalists because we have not had an adequate opportunity to work out a clear position on the energy crisis. These are my personal views which I believe reflect the general views of those who I represent.

The Energy Crisis Is a Positive Event

The energy crisis has given the country a unique opportunity. It is not just a crisis; it also can be a long range positive event. The immediate crisis will cause some disruption and needs to be dealt with decisively. We, however, must not blow the chance to redirect and reshape our lifestyles to actually reflect the earth's finite carrying capacity for supporting Mainers, Americans, and all mankind. You, Mr. Simon, and President Nixon; and you, Congressman Steele, and Congress generally have the opportunity to lead the nation to a new age which has man as a custodian rather than an exploiter of the earth. If you fail and if we fail, then future generations will suffer because of our folly. We should welcome the transition and not try to hold onto the past two decades of explosive growth and a more, more, more philosophy.

In short, the energy crisis gives us time to plan. It gives Maine a breathing space because it will slow up the incredible development pressure that was about to overwhelm us. Maine and the nation must not only plan a long range energy policy — it must also develop sensible land use plans which reflect the land's capacity.

The energy crisis clearly demonstrates the difference between states. These differences create complex answers. For example, most everyone agrees that more mass transportation is needed. But Maine is a rural state and the mass transportation system we need will be different from the one Connecticut needs. We urge you to keep this complexity in focus.

Maine as a Sacrificial Lamb

The energy crisis can be a direct threat to Maine as well as a positive opportunity. We have only .5% of the nation's population and a corresponding national political power. Great numbers of people live just south of us. It may be, and in fact has been suggested, that Maine become the energy bank for the East. Maine may, therefore, be threatened by numerous nuclear power plants on its coast; by oil wells off its coast with refineries on the mainland; by large hydro-power facilities on our rivers that flood our land. Maine does not want to become the sacrificial lamb of the energy crisis. We do not know what the final details of "Operation Independence" will include so we strongly emphasize that international energy independency should not be achieved by sacrificing the environment of our rural states.

Maine has passed several nationally recognized landmark environmental laws. These are, of course, subject to Federal pre-emption. We firmly believe that Maine has a national and regional responsibility but we do not believe that any rural state should be sacrificed for the more populated and politically powerful states. Therefore, we suggest a federal/state partnership where states, such as Maine, can continue to review and regulate development projects under its own laws. We believe the partnership is possible. We just don't want something pushed on us for the exclusive benefit of others.

In conclusion, the nation must not be blinded by the immediate crisis. We now have the opportunity in this generation to adapt ourselves to the finite capacity of our planet. This opportunity makes the crisis an exciting as well as a difficult transitional period. We are all in the same fix and we must be cautious not to sacrifice the weak for the strong.

RETROSPECT '73—BIBLICAL LESSONS WE CAN LEARN FROM WATERGATE
by John A. Huffman, Jr.

[John A. Huffman, Jr., is the young (age thirty-four) pastor of the 2,800-member First Presbyterian Church of Pittsburgh. His sermon, "Retrospect '73—Biblical Lessons We Can Learn from Watergate," was preached to the First Presbyterian Congregation at the 10:45 A.M. service on Sunday, December 30, 1973, and broadcast on radio station KDKA at 10:00 P.M. His interest in the subject is intensified because his previous pastorate was at Key Biscayne, Florida, where President Nixon was a worshiper.

How effective do you believe the first four paragraphs of his sermon were in interesting and orienting the congregation and the radio audience? How does his phrase, "to declare the word of God," serve to distinguish a sermon from other forms of speaking? In what ways might his "seven lessons" be called controversial among non-Christians? Was the following of his text (Matthew 5:37) a help or a hindrance? Was its use a necessity in the pulpit? Why or why not? What were some of his techniques used in persuading his listeners to apply the lessons to themselves? Note the numerous forms of support used. How effective do you believe they may have been in making clear his meaning and in persuading his listeners?]

Search for a word to capsule the past year and you'll quickly find it—WATERGATE! By an overwhelming margin American editors have chosen the Watergate disclosures and the challenges they raise to the presidency as the top news story of 1973. This year we have seen a president boasting an overwhelming electoral victory, inaugurated only to move on to a higher pinnacle of success as he disengaged our nation from the longest war in the history of the United States. We paused. We prayed. We breathed a sigh of relief as the cease fire went into effect. We watched the POW's come home. Many of us saluted the efforts of the man, Richard M. Nixon, who stood at the apex of his career.

Today, less than a year later, we observe the tragic, isolated figure of our President. Swept from positions of highest influence are dozens of public officials accused of betraying our trust. Bludgeoned by fuel shortages, rising costs, and international unrest, our President and nation seem paralyzed to cope creatively with these problems as we are held in the clutches of this unresolved Watergate.

As a minister of the Gospel, I am not here to attack persons or assign guilt. Nor am I here to defend certain people declaring their innocence. I have a deep love for President Nixon and value highly his personal graciousness to me during my six Key Biscayne years. I greatly appreciate my friendship with him, his family, and others of his White House associates. For me to make fallible human judgments on incomplete data would be both foolish and unwise. Fortunately, we have a due process of law which hopefully will proceed deliberately convicting those who are guilty and acquitting the innocent. Only additional months will reveal the full extent and nature of personal involvement of the various Watergate parties. And you are familiar with all the details.

Today, I'm here to declare the Word of God as we take a retrospective look at 1973 and we discover biblical lessons. You and I can learn from the tragic events called "Watergate." The problem is bigger than any one president, any one administration. It is your problem and my problem. We have a responsibility to learn from these sad events in order to free ourselves by God's grace from the bondage and inertia of such tragedies. As Howard F. Stein writes in a recent issue of *The American Scholar*, "There is a kind of silent complicity in which we are all a part of Watergate. We have created the society in which these events can happen."

God's word calls for transparent integrity on the part of every single believer in Jesus Christ. It leaves no room for easy accommodation with wrong doing. It calls for a frankness, an honesty, an open-discussion of difficult problems within the context of biblical faith. Here are some of the biblical lessons which we can learn from Watergate.

Lesson One—*"Let your 'yea' be 'yea' and your 'nay' be 'nay'."*

Endemic to human nature is our capacity to shade truth to our own benefit. Little do we analyze at the time the future cost. Many of the principal figures in this whole Watergate matter I have had as personal acquaintances. Some of these men have either confessed their dishonesty or can be shown dishonest by a comparative look at their public statements over a several months' span. I am convinced that some of them did not originally intend to get caught up in such a complicated web of dishonorable activity, such dishonest cover-up. Somewhere along the line they had rationalized that "little white lies don't make any difference. In fact, they protect many people from hurt. What's wrong with a little cover-up? After all, our nation's security is at stake."

How about you. Have you ever instructed your secretary to get rid of that nuisance phone caller by saying, "Tell him I'm not in?" If so you have begun a compromise of your own personal integrity. You've involved yourself in a life style of cover-up. How much better to say, "Tell him I'm not available now." Or, "I'll return his call later." Or, if necessary, "I'll not be able to talk with him at all." Jesus said "Let what you say be simply 'Yes' or 'No'; anything more than this comes from evil." (Matt. 5:37 RSV)

Let your 'yea' be 'yea' and your 'nay' be 'nay'. Clean, crisp honesty. Pay some prices right now. But in a strictly pragmatic sense it releases you from the horrendous penalties of your own personal Watergate. Cover-up functions not only in public life but so subtly in our own interpersonal relations in business, husband-wife, parent-child relationships. Yet God wants you and me to be stripped of our phoniness. To be authentic people whose word can be trusted.

Lesson Two—*The New Morality does not stand up.*

Since the early 1960's there have been a lot of discussions about Situational Ethics which also goes under the name of Contextual Ethics or the New Morality. Joseph Fletcher, the Episcopal theologian, has been one of the main articulators of this concept. Granted, the New Morality means different things to different people. In its purest form it appears to me that Joseph Fletcher and other proponents of this position are calling for us to be ethically motivated by love instead of arbitrary detailed laws. A mature person who desires the best for someone else in love is set free to make his ethical decisions, not on the basis of what is set down in the Bible or some legal system, but on the basis of what is really best for all parties involved. An appeal is made to Christ's statement that love should be our motivation for everything. The greatest commandment of all is to love the Lord thy God with all thy heart, soul and might and to love thy neighbor as thyself. Following this logic, proponents of the New Morality would release us from the arbitrary bondage of rules. For example, some would say there are circumstances in which an altering of the truth or adultery would be permissible.

I believe that Watergate teaches us that this kind of New Morality does not stand up. In fact, it leads me to the Old Testament statement which underlines the plight of Israel caught up in moral and political anarchy. Judges 21:25 reads, "In those days there was no king in Israel; every man did what was right in his own eyes."

God has revealed to us, through the Scriptures, how you and I function best. No, we're not bound by law. We live in the grace of our Lord, Jesus Christ which promises God's forgiveness for everything you and I have done wrong. At the same time this does not free us to live in the bondage of wrong activity. Some highly intelligent, capable men felt that the reelection of the President of the United States was for the highest ethical good of our nation. They did all kinds of wrong, which they called right, to see that he was reelected. In the context of their value system, for him not to be reelected was evil. Therefore, their defiance of the law, in the pursuit of what they considered to be the ethical good, was permissible. This explains why they could self-righteously point their finger at criminal and immoral activities carried out by other elements in society without for a moment realizing that their activities, both in the initial acts and the cover-up, were wrong. God's word calls you to an ethical discipline to live obedient to the guidelines the Lord has revealed in Scriptures. The order which we have in society is the fringe benefit coming from people who took the moral or divinely revealed law seriously. The relativistic approach in which you live above God's law will only cause you trouble, and hurt the lives of those you are trying to help.

Lesson Three—*Two wrongs don't make a right.*

How often have you heard someone say, "But that's politics. Everybody else does it. The only thing wrong here was these men got caught!" Yes, it is tragic that elections can be stolen in America. Yes, it is true that a study of our American political process points out some enormous ethical inconsistencies. Does this give us any right to "fight fire with fire?" Absolutely not! We should do all we can to uncover other cover-ups. We have a God given responsibility to see that justice prevails. We are in dangerous waters when we presume to take divinely revealed law into our own hands, using it to our own advantage when it is convenient and dismissing it when when we are trying to get even with those who function in a lawless manner.

To insist, "They all do it" will mean that the horrible experience of Watergate will not purge our society but only make us look for more subtle ways to defy what is right.

Lesson Four—*Success in a Christian context is determined by eternal not temporal standards.*

By this I mean a secular pragmatist is interested in getting results and getting them now. Nothing succeeds like success. To lose an election is to fail if your highest priority is winning. The Christian has the exhilarating opportunity to see beyond the immediate external success syndrome. He is able to realize that in losing he may make a moral and spiritual impact much larger than that made if he wins (especially if he wins using illegal methods.) For example, take the election of 1972. As we look back we can say it was inevitable that Richard Nixon would win. Why were any dirty tricks needed? Yet it was not always inevitable that he would win. These illegal activities were carried out long before the election was secured. The highest priority, according to some involved in the campaign, was to win the election. One man even stated that he would walk over his own grandmother to assure the President's reelection. How much happier all the parties would be today if the election had been lost with personal honor and integrity kept intact. Joseph lost when he rejected the seductive advances of Potiphar's wife. Doing what was right sent him to jail. Now he stands in the pages of history as an eternal winner, a man of character who would not adapt to the expedient.

The man of God is going to lose at many points in this world. Jesus warns us that the Christian life is a difficult life. Yet He says, "He who loseth himself shall find himself. He that would be first shall be last. The last shall be first." Christ sets our success-failure motivations into a context of the eternal. In reality, Jesus is saying, "God's payday is not always Friday." To put it more crassly, it is better to win on the day of judgment as you stand before Almighty God than it is to win down here.

Pragmatic, non-spiritual man has no scales on which to measure success or failure except those of the immediate. The *Christian Century* magazine, in a December 12, 1973 editorial states it so crisply, "The functional man dares not to view his immediate victories in the light of a thousand years, because his entire life is dependent upon that victory. Not to have it treated as ultimate is to require that all our victories be measured against the victory of Advent, which promises us a hope that is not seen. And the moment we are driven into an arena of waiting for something not to be seen, we lose the win-or-lose certainty that powers functional man."

Now I realize that this kind of conversation has been used as a narcotic to dull the senses of those who suffer. Give people promises of the future life and they are much more exploitable in this life. God forbid that we twist this to our own purposes.

Lesson Five—*Don't put your faith in America, but in Jesus Christ.*

During the past several months more people have said to me, "I've just lost my faith in politicians." Why in the world did they have their faith in the politicians in the first place? "I've lost my confidence in our public leaders." The Christian's confidence is to be in God Almighty not in human leaders. You have heard people say "I believe in the United States." Let me ask you this. Imagine that the United States should disappear tomorrow just like Rome crumpled and disappeared from the position of world leadership. What would that do to your faith? Would God be any less alive tomorrow evening than He is today? Granted, your circumstances of life would be quite different. But would Jesus Christ be any different? A November, 1973 editorial in *Eternity* magazine states,

"Hopefully, the revelations of Watergate have brought us back to reality. Unpleasant as the facts were, we can be grateful for the jolting reminder that no man, no party, no administration can give us assurance of righteousness in government.

Thousands of conservative Christians across the land consciously or unconsciously, felt that the conservative politics of the administration, coupled with Mr. Nixon's religious roots and associations, pointed toward a high moral tone in government. The facts have demonstrated otherwise, and we are driven back to the total dependence and trust in God that should characterize us at all times, under all administrations, Democratic, Republican, or otherwise."

I thank God that in the United States at least there is still some concern about right and wrong. There are countries in this world where corruption in government would never be aired. At least there is a kind of residual, ethical impulse that makes us recoil from abuse of the public trust. Former Vice President Agnew has talked about a post-Watergate morality, using this as a rationalization for his criminal actions. Thank God that there is a kind of post-Watergate morality. And let's hope that it sticks. Let it never be forgotten.

Lesson Six—*Watergate gives us a correcting confrontation with the true nature of man.*

No one is perfect. Crime must pay. Yet unfortunately a strange kind of double standard has developed. Some of us have the capacity to speak into microphones at public hearings, political rallies, or religious gatherings, assuming self-righteous postures. A young senator accuses an incumbent president of all kinds of immorality when he himself cheated on an exam and at the very least was guilty of fleeing from the scene of an accident. One political party points its finger at the morals of another when that same party covered up the corruption of the Bobby Baker scandal. The evening after the resignation of the Vice President, I had dinner in Washington with a prominent congressman. He said, "Many a governor and ex-governor is shaking in his boots as a result of these Maryland allegations against Agnew. Those same companies which gave him kick-backs are functioning in a number of other States. That's the way this political business functions."

Unfortunately, there is a tragic disjuncture between personal and social morals. Some of the very men and women who are most quick to accuse the President and others of dishonesty are right now totally disregarding the marriage vows of fidelity which they made "till death do us part." The Bible says, "All have sinned and come short of the glory of God." Watergate alerts us to our own human weakness, our need of a Saviour. Watergate puts a mirror in front of me, alerting me to cover-ups in my own life. My subtle shadings of the truth. My unfaithfulness to the confidence people have put in me. Jesus had some terse words for those who tossed that pathetic adulteress at His feet. With the penetrating expression which could come only from one who had ultimate authority He said, "He who is without sin cast the first stone." Suddenly, there weren't many accusers. The self-righteous became guilty. The guilty one was set free with the words, "Go and sin no more."

Lesson Seven—*Remember these are people.*

There's a danger for us in trying to find a scapegoat for everything that goes wrong. I do not for a moment mean to excuse illegal activities. Those who have done wrong should be held responsible. At the same time a man should be considered innocent until proven guilty. And even if he is found guilty, he should be treated as a person who is created in the image of God and still loved by Him. Hopefully, Watergate will help us reanalyze our whole attitude toward the criminal, help us to show a greater compassion to people who have sinned against society.

Thank God that the cover-up is being uncovered. Thank God that the breaking of laws has been discovered. Thank God that our Country at least for the moment, has been halted in its direction toward a totalitarianism in which the few see fit to live above the law. Let's remember that these men have children and wives. Many of them were misguided zealots who thought they were serving their country. Some of them, in the process of trying to do their best—failed. There needs to be a love, grace, a compassion, a concern which says, "But for the grace of God there go I."

Too long have we taken pornographic delight in the misadventures of someone else. For too many months now we have eaten away at the vitals of our own political and moral system enjoying Watergate for its entertainment value. Let us love. Let us care. Let us make certain that justice prevails. But let us temper it with mercy for all in our society who have failed. Perhaps this is the moment for a kind of amnesty in which we make 1974 a year of forgiveness, both for those who failed to serve their country in military service, and those who failed to serve their country in the highest levels of leadership. Let us get off the backs of those humans like us who are trying to do their best. Let us be sensitive to the heart throb of men and women in all levels of our society, including our very selves, who are the tragedies of failure. Let us reach out with a gesture of love as we have been loved. The gesture of forgiveness wherein we have been forgiven in the name of Jesus Christ, our Saviour.

Conclusion

Retrospect '73—yes, there are biblical lessons we can learn from Watergate. How tragic that it ever happened! But let us learn from it lessons never to be forgotten.

SPEAKER OF THE YEAR AWARD
by Honorable David L. Lawrence

[David L. Lawrence, then governor of Pennsylvania, was given the Pennsylvania Speech Association 1962 Speaker of the Year Award. At the conclusion of his speech the author of this book asked Governor Lawrence for permission to print the speech in *Today's Speech,* which Dr. Tacey was then editing. It appeared in volume 11, number 1 (February 1963), pp. 2–3, under the title, "The Power of Good Speech." The Lawrence speech is here reproduced in its original manuscript form (with its print size reduced by one-third), including the governor's penciled notes which guided him in giving greetings to officers and members of the Pennsylvania Speech Association.

What evidence is there in this speech to show that the governor had made a study of his subject in order to be able to talk intelligently with the professionals whom he was addressing? How successful do you believe that he was in uniting his field—politics—with the discipline of speech?

Why do you suppose that he chose freedom of speech as a basic theme? Might he have been paying tribute to the academic freedom which every teacher must have if he is to teach successfully rather than to indoctrinate?

Why do you suppose he quoted Aristotle and Socrates rather than more modern philosophers? Why was he not more specific in discussing modern demagogues? Would it have helped achieve his purpose to have done so?

What standards for a courtesy speech (accepting an award) do you think that he upheld? Do you believe that Governor Lawrence, one of the most powerful politicians of his time, was sincere in what he said in this speech? Why?]

REMARKS OF GOVERNOR DAVID L. LAWRENCE
IN ACCEPTANCE OF THE "SPEAKER OF THE
YEAR AWARD" OF THE 23D ANNUAL CONVENTION
OF THE PENNSYLVANIA SPEECH ASSOCIATION,
PENN HARRIS HOTEL, HARRISBURG,
PENNSYLVANIA, 12:30 P.M., FRIDAY,
OCTOBER 12, 1962. *Miss McFarland* *Rev. —*
Dr. Hopkins *Clergy —*
Sisters —

WHEN THE ANNOUNCEMENT WAS MADE

THAT THIS ASSOCIATION HAD CHOSEN ME TO

RECEIVE ITS ANNUAL AWARD THE THOUGHT

CROSSED MY MIND THAT, THIS YEAR AT LEAST,

YOU MUST BE BASING IT UPON QUANTITY

RATHER THAN QUALITY.

ON THOSE TERMS YOU WOULD SEEM TO

BE ON FAIRLY SOUND GROUND, FOR I DOUBT

THAT ~~TOO~~ MANY CITIZENS OF THIS STATE HAVE

MADE MORE SPEAKING ENGAGEMENTS DURING THIS

PAST YEAR, TRAVELED MORE MILES TO AND

FROM THOSE ENGAGEMENTS, OR BEEN PRIVILEGED

TO TALK WITH A WIDER VARIETY OF AUDIENCES.

I AM DEEPLY HONORED TO HAVE THIS
AWARD -- NOT BECAUSE OF THE PERSONAL
TRIBUTE IT PAYS ME, BUT BECAUSE IT
INDICATES THE PRIDE YOUR MEMBERSHIP FEELS
IN THE GOVERNMENT OF THIS STATE AND ITS
RESPECT FOR A PUBLIC SERVANT WHO IS --
AND QUITE PROUDLY SO -- A POLITICIAN.

THE ART OF PUBLIC SPEAKING AND
THE FIELD OF POLITICS HAVE BEEN BOUND
TOGETHER SINCE THE BEGINNING OF TIME. FAR
MORE IMPORTANT, THE EVOLUTION OF FREE PUBLIC
SPEECH IN AN OPEN FORUM GAVE BIRTH TO
DEMOCRACY AND, IN THE LAST ANALYSIS,
LIBERATED MANKIND.

THE LONG MARCH OF HUMAN PROGRESS HAS
MOVED, STEP BY STEP WITH THE SOUND OF THE
DRUM OF FREE, RESPONSIBLE RHETORIC.
TWENTY-THREE CENTURIES AGO, ARISTOTLE SET
DOWN THE FUNDAMENTAL TENET OF DEMOCRATIC

SOCIETY WHEN HE SAID:

"IF LIBERTY AND EQUALITY, AS IS
THOUGHT BY SOME, ARE CHIEFLY TO BE FOUND
IN DEMOCRACY, THEY WILL BE BEST ATTAINED
WHEN ALL PERSONS ALIKE SHARE IN THE
GOVERNMENT TO THE UTMOST."

THE PASSAGE OF TIME HAS NOT DIMMED
THE TRUTH OF THAT STATEMENT -- NOR HAS IT
LESSENED THE NEED FOR GREATER
PARTICIPATION BY THE PEOPLE IN THEIR
GOVERNMENT.

TODAY, BOTH MAJOR POLITICAL PARTIES
AND A WIDE ARRAY OF PRIVATE CIVIC
ORGANIZATIONS CARRY ON AN UNCEASING DRIVE
TO GET AMERICAN CITIZENS TO REGISTER AND
TAKE PART IN THE FREE SELECTION OF THE MEN
AND WOMEN WHO BECOME THEIR PUBLIC SERVANTS.

THE PRIVILEGES THAT ACCOMPANY
FREEDOM ARE SO MANY AND SO GREAT THAT,
ALL TOO OFTEN, THEY ARE SACRIFICED BY
COMPLACENCY AND APATHY.

YET IT IS A MEASURE OF THE GREATNESS
OF OUR FREEDOM THAT, DESPITE THIS FAILURE,
DEMOCRACY SUCCEEDS.

IT IS IN THE PURSUIT OF FREEDOM'S
FULL POTENTIAL THAT THE MODERN-DAY
POLITICIAN SHARES HIS GREATEST KINSHIP WITH
THE TRULY GREAT ORATORS OF THE PAST.

FOR EACH OF THESE MEN -- SOCRATES
AND ARISTOTLE, DEMOSTHENES AND PLATO --
WERE MEN OF DEEP AND ABIDING CONVICTION.
THEY BELIEVED IN THE DIGNITY OF MAN; THEY
PREACHED A DOCTRINE OF RESPONSIBLE LIBERTY
AND RESPONSIVE GOVERNMENT.

THEY WERE ORATORS AND LEADERS OF
MEN. THEY HAD COURAGE AND DETERMINATION.
THEY CHANGED THE COURSE OF THE WORLD.

MANY OTHERS HAVE FOLLOWED IN THEIR
FOOTSTEPS -- AND, ESPECIALLY IN AMERICA,
THEY HAVE BROUGHT THE DREAM OF INDIVIDUAL
LIBERTY FROM THE TWILIGHT OF MAN'S HOPE
TO THE BRIGHT DAY OF REALITY.

THEY HAVE BEEN ALLIED IN MANY WAYS --
IN THEIR ABILITY TO USE WORDS, IN THEIR
CAPACITY TO MOLD THE OPINIONS OF MEN AND
USE THOSE OPINIONS CONSTRUCTIVELY.

BUT THERE IS ONE QUALITY ABOVE ALL
OTHERS THAT HAS MARKED THE WORK OF THE
WORLD'S GREAT PUBLIC SPEAKERS. THAT
QUALITY IS TRUTH. AND THEY HAVE RESPECTED
IT AND REVERED IT AS THE MOST POWERFUL OF
ALL THE WEAPONS OF SPEECH.

DESPITE THIS OVERWHELMING EVIDENCE THAT TRUTH -- AND ONLY TRUTH -- SURVIVES THE ONSLAUGHT OF TIME, THE PECULIAR SENSE OF THE DEMAGOGUE STILL RISES ALL TOO OFTEN IN THE DEBATE AND THE DIALOGUE OF MODERN POLITICS.

AGAINST THOSE WHO TRY TO SPEAK THE TRUTH AND TALK COMMON SENSE TO THOSE WHO WILL LISTEN, THERE ARE ALWAYS OTHERS WHO SEEK ONLY TO PLAY UPON THE FEARS OF THE PEOPLE BY DECEIT AND DELUSION. IN THIS DETERMINED -- AND OFTEN DESPERATE -- DRIVE TOWARD POWER, THE LISTENER IS DELUGED WITH FANCIFUL ALLEGATIONS, HE IS SNOWED UNDER BY STATISTICS, HE IS TORN BY INSECURITY AND SURROUNDED BY EMOTIONAL IRRELEVANCIES.

OUT OF THIS TRAGIC AFTERMATH OF CONFUSION, THE DEMAGOGUE HOPES ONLY TO GAIN HIS OWN END. HE CARES LITTLE FOR THE CONSEQUENCES -- UNTIL HE IS FORCED TO FACE THEM.

IF SUCH MEN EMERGE TRIUMPHANT, HOWEVER, THEIR CONSOLATION IS SMALL. FOR THEY HAVE WON A PYRRHIC VICTORY -- AND ITS COST IS PAID ONLY AFTER LONG YEARS OF SACRIFICE AND UNCERTAINTY.

THERE IS A NAME -- AND NOT A VERY HONORABLE ONE -- FOR THIS KIND OF PUBLIC SPEAKER. HE IS A MUCK-RAKER AND JOHN BUNYAN TELLS US, IN PILGRIM'S PROGRESS, THAT HE IS A MAN WHO LOOKS IN ONLY ONE DIRECTION -- AND THAT IS DOWNWARDS.

HE IS A MAN OF NARROW VISION WITHOUT REGARD FOR TRUTH -- A MAN WHO BELIEVES, WITH TRAGIC OBSESSION, THAT THE END JUSTIFIES THE MEANS.

A GREAT AMERICAN PRESIDENT ONCE HELD OUT THIS SOBER PIECE OF ADVICE ABOUT SUCH MEN.

"MEN WITH THE MUCK-RAKE ARE OFTEN INDISPENSABLE TO THE WELL-BEING OF SOCIETY," THEODORE ROOSEVELT SAID, AND THEN HE ADDED: "BUT ONLY IF THEY KNOW WHEN TO STOP RAKING THE MUCK."

THE CONCERN HONEST MEN HAVE SHOWN WITH THE TERRIBLE PRICE THE MUCK-RAKER EXACTS FROM HIS PUBLIC DATES BACK TO THE BEGINNING OF FREE SPEECH. FOR IT WAS SOCRATES WHO SAID, IN THE FOURTH CENTURY BEFORE CHRIST WAS BORN, THAT:

"THE PARTISAN, WHEN HE IS ENGAGED IN A DISPUTE, CARES NOTHING ABOUT THE RIGHTS OF THE QUESTION, BUT IS ANXIOUS ONLY TO CONVINCE HIS HEARERS OF HIS OWN ASSERTIONS."

AND TO THIS HE SET DOWN A
REMARKABLE ADMONITION:

"FALSE WORDS," HE SAID, "ARE NOT
ONLY EVIL IN THEMSELVES, BUT THEY INFECT
THE SOUL WITH EVIL."

READING THOSE WORDS, THE AVERAGE
CITIZEN MAY BE FORGIVEN IF HE WISHES,
VEHEMENTLY, FOR A GREATER CONCERN FOR THE
TRUTH ON THE PART OF PUBLIC FIGURES AND
THOSE WHO ASPIRE TO SERVE THE PUBLIC.

THE FACT OF THE MATTER IS THAT
THE VAST MAJORITY OF THE AMERICAN PEOPLE
TRULY WANT TO DECIDE THE MAJOR POLITICAL
AND SOCIAL CONFLICTS OF THEIR TIME ON THE
ISSUES.

THE FURTHER FACT IS THAT THEY ARE
VERY OFTEN DENIED THAT OPPORTUNITY.

I BELIEVE WHEN THE SOUND AND THE FURY DIE AWAY, THE PEOPLE OF THIS COUNTRY AND THIS STATE REJECT THOSE WHO WOULD DELIBERATELY MISLEAD THEM FOR THE SAKE OF PERSONAL GAIN.

IT IS FOR THAT REASON THAT I HAVE TRIED -- TO THE BEST OF MY ABILITY -- TO MAKE THE TRUTH, AS I SEE IT, THE HALLMARK OF MY PUBLIC UTTERANCES.

THE RESULT HAS BEEN, I SUPPOSE, PREDICTABLE -- FOR THE TRUTH IS NOT SENSATIONAL AND IT IS NOT CALCULATED TO GRAB HEADLINES.

IN THIS REGARD, I SUSPECT THAT WE ARE ALLIED IN A GOOD MANY WAYS. FOR A MAN WHO SEEKS ONLY TO SERVE THE CAUSE OF TRUTH IN GOVERNMENT IS VERY LIKE A TEACHER WHO STRIVES ONLY TO DO THE BEST JOB HE CAN IN THE WORK HE IS DOING.

THERE HAVE BEEN FEW BANNER
HEADLINES CALLING ATTENTION TO YOUR WORK,
FOR YOURS IS A FIELD IN WHICH
ACCOMPLISHMENTS COME QUIETLY, AFTER LONG
MONTHS, PERHAPS YEARS OF PAINSTAKING
EFFORT.

IF WE HAD IT TO DO ALL OVER AGAIN,
I DOUBT THAT WE WOULD CHANGE THAT APPROACH
TO THE RESPONSIBILITIES OF OUR WORK. YOU
WOULD ELECT TO HELP YOUNG MEN AND WOMEN
BECOME USEFUL MEMBERS OF SOCIETY, ABLE TO
VERBALIZE THEIR FEELINGS AND MOLD THE
OPINIONS OF THEIR NEIGHBORS. YOU WOULD
DO SO WITHOUT FANFARE -- AND YOU WOULD
NOT CARE IF LITTLE ATTENTION IS PAID TO
THE TRIUMPH OF YOUR ACHIEVEMENTS.

YOU HAVE A RIGHT TO FEEL DEEP,
PERSONAL PRIDE IN THE WORK YOU HAVE DONE
AND ARE NOW DOING.

THE MEMBERS OF THIS ASSOCIATION
WILL HAVE A LASTING AND PROFOUND EFFECT
UPON THE COURSE OF THIS STATE AND THIS
COUNTRY -- FOR THE POWER OF GOOD SPEECH,
EFFECTIVELY AND CREATIVELY DIRECTED, IS
AMONG THE FOREMOST GLORIES OF A FREE
SOCIETY.

I AM DEEPLY HONORED THAT YOU FEEL
MY EFFORTS IN PUBLIC SPEAKING HAVE BEEN
WORTHWHILE -- AND I ACCEPT THIS AWARD
WITH HUMBLE HOPE IN MY HEART THAT YOUR
FAITH IS JUSTIFIED.

BEYOND THIS, I CAN SAY ONLY THAT I
COMMEND THIS ASSOCIATION FOR ITS UNTIRING
WORK IN A VALUABLE FIELD OF EDUCATION.

THE STRENGTH OF A DEMOCRACY LIES
IN THE ABILITY OF ITS CITIZENS TO EXPRESS

THEMSELVES, TO MAKE THEIR WISHES KNOWN, TO INFLUENCE THOSE WHO SERVE THEM AND EACH OTHER FOR THE BETTERMENT OF MANKIND.

WE ARE A NATION OF FREE MEN AND WOMEN -- FREE TO SPEAK OUR MINDS, TO WORSHIP AS WE PLEASE, TO ENLIGHTEN AND INFORM THOSE ABOUT US WITH THE WEAPONS OF LIBERTY AT OUR COMMAND.

THOSE WEAPONS ARE MANY -- A FREE PRESS, AN OPEN PUBLIC FORUM AND A GOVERNMENT WHOSE ONLY LEGITIMATE OBJECT, IN THE WORDS OF THOMAS JEFFERSON, IS "THE CARE OF HUMAN LIFE AND HAPPINESS."

WHEN WE USE THOSE WEAPONS WISELY -- WHEN WE GIVE THEM THE RESPECT AND THE REVERENCE, THE DISCRETION AND THE DISCIPLINE OF RESPONSIBILITY THEY MUST HAVE -- WE RAISE THE LEVEL OF MAN'S DIGNITY TO THE GREATEST PEAK IT HAS EVER

KNOWN.

AMERICA STANDS, TODAY, AT THE TOP OF A MOUNTAIN OF HUMAN LIBERTY FOR ALL MEN. IT IS THE TRUTH THAT HAS BROUGHT US THERE. IT IS THE TRUTH THAT WILL KEEP US THERE IN THE PERILOUS, CHALLENGING YEARS THAT LIE AHEAD.

- END -

COMMENCEMENT ADDRESS

by Letty Cottin Pogrebin

[Letty Cottin Pogrebin of *MS* magazine is an accomplished extemporaneous speaker. She writes: "The only speech I have ever prepared verbatim was the Commencement Address I delivered to last year's graduating class at Douglass College, Rutgers University. I was paralyzed by an attack of humility at the idea of speaking to a huge graduating class in the presence of robed scholars, and so I prepared and rehearsed every word in advance." The following speech is the one the graduates and "robed scholars" heard.]

Friends and Sisters:

It is an extraordinary honor for me to be here today — to speak to the women of the class of 1973. I believe yours is a very special class, because your university experience has precisely paralleled the progress of a vast and historic social movement.

When you came here in September 1969, Women's Liberation was far from a national concern. It was the work of a few brave women, veterans of the politics of the left, who were tired of fighting for everyone's freedom but their own; or else it was a comedian's punchline. But concurrent with your four years of school, women everywhere have been educating themselves to a new purpose — and you have been with us and of us in this time of immense vigor and apocalyptic change. And today, as you are graduated, the New Feminism has also matured into a broad, sweeping and life-enhancing ideology with which many of us are reinvesting ourselves and redesigning our lives.

Because of this remarkable parallel in space and time, your commencement ceremonies represent a symbolic rite of passage for me as well. It is a fine moment for us to reflect back together.

When I was graduated from Brandeis University in 1959, Pierre Mendes France, a French statesman and Edward R. Murrow, a news commentator, spoke of lofty goals and remote global problems. They were addressing the young men in our class who were expected to forge out and do the world's work. Even if we women had been included in their remarks, we would have exempted ourselves. The price of excellence and accomplishment for a woman was simply too great. As Matina Horner demonstrated in her study on "Why Bright Women Fail," the fear of success has a chilling effect on young women. We would rather be popular than President. We would rather marry power than possess it.

Four years ago when you entered Douglass, many women like myself had not yet entered consciousness. We called ourselves ladies or gals and we dressed to attract men. If we were smart or strong, if we were artists or thinkers, we worked hard to hide it because we knew perfectly well that smart women terrify men.

And we *needed* men — to choose us, to reaffirm us by taking possession of our small, self-effacing lives. As Cynthia Ozick has written in her essay on "Women and Creativity" — "female infantilism is a kind of pleasurable slavishness. Dependency, the absence of decisions and responsibility, the avoidance of risk, the shutting out of the gigantic toil of art — all these are the comforts of the condoning contented subject."

But now we've begun to *reject* the diminutive, female ideal. Male standards and the collective male ego no longer coerce us into pretended inferiority. We are refusing to be trivialized. We are insisting on autonomy and dignity whatever the risk.

Four years ago, we wore derivative indentities with pride. We were our father's daughter, our husband's wife and then our children's mother. There was no need for any debate about the use of Ms. Most of us were desperately trying to convert Miss. into Mrs. so that we could wear the label as a badge. We never noticed that when we were pronounced man and wife, he was pronounced a person and we were pronounced a role.

George Bernard Shaw described woman's Children-Kitchen-Church pattern with his famous parrot analogy. He wrote: "If we have come to think that the nursery and the kitchen are the natural sphere of woman, we have done so exactly as English children come to think that a cage is the natural sphere of a parrot — because they have never seen one anywhere else."

Today we call this phenomenon "the absence of female role models" and we are fast filling in the gap. Brilliant, active women are becoming visible in every field and they're clearing a path for the rest of us. We are re-evaluating history and rediscovering women whose lives could have inspired us all along.

Marriage and motherhood are becoming voluntary options rather than a manifest destiny for anyone born female. If marriage is no more than institutionalized male supremacy in the home then women must either avoid it or reform it. We all know that one out of three marriages ends in divorce. Margaret Mead has said that one of the reasons marriage worked well in the 19th century was because people only lived about fifty years. But now, we are expected to live *together* for fifty years. If we are indeed perfectible, loving human beings and marriages still turn sour so often, then there must be something wrong with the myth that promises us that the key to the hope chest opens a rich, complete life.

Women of my age and older are struggling now to remake real lives out of false expectations. We are renegotiating the contract with the ones we love. We are revising our values, reorganizing our homes and re-entering the world. But *you* can, at the very outset, get right to the business of making considered and careful choices from among a great many alternatives.

Though it may be difficult, you can live alone or with someone; marry or not; conceive or adopt a child or choose not to be parents; work or study; travel or put down roots; build a career or make the revolution.

And it is nothing short of revolution that has been in the making during these years.

Because of it, you are the first generation of grown women who — I hope — has not swallowed the lie. You *know* too much.

You know that women with children, even college-educated, white women, are not economically secure. They are only one man away from welfare.

You know that society can't really be committed to women's self-actualization when hopes of a national child care program can be destroyed with a President's veto declaring that it would "weaken" the family.

You know that if you choose full-time motherhood you will work a 99-hour week at no pay, with no sick leave, fringe benefits or vacations. And the only way anyone besides your family will recognize the enormity of your job is if you die — and the surviving father complains about having to pay nearly $10,000 a year to replace your services.

You know that childbearing is not every woman's "ultimate fulfillment" — and that the promise of fulfillment through other lives is no substitute for a life that is full.

The average woman who does have children has sent her last child to school by the time she is 35. With women's greater life expectancy, you're still faced with forty more years of living. You may as well decide now whether you will live them as Portnoy's mother or as your own person. Today, you can make that choice.

Four years ago, when you were Freshwomen, I was out in the business world thanking people when they said I think like a man. I remember that year well, because it was then I wrote a book that today — to my feminist sensibilities — reads like an anachronism.

But at that time, counseling women on how to make it in a man's world, seemed reasonable. Questioning *why* it was a man's world, or whether it had to remain so, seemed moot and unproductive. Women such as myself were having enough trouble with accusations that we were unfeminine, castrating monsters. We were challenging the mythic female stereotype simply by being active participants rather than docile observers or handmaidens to the male hierarchy in business or political life.

We thought it was hard enough to get into the board room without having to carry in the coffee — and to be taken seriously, not chased around the desk, once we got inside.

We were making a career out of being token women because there was no honor in joining with the oppressed mass of secretaries and saleswomen, who were only doing women's work for women's wages. Why blow the whistle on male chauvinists in the office, we thought, when with a little good behavior we could be treated like one of the boys.

Sure, we had read *The Feminine Mystique*. And in 1966 we were aware that The National Organization for women had been founded on our behalf. But we still laughed along with men in 1968 when the protest against the Miss America pageant brought the word "bra burner" into the language (though no underwear was ever incinerated; bras were actually tossed into a Freedom Ash Can). Still, with all this early activity, by the end of your first semester, most of us believed that Women's Liberation was sour grapes from frustrated, homely women. We all knew what they really needed.

Four years ago, we were still clinging to the survival behavior of any second-class group. We were collaborating with the oppressor to avoid being identified with the despised caste. Like good Aunt Toms — or perhaps like good Watergate functionaries — we still followed orders from The Man.

Today, those of you who are entering careers, face an entirely different challenge. Much of society's sexist injustices have been named and catalogued. Equality for women is supposedly a national priority, and tokenism has been publicly condemned. The statistics are in. Many legislative tools are available. Beyond the courts, women know we must use other tactics and so we are getting organized in workplace caucuses and we are demonstrating. We have our leaders and our strategies; we have our landmark cases, and our documentation, and our overwhelming numbers. Your challenge now is to become working feminists and feminist workers — informed of your rights and spiritually resolved to fight for them. The battle has begun but the war is far from over.

Equal pay for equal work is an absurd oversimplification of our goal. It is a concept that no one argues with, and no one lives up to. For what we are really talking about now is a major economic upheaval and a total redistribution of wealth and power. It should be clear that there can be no equal pay for equal work if there is dehumanization of Woman and devaluation of whatever work she performs.

Therefore we are not only demanding fair opportunity for the exceptional female but equity for all women. This seems a disturbing concept to many men — that the mediocre woman be as readily rewarded as is the mediocre man. We know why it is disturbing. Because a lot of men feel threatened. They have already sneaked off with the privilege of paid mediocrity, and now they believe it belongs to them exclusively.

We have a long way to go to reach parity. Right now, a black woman with a college degree earns as much as a black man with an eighth grade education; a white woman with a college degree earns as much as a minority man with a high school diploma.

While this statistical comparison inevitably seems to pit working women against minority men, we must not be so myopic that we fall into that political trap. The lesson is only that whomever is neither white nor male is the lowest in the caste system. We see this most clearly at the top levels: of all the jobs paying $15,000 a year or more only six per cent are held by women-and-minority-men combined.

And still, among the have-nots, women have least. The gap between men's and women's wages has actually widened in recent years: in 1955 we made 64 cents for every dollar a man earned; today we're down to 59 cents.

This should not surprise us. Right from the beginning of life, females have not been worth very much by anyone's financial yardstick. For instance, because of the difference in our earning potential, the Social Security Administration has valued a newborn girl at about $34,000. Her baby brother, however, is worth $60,000.

Another study may give you a different perspective on the diploma you receive today. If you work throughout your lifetime, that certificate is worth an extra $56,000 to you. But your male counterpart over at Rutgers, will gain $118,000 over a lifetime from the earning power of his sheepskin.

And so, "equal pay for equal work" does not begin to reach the problem. Women will always be worth less if whatever women do is devaluated, and whatever men do is rendered primary. Thus, in primitive societies where men are responsible for the weaving and women for the food-gathering — it is weaving that is considered the prestigious labor. It is the same as it has always been. For centuries, value has been assigned according to *who* does the job, rather than the job to be done.

That is why we're talking about deep and telling change — not just a facile slogan. Today, when we speak in terms of affirmative action, we are neither defensive nor placatory. We mean reparations and compensation for blatant and cruel mistreatment — and we must not shrink from the concept of full parity.

It's tempting to be encouraged by showy signs of progress. Rhetoric can easily pass for reform. Madison Avenue provides ample illustration of how this can work. If the admen can rip off the movement with headlines like "Ma Griffe apologizes for unliberating the liberated woman — or with perversions like "Freedom of choice — for lips" — then imagine what distortion and exploitation can be masquerading as progress inside some of our august institutions and patriarchal corporations.

Which leads us to the plain fact that living as an autonomous, self-respective human being inevitably boils down to the daily discussions, arguments, conversations and confrontations that will soon be your everyday life. Even in this age of consciousness, it isn't easy. The impulse to "femininity" and agreeableness dies hard. Think about it.

You are in a job interview. The personnel man asks you if you use birth control. He wants to make sure you're not going to get pregnant and waste the company's investment in your training.

Do you tell him that his question is both offensive and illegal? Do you inform him that according to the U.S. Department of Labor — hardly a radical source — women's turnover and absenteeism rate is no greater than men's even including pregnancy leave? Do you remind him that most women — like most men — work because of economic need, and that few of the 13 million working mothers can afford the luxury of staying home, whatever their preference. — Or do you just smile demurely and answer that you take The Pill?

You are at a career conference. A woman who made it in the old days, with the old ways, is lecturing to aspiring women managers. She tells you to wear skirts, speak softly and be sure you're twice as good as any man. Do you suggest to her that women — like men — should be judged strictly on talent and performance. Or do you quietly resolve to become a Queen Bee?

Interviewers are *still* asking those questions and career advisors are still counseling pretense. But no one has the right to expect any woman to become "a credit to her sex." And we are not going to be placated for long by breakthrough women — any more than blacks were placated by Jackie Robinson or Ralph Bunche. We are all aspiring women now.

When women push and petition for themselves, we call them aggressive; but when men do it, we call them assertive and we make them our leaders. Well, the assertive woman is an idea whose time has finally come. She is the determined woman within you, and only you can give her permission to come out. I fervently hope that you have decided to release her and let her work for you and all of us.

Because so much work is still to be done and we must prepare to be resilient in the face of disappointment. We've learned *that* already. Courts have ruled unconstitutional all the State Protective Labor laws that restrict women's working hours and the kinds of jobs women can perform. And yet there are still states where the laws are on the books and women are still locked out of remunerative occupations.

We have judicial decisions that articulate a woman's right to work throughout her pregnancy with her doctor's approval, and to return to work after her baby is born. And we have a recent paternity leave ruling that acknowledges a father's right to share his child's infancy. And yet it still takes case after case to reaffirm those rights for each individual.

It has taken fifty years for Congress to pass the Equal Rights Amendment and yet we are having to fight a rightwing backlash to achieve ratification by the required 38 states.

One year ago The Equal Pay Act was extended to include protection for 15 million additional workers, most of them white collar executives, teachers and administrators. Yet, in the first three months after this legal remedy was made available, only 35 people bothered to file charges of wage discrimination based on sex.

Title VII has also been interpreted to prohibit sex-segregated classified ads — because listing jobs for males and females is not so different from listing jobs for Coloreds and Whites. The Equal Employment Opportunity Commission has issued guidelines that specify sex as a *bona fide* occupational qualification in only the narrowest sense. Or as the outspoken Florynce Kennedy has put it: "The only *bona fide* sex-typed jobs are — wet nurse, for a woman, and sperm donor, for a man."

And yet, despite all this, many newspapers and employment agencies perpetuate the female job ghetto, and so, the issue must now be heard by the Supreme Court.

How many of us will file the charges, demonstrate, write letters, go to court or pursue a job that asks for "a man who is a go-getter."

The answer is — all of us *must* do all of that; Not simply jump the barriers, but tear them down. And we must do it together — as women.

One recent case is a bellwether. It is costing A T & T nearly $30 million to rid itself of sexism and racism. Why did it take a costly government study and the threat of suit to persuade A T & T of what a dime in the phone slot could have made clear to anyone. Telephone operators are women. And most of them are minority women, with limited options — women on the boards of tedium, plugged in to one of the lowest wage scales in the labor market; closed out of the craft jobs, the management jobs, the computer jobs; the jobs that pay and the jobs that lead somewhere. Those women will get their back wages and a new chance. But who can compensate them for their lost self-esteem?

Four years back, we believed that as privileged, educated women, we had little in common with that telephone operator. It has taken more than a college degree to teach us *all* about the commonality of women's experience. We've been learning together — and many of *you* have been our consciences. We've learned that the woman lawyer, who is denied a partnership because corporate clients supposedly won't take legal advice from a woman — is suffering the same sexist bias as the household worker, who is exempt from the minimum wage law, because domestic labor is women's work and after all, housewives do it for nothing.

In these last four years we've seen Columbia University women students picketing side-by-side with campus cleaning maids; we've seen legal secretaries being unionized with the help of feminist lawyers; we've seen brave older women, well past the age of childbearing, who have marched with high school women in support of abortion and every woman's right to control her own body.

We've seen women who are single and married, teenagers and grand-mothers, rich and poor, black and white, meeting weekly in consciousness-raising groups — sharing secret fears and finding them merely women's gen-eric heritage; unlocking the prison of our sexuality and understanding the politics of second-sexness; learning from one another, and listening to one another — because we are all experts at living life as a woman.

Four years ago, too, we had not yet witnessed the horror of Cambodia and Kent State, Jackson State and carpetbombing, My Lai and Watergate. We had not yet seen how much inhumanity could be justified by the passion for "peace with honor" — and by the national obsession with being Number One.

None of these concepts or events are born of Women's Culture. And so we must say a word about the traditional conditioning of the sexes and the invidious roots of the masculine mystique which bathes all our lives in war and violence.

One side of that conditioning, we know well. The "Sugar and Spice" part. We remember the restrictions on us as little girls, restrictions imposed in the name of sexual identity. We remember being admonished to keep clean rather than climb trees. We remember the platitudes — "act like a lady" and "girls don't do well in math" and "women can't be doctors."

But the little boys' "Snips and Snails" conditioning has turned out to bear even more bitter fruit than our frustration and our rage. It is little boys who must prove their manhood and exploits of violence and brute strength. It is little boys whose emotional lives are systematically stunted — and who are forbidden to cry. And so it is that we see in power, grown men who have learned to repress their feelings so "manfully" — men who stand impassive when the only decent human response is to weep. Little boys raised on a must-win policy have become men who cannot pull out of a game of death.

Would women do it all differently?

None of us can say for sure. We can only say that we have not been conditioned to sacrifice compassion for honor. Or decency for victory. We can only recognize that we have not *yet* been corrupted by power. And we can only hope that when women assume our proper share in decision-making, — we will have learned from men's mistakes.

If we are to work changes in society, we will have to be visible and vocal. And so, the new assertive woman must become an undeniable fact of life — and she must be internalized in our cells.

Where my generation of women depersonalized its political battles, licking stamps for politicians who patted our heads and neglected our issues — your generation can be clearheaded, focused and committed to nothing short of a humanist revolution.

Where women like myself have to unlearn the habit of *asking* for jus-tice, you have known all along, that freedom and power are never given, — they must be taken.

You are a unique class commencing adult life at a remarkable time. You have had access to an incredible wealth of information about yourselves as women — about your economic potential, about choices and limitations, about the price of accommodation and the consequences of rebellion. Four-teen years ago, when I last wore a cap and gown, I had a B.A. in English and American literature — and a set of sterling silver.

I suspect that even four years ago, the **Senior** women who sat in these chairs were dreaming still of finding husbands who were doctors, scientists, scholars or artists, architects or revolutionaries.

It would be my hope that the women of this class are dreaming of *becoming* the people that my generation of women wanted to marry.

No — I am not saying that today you are a man. None of us want to trade places with man, not to imitate them. What we want is what we've learned is our birthright all along: choice, self-determination and human dignity.

I have tried today to say to you what I wish someone had said to me fourteen years ago. And so, as I wish every joy to this very special class, I share deeply in this ritual. Because we are peers and colleagues, sisters and fellow students of the organic anthropology of these last four years.

We have come of age together. And together we shall flourish.

FOR DISCUSSION

1. Of what value to a listener or reader is the critical study of a speech?
2. Can a speaker improve his own performance through the study of the speeches of others? Why or why not?
3. Upon what grounds is the critical appraisal of a speech properly based? Why?
4. What determines whether or not any speech is effective?
5. Why or why not can a speaker rely exclusively upon appeals to reason?
6. What are some common forms of motivating appeals which are useful in persuading an audience?
7. What differences in style of speech composition are noticeable between current speeches and those of the early 1900s? Or of the mid nineteenth century?
8. In the speeches quoted in this chapter what evidence of *audience adaptation* may be noted?
9. Which of the several speakers quoted in this chapter spoke on controversial topics? What means did each use to avoid further alienating opponents?
10. Which of the speakers seemed to be trying to reach people other than those in the immediate audience? What evidence can you cite?

PROBLEMS AND EXERCISES

1. Outline two or three short or medium-length speeches. Write the probable subject sentence of each. Did the structure of the speech lead the listener to the main idea?
2. Study the introduction of several speeches. What technique or method of catching the listener's attention did each speaker use? How did he orient his audience?

3. What forms of support were most frequently used in the speeches used in number 2? Comment on their probable value.
4. How reliable do you believe that each speaker's information was? What tests did you apply?
5. Did you detect any errors in logic? Cite examples.
6. For the same group of speeches study the conclusions. What techniques or methods were used? How successful do you think that they were in clinching the speakers' main idea?
7. Arrange with a speaker to conduct a survey after he finishes speaking. Distribute a questionnaire among a random sample of the audience to test listener comprehension and recall.
8. Following one of your own speches make a similar survey. As a result what changes may be needed in your methods of speech preparation and delivery?
9. Study the speaking style of experienced speakers in several different professions or businesses. What similarities or differences did you note? What practices that you noted would you want to emulate or avoid? Why?
10. Study a speech that was designed primarily *to inform* the audience. What method or methods did the speaker use in developing his factual information?
11. Study in the same way a speech *to persuade*. What motivational appeals did the speaker use?
12. Study a speech in which a problem is presented (with or without a suggested solution). What means did the speaker use to involve the audience in the problem?

BIBLIOGRAPHY

Books

ALY, BOWER, and ALY, LUCILE. *American Short Speeches.* N. Y.: The Macmillan Company, 1968.
ARNOLD, CARROL C.; EHNINGER, DOUGLAS; and GERBER, JOHN. *The Speaker's Resource Book.* Rev. ed. Glenview, Ill.: Scott, Foresman and Company, 1966.
BAIRD, CRAIG A. "Why Study Speeches?" *American Public Addresses 1740–1952.* N. Y.: McGraw-Hill Book Company, 1956, pp. 1–14.
BERQUIST, GOODWIN F. JR. *Speeches for Illustration and Example.* Chicago: Scott, Foresman and Company, 1965.
BOYER, WILLIAM W., ed. *Issues 1968.* Lawrence, Kans.: The University Press of Kansas, 1968.
BRIGANCE, WILLIAM NORWOOD. *Classified Speech Models.* N. Y.: Appleton-Century-Crofts, 1928.
HARDING, HAROLD F. *The Age of Danger: Major Speeches on American Problems.* N. Y.: Random House, 1952.
HILDEBRANDT, HERBERT W. *Issues of Our Time: A Summons to Speak.* N. Y.: The Macmillan Company, 1963.
HOPKINS, THOMAS A., ed. *Rights for Americans: The Speeches of Robert F. Kennedy.* Indianapolis: The Bobbs-Merrill Co., Inc., 1964.

LOMAS, CHARLES W. *The Agitator in American Society*. Englewood Cliffs, N. J.: Prentice-Hall, Inc., 1968.

OLIVER, ROBERT T., and WHITE, EUGENE E. *Selected Speeches from American History*. Boston: Allyn & Bacon, Inc., 1966.

THONSSEN, LESTER, and BAIRD, A. CRAIG. *Speech Criticism: The Development of Standards for Rhetorical Appraisal*. N. Y.: The Ronald Press Company, 1948, chap. 1.

Periodicals

BAILEY, M. C. "Communication." *Vital Speeches* 39 (July 1, 1973):565–67.

BAIRD, A. CRAIG, and THONSSEN, LESTER. "Methodology in the Criticism of Public Address." *Quarterly Journal of Speech* 33 (April 1947):134–38.

BARRETT, HAROLD. "The Lamp of Henry Grady." *Today's Speech* 11 (September 1963):19–21.

HARDING, HAROLD F. "The College Student as a Critic." *Vital Speeches of the Day* 18 (September 15, 1952):733–36.

NILSEN, THOMAS R. "Criticism and Social Consequences." *Quarterly Journal of Speech* 42 (April 1956):173–78.

PADROW, BEN. "Norman Vincent Peale: The Power of Positive Speaking." *Today's Speech* 10 (February 1962):8–10.

ROSENFELD, L. W. "A Case Study in Speech Criticism: The Nixon-Truman Analog." *Speech Monographs* 35 (November 1968):435–50.

THOMPSON, WAYNE. "Contemporary Public Address: A Problem of Criticism." *Quarterly Journal of Speech* 40 (February 1954):24–30.

ZELKO, HAROLD P. "Books and Materials for Business and Professional Speech Training." *Today's Speech* 11 (November 1963):12–13.

index